AF600069

THE LAWS OF THE STATE OF MISSISSIPPI AFFECTING CHURCH PROPERTY

This dissertation was approved by the Reverend John J. McGrath, A.B., LL.B., J.C.D., as director, and by the Reverend John Rogg, Schmidt, A.B., J.C.D., LL.B., and the Reverend Bernard F. Deutsch, J.C.D., I.C.D., as readers.

THE CATHOLIC UNIVERSITY OF AMERICA
CANON LAW STUDIES
NO. 417

The Laws of the State of Mississippi Affecting Church Property

A DISSERTATION

SUBMITTED TO THE FACULTY OF THE SCHOOL OF CANON LAW OF THE CATHOLIC UNIVERSITY OF AMERICA IN PARTIAL FULFILLMENT OF THE REQUIREMENTS FOR THE DEGREE OF DOCTOR OF CANON LAW

BY
JAMES PATRICK McGOUGH, J.C.L.
PRIEST OF THE DIOCESE OF NATCHEZ-JACKSON

THE CATHOLIC UNIVERSITY OF AMERICA PRESS
WASHINGTON, D.C.
1962

NIHIL OBSTAT:

JOHN J. MCGRATH, A.B., LL.B., J.C.D.
Washington, D.C., May 20, 1961

IMPRIMATUR:

✠ RICHARD O. GEROW, S.T.D.
Bishop of Natchez-Jackson

Jackson, Mississippi, May 24, 1961

Printed by The Abbey Press, St. Meinrad, Indiana, U.S.A.

FOREWORD

As a visible society, the Church seeks from the state recognition of certain rights which are essential to its well being and the attainment of its sublime purpose. Among these is the right of acquiring, holding and administering property in accordance with its own discipline. Through the centuries civil authority has recognized this right in varying degrees.

While the Church's right to acquire, hold and administer property is not recognized as an inherent right of the Church by federal and state law in the United States, nevertheless, the law will grant such a right to the Church upon its incorporation. Moreover, the policy of the several states, in accordance with their constitutional provisions to guarantee freedom of religion, in general, has been to frame legislation so that each denomination may have an equal right to exercise religious profession and worship and to support its ministers, teachers and institutions in accordance with its own practice, rules and discipline. Unfortunately, however, not all states have pursued this liberal policy. While freedom of worship without preference to any sect is guaranteed by the Constitution of the State of Mississippi, nevertheless, in the opinion of this writer, there is legislation which, while not purposely so, is in fact an abridgement of the religious freedom guaranteed by the Constitution. The religious corporation statute is certainly partisan, for while it adequately provides for religious societies which are congregational in form, it makes no provision for those which are hierarchical in form. All religious societies are discriminated against by the limitations imposed on their proprietary capacity as well as on their capacity to receive property by devise. While mortmain provisions may have been justified in Feudal England, they should have no place among the legal institutions of our Democracy.

To acquaint the reader with the historical background of the Catholic Church in Mississippi, a brief history of the

Church with reference to the civil powers under which it developed is contained in the first chapter. In the subsequent chapters an effort has been made to make a comparison of Canon law and the present civil law of the State of Mississippi regarding acquisition, tenure and administration of Church property to determine how, and to what degree, the Church is affected in those instances where this parallel does not exist. No attempt has been made to discuss all the aspects affecting Church property involved under these titles; rather, it is hoped that those aspects will be discussed which may be of practical importance to the ecclesiastical administrator.

The writer is deeply grateful to His Excellency, the Most Reverend Richard O. Gerow, M.A., S.T.D., Bishop of the Diocese of Natchez-Jackson, for the opportunity to undertake graduate studies in Canon law, and to the faculty of the School of Canon Law of the Catholic University of America for their kind assistance during the course of these studies and in the preparation of this work.

TABLE OF CONTENTS

CHAPTER III

CHAPTER IV

CHAPTER I

THE CHURCH IN MISSISSIPPI WITH REFERENCE TO THE CIVIL POWERS UNDER WHICH IT DEVELOPED

ARTICLE 1. DISCOVERY AND FIRST MISSIONARIES (1528-1698)

Nearly a century before the Mayflower anchored at Plymouth Rock in 1620, Mississippi's history began. Spanish treasure ships linking the western hemisphere to the dynastic empire of Charles V made the Carribean and the Gulf of Mexico a Spanish Main.

Of the early Spanish expeditions, however, probably only one, that of De Soto, touched the soil of the present State of Mississippi. After wandering through the wild of what is now the States of Florida, Georgia and Alabama, he entered Mississippi in 1540. Somewhere below the site of Memphis, Tennessee, he discovered the Mississippi River in May, 1541. After veering westward, De Soto, dejected and near death, returned to the river; upon its banks he died on May 21, 1542.

Such was the secular significance of the De Soto expedition; however, it also had an ecclesiastical significance, for in all probability the Dominican chaplains of the De Soto expedition were the first missionaries to enter Mississippi. History records that these priests did all in their power to convert the natives and succeeded in baptizing many of them. After the death of De Soto and the failure of the expedition, however, it is not known whether the missionaries remained with their converts or accompanied the remainder of the expedition into Mexico.[1]

[1] Claiborne, *Mississippi as a Province, Territory and State with Biographical Notices of Eminent Citizens* (Jackson, Miss., 1880) pp. 1-11 (hereafter cited Claiborne); Kenny, *The Romance of the Floridas* (Milwaukee: Bruce Publishing Co., 1934), pp. 1-52 (hereafter cited Kenny); Baudier, *The Catholic Church in Louisiana* (New Orleans, 1939), p. 14 (hereafter cited Baudier).

From the death of De Soto in 1542 to 1608, Mississippi remained unexplored. However, with the discovery of Quebec by the French navigator Champlain, and the subsequent discovery of the "Great River," the Mississippi, efforts were made to penetrate the unknown wilderness.[2] The first expedition was carried out by Louis Joliet, who was accompanied by a Jesuit, Father Marquette. This expedition probably did not enter the State of Mississippi, as it returned after reaching the Arkansas River.[3]

The next effort to explore the "Great River" was undertaken by Robert Cavelier, Sieur de la Salle. On December 21, 1681, he set out on his memorable voyage, accompanied by his faithful friend Tonti and Father Zenobius Mambre, a Recollect Father, as Chaplain. The whole party numbered forty-nine persons. They floated down the river for days, occasionally stopping along the shore to make friends with the Indians and to study the surrounding country. Finally, on April 6, 1682, they arrived at the mouth of the river and there La Salle took formal possession of the territory of the Mississippi valley for France under the name of Louisiana in honor of Louis, King of France.[4]

During the voyage Father Mambre endeavored to give the Indian tribes a knowledge of the faith. However, as he remarked himself, he did not accomplish any direct result for the Church, baptizing merely two infants whom he saw struggling with death. Nevertheless, he prepared the way for future missionary activity. Only once does he mention in his memoir the celebration of Mass, and this is in reference to Easter Sunday, March 28, 1682. This great event probably occurred in the neighborhood of the present Fort Adams in southwestern Mississippi.[5]

[2] Claiborne, p. 12.

[3] Claiborne, p. 12; Shea, *History of the Catholic Missions Among the Indian Tribes of the United States (1529-1854)* (New York: Edward Dunigan & Brother, 1885), p. 437 (hereafter cited Shea, *Catholic Missions*).

[4] Cf. Claiborne, pp. 13,14.

[5] Shea, *The Catholic Church in Colonial Days* (New York: John G. Shea, 1886), pp. 326, 327 (hereafter cited Shea, *Colonial Days*).

When Governor Frontenac of Canada was informed of the immense territory explored by La Salle and claimed in the name of France, he decided to attempt the evangelization of the natives in accordance with the wishes of the French King. Consequently, he induced the French government to ask the Holy See to erect one or more Vicariates Apostolic in the immense territory of the valley, as the territory was thought too extensive for the Bishop of Quebec. Rome looked with favor on the project and on December 8, 1685, Father Hyacinth Le Febvre of the Recollect Province of St. Denis in France was named prefect of the mission *in the island,* popularly called Louisiana in America. The faculties were given *ad Septennium* with the condition that four more Fathers be sent to Louisiana, but after this no more, unless the Sacred Congregation be consulted. The four additional Fathers who were assigned to the Recollect Vicariate were Fathers Zenobuis Mambre, Maximus Le Clerq, Anastasius Douay, and Dionysius Morguet.[6]

The Prefecture of the Recollects was, however, shortlived, because of the opposition of Bishop Saint Vallier of Quebec, who claimed the territory of Louisiana as part of his diocese.[7]

ARTICLE 2. THE FRENCH PERIOD (1698-1763)

Bishop Saint Vallier was now entrusted with the spiritual welfare of the territory of the Mississippi valley. In the discharge of this duty he was assisted by the priests of the seminary of the foreign missions in Quebec. As pioneer for the new missions the seminary chose Father Francis Joliet de Montigny. Invested by the Bishop with the powers of Vicar General, Father Montigny set out with Father Anthony Davion, a priest of the same seminary, in the Ottawa flotilla of 1698. Descending the Mississippi, Father Montigny chose the Taenzas tribe for his labors and placed Father Davion

[6] Marcellino, *Storia Universale delle Missioni Francescane* (XI Vols., Firenze, 1895), XI, 24, 25 (hereafter cited Marcellino); Cf. Baudier pp. 17, 18.

[7] Vogel, "The Capuchins in French Louisiana, 1722-1766," *Franciscan Studies,* VIII (August, 1928), 4, 5 (hereafter cited Vogel).

among the Tonicas Indians on the Yazoo River. Father Davion thereby became the first resident priest of Mississippi.[8]

In the meantime, the activities of the Spanish in the Gulf of Mexico and the threat of the English from the Atlantic seaboard, with their infiltration among the Indian tribes in the valley of the Mississippi, finally aroused France to a greater interest in her vast domain of Louisiana. As a result, Count de Maurepas, the French minister, chose Pierre Le Moyne, Sieur d'Iberville, to establish the power of France at the southern end of the colony of Louisiana, and to establish communications with Canada in the valley. He was joined by his brother, Jean Baptiste Le Moyne de Bienville, and with four ships they sailed from France on October 24, 1698. After exploration of the Mississippi coastline, the place now known as Ocean Springs was finally chosen as the site for the new settlement. Here a fort was built, which became known as Fort Biloxi, a name derived from the Indian tribe of that area.[9]

Having provided the settlers with all necessary supplies, D'Iberville sailed for France on May 3 to report to the King and also to gather more colonists and provisions. Before his departure he appointed Sauvolle Commander of Fort Biloxi, and Bienville, Lieutenant and second in command. Father Bordenave was appointed chaplain to the little settlement.[10]

At the Red River, Fathers Davion and Montigny heard of this French settlement and resolved to visit it. After ten days of sailing, they arrived at Biloxi but only remained a short time, returning to their mission with wine for Mass and flour and tools. It is probable that Father Montigny, on his return journey, went to the villages of the Natchez tribe, where he

[8] Shea, *Catholic Missions*, p. 440.

[9] Claiborne, pp. 18, 19; Gayarre, *History of Louisiana; The French Domination*, (4 Vols., New York, 1866) I, 57, 58 (hereafter cited Gayarre).

[10] Baudier, pp. 24, 25; Gerow, *Catholicity in Mississippi* (Natchez, 1939) pp. 8, 9 (hereafter cited Gerow).

proposed founding a new mission for which another priest had arrived. This was the Canadian, Father John Francis Buisson, commonly called de St. Côsme.[11]

The activity of the seminary priests of Quebec among the tribes of Mississippi did not bear much fruit at this time. Father de St. Côsme had little success in converting the Natchez, but he struggled on for some years. Father Davion visited the villages of the Chicasaws, but no mission could be attempted in this tribe, already devoted to the English. Father Geoffrey Thierry Erborie, who is also mentioned as a companion of the Vicar General, tried to evangelize the Choctaws and labored among them and the Natchez until 1709 when he returned to Illinois.[12]

On the return of 'Iberville to the Biloxi settlement at the end of 1699, he was accompanied by a Jesuit, Father Paul Du Ru, who was to found missions among the Indians on the Mississippi River. However, after some efforts to establish these missions, he retired to Biloxi, realizing that the seminary priests were already laboring among the Indian tribes. Here he acted as chaplain to the French garrison and as missionary to the Pascagoulas, Chicasaws, Pensacolas, and Biloxis.[13]

Soon afterwards Father Du Ru was joined by two other Jesuits, Fathers Joseph de Limoges and Peter Dongé. Father de Limoges, whom we find at a subsequent period laboring in Illinois, now proceeded to the Oumas on the Red River and began a mission among them which apparently lasted several years.[14] Father Dongé remained with Father Du Ru and labored in the districts of Mobile and Biloxi.[15]

These Jesuits now applied to the Bishop of Quebec to assign them an exclusive district, but the Bishop paid no heed to their request. In 1703 they had recourse to the Pope,

[11] Shea, *Catholic Missions,* p. 441.

[12] Shea, *Catholic Missions,* p. 441.

[13] Cf. *Journal of Father Paul Du Ru, Feb. 1-May 8, 1700; Missionary Priest to Louisiana* (Chicago, 1934), pp. 1-72.

[14] Shea, *Catholic Missions,* p. 442

[15] Vogel, p. 9.

asking that instructions be sent to the Bishop of Quebec for a permanent division of Louisiana between the Jesuits and the seminary priests of Quebec. On September 24, 1703, the Sacred Congregation for the Propagation of the Faith granted their petition.[16] Bishop Saint Vallier of Quebec, however, did not approve of this division. Consequently, on March 7, 1704, the Jesuits were recalled to France by their Provincial, and thus the labors of these zealous missionaries were lost for twenty years.[17]

After the withdrawal of the Jesuits, there remained in the Mississippi territory only Father Davion at the Tonicas and Father de St. Côsme. Father Geoffrey Thierry, as already indicated, labored among the Choctaws until 1709. Father Davion left the Tonicas for a time after the murder of Father Nicholas Foucalt in 1702. However, at the request of the Tonicas in 1704, he returned to his mission and in 1706, when the Tonicas moved their village down the river to the Fort Adams section, he accompanied them and remained there until 1722 when the Capuchins took over the southern part of the Mississippi valley as their mission field.[18] Father de St. Côsme was not so fortunate. On descending the river in 1707 with three Frenchmen and a little slave, he was murdered by the Sitmachas Indians.[19]

In the meantime, the French made efforts to consolidate their position in the colony. In 1702, England having declared war on France, the French King gave orders to Iberville to build a fort on the Mobile River and to remove the Biloxi colony there. Thus, in case of trouble with the English who were moving westward from the Carolinas, the French settlers would be near their Spanish friends at Fort Pensacola. The seat of government was removed eighteen leagues up the river to the new fort, named Louis de la Mobile, and

[16] Hughes, *History of the Society of Jesus in North America* (4 Vols., New York, 1917) II, 257 (hereafter cited Hughes).

[17] Biever, *The Jesuits in New Orleans and the Mississippi Valley* (New Orleans, 1924), p. 17 (hereafter cited Biever); Baudier, p. 32.

[18] Gerow, p. 15; Baudier, pp. 32, 33.

[19] Shea, *Catholic Missions*, pp. 443, 444.

the first white family arrived there in May, 1702. In 1711, the settlement of Mobile was inundated, causing the removal of the colonists to the present Mobile.

Biloxi, however, was not abandoned. From this settlement Iberville and Bienville penetrated the surrounding country, establishing trading posts and forts, among which was Fort Rosalie, founded on the bluffs of Natchez in 1714. In 1704, twenty or more young women, destined for marriage with the colonists, landed at Mobile and Biloxi. This was the first of several shiploads of "Casket Girls," French orphans and peasants who came voluntarily to the New World as prospective wives of the settlers.[20]

The condition of the colony, however, was far from prosperous. In an effort to promote its growth, the King of France devised a new scheme. He granted to Anthony Crozat, a rich merchant, the exclusive privilege of trading for fifteen years in Louisiana. The country was actually farmed out to Crozat who was to possess and work all the mines that might be discovered, provided that one-fourth of the proceeds be reserved for the King. He had also the privilege of owning forever all the lands he would improve by cultivation and all buildings he might erect. His principal obligation in exchange for these advantages was to send annually to Louisiana two shipments of colonists, and after nine years to assume all the expenses for the administration. For the present, the yearly sum of fifty thousand livres was allowed Crozat for the King's share of the expenses entailed by the venture.[21] The King also agreed to maintain the necessary military forces in the country, while its government was to be entrusted to a council as in the islands of San Domingo and Martinique.

Bienville, who on the death of his brother, Iberville, in 1706 had assumed command of the colony, did not approve of this new scheme, believing that the welfare of Louisiana lay in agriculture rather than in trade. Consequently, he

[20] Claiborne, pp. 27, 28.

[21] Gayarre, *History of Louisiana, the French Domination*, I, 79-115.

was assigned to what might be called the Indian department, and La Mothe Cadillac, a kind of partner to Crozat, was sent to rule as governor.[22]

The chief object of Crozat was trade, not with Louisiana, but rather with Mexico and the Spanish possessions. His plans, however, miscarried. The Mississippi valley yielded neither gold nor silver and when he attempted commercial relations with the Spaniards they persistently closed their ports to French ships and kept a strict guard over their Texas frontier.[23]

As a result of Crozat's failure to carry out his scheme, the condition of the colony did not improve. Consequently, on January 13, 1717, the Council, recognizing that the improvement of Louisiana was too great an undertaking for one private individual, decided to organize a company powerful enough for this enterprise. Accordingly, Crozat surrendered his lease to the Duke of Orleans, Regent of France after the death of Louis XIV, and the Company of the West, later known as the Company of the Indies, was formed in August, 1717.[24] The Company was given a lease for twenty-five years but, as it turned out, it was forced to give up the colony in 1731.[25]

On February 9, 1718, Bienville again returned to favor and was nominated governor. His first proposal for the welfare of the colony was the transfer of the capital from New Biloxi, which had been established in 1713 by his predecessor, Governor Cadillac, to the mouth of the Mississippi River. The company did not support the governor in his policy; however, Bienville prevailed and in 1722 the capital was transferred to the district now known as New Orleans.[26]

With the organization of the Company of the Indies and

[22] Claiborne, pp. 32, 33.

[23] De Villiers, "A History of the Foundation of New Orleans (1717-1722)," Warrington Dawson transl., *The Louisiana Historical Quarterly*, III (1920), 175 (hereafter cited De Villiers).

[24] Claiborne, p. 35.

[25] *Loc. cit.*

[26] Claiborne, pp. 35-39.

the extravagant advertising of John Law, its comptroller general, new impetus was given to immigration and most of the posts where settlements had been projected were increasing in population. The company now divided Louisiana into nine districts, namely, New Orleans, Mobile, Biloxi, Alibamos, Natchez, Yazoo, Natchitoches, Arkansas and Illinois.[27]

One of the outstanding obligations of the company was the provision of missionaries and churches for the settlers. The fifty-third clause of the contract read as follows:

> As in the settlement of the countries granted to the said company by these presents, We regard especially the glory of God by procuring the salvation of the inhabitants, Indians, savages and negroes, whom we desire to be instructed in the true religion, the said company shall be obliged to build, at its expense, churches at the places where it forms settlements; as also to maintain there the necessary number of ecclesiastics, either with the rank of parish priest or such others as shall be suitable, in order to preach the Holy Gospel there, perform divine service, and administer the sacraments all under the authority of the Bishop of Quebec.[28]

During this period, religion was at a low ebb. In accordance with its obligation, the Company of the Indies had endeavored to furnish priests, but the system was badly organized. Great grants of land were given in the colony and great colonization schemes were undertaken. Settlements began to spring up on the grants, known as concessions, and chaplains were assigned to them. Among the concession chaplains who served Mississippi were Father du Hal de St. Malo at the Concession of Devecher and Coestegon, probably along with the Sainte Reine of the Tonicas; Abbe Claude Juif, who became chaplain of the Post of the Yazoos; Abbe d'Arquevaux, who also served the Yazoos and died there; Abbe de Brabant, chaplain at the Sainte Reine con-

[27] Hamilton, *Colonial Mobile* (New York, 1897), p. 106 (hereafter cited Hamilton).

[28] Shea, *Colonial Days*, p. 562.

cession; Father Richard, chaplain of Madame de Chaumont's concession at Pascagoula.

Ship chaplains also officiated on the Mississippi Gulf Coast. In 1720, Father Paulin, chaplain of the ship L'Alexandre, performed pastor's functions at Old Biloxi.[29]

The system of concession chaplains, however, proved a failure. As a result, efforts were made to secure the services of religious orders whose systematic organization lent itself excellently to the conduct of work such as was needed in the colony, especially in view of the absence of a bishop in the territory.[30]

The Discalced Carmelites of France were the first to accept the invitation of the Company, and on March 1, 1720, the Company issued letters patent to Father James de St. Martin, Father Charles de St. Alexis and Father de St. Mary Magdelene for their establishment in Louisiana.[31] The Carmelites, however, did not leave for the mission until they had secured from Rome a brief of Apostolic Prefecture. On June 20, 1720, Rome published the desired brief deputing Father James de St. Martin prefect, and declaring his companions missionaries of Louisiana.[32] This action of the Carmelites was later to occasion their expulsion from the colony, as will be seen.

Concerning the activities of the Carmelites in the territory of Mississippi, there is little information. Father Matthew de Saint Anne, who succeeded Father James de St. Martin on the latter's death, took up work at Old Biloxi in the Fall of 1720, but in November of that year he went to Mobile. He was followed by his confrere, Father Charles de Saint Alexis who officiated at Old Biloxi until the middle of 1721 when he took up duties at New Orleans. Vogel maintains that Father Maximin, who labored at Natchez at this time, was also a Carmelite.[33]

[29] Gerow, pp. 21, 22.

[30] Baudier, p. 51.

[31] Vogel, p. 16; Baudier, pp. 31, 32.

[32] *Prop. Arch.*, *Atti.*, 1720, ff. 308, 309 in Vogel, p. 15.

[33] Vogel, footnote p. 445; Cf. Baudier, pp. 51, 52.

Having obtained the services of the Carmelites, the Company next invited the Capuchins of Champagne to labor in the Louisiana territory. Accordingly, on April 13, 1722, the Capuchin Provincial of Champagne appealed to the Propaganda for a Prefecture in Louisiana. This request was, however, refused by the Sacred Congregation for the Propagation of the Faith after consultation with the Papal Nuncio in Paris, on the ground that "there are enough missionaries on the spot."[34]

The Company, however, seemed to have ignored the refusal of the Sacred Congregation. On May 16, 1722, its commissioners, with the consent of the Bishop of Quebec, divided the Province of Louisiana into three ecclesiastical jurisdictions. The first comprised all the district to the West of the Mississippi from the Gulf of Mexico to the point of entry of the Ohio River. The churches and missions of this district were to be in charge of the Capuchins whose superior was to reside in New Orleans and be a Vicar General of the Bishop of Quebec. The second district was that extending over all the country above the Ohio River. It was given to the Jesuits who were already established in that district, and their superior officer residing in Illinois was to be a Vicar General of the Bishop of Quebec in this district. The third district included all that territory to the East of the Mississippi, and it was assigned to the Carmelites whose superior was to reside at Mobile and be a Vicar General of the Bishop of Quebec in that territory.[35]

The Carmelites, as already indicated, were laboring in the territory when the above arrangements were made. Their stay in the colony, however, was of short duration. The document of partition had scarcely appeared when the French government objected to the Carmelite mission of Mobile. No one was at a loss for the reason. Against the wish of the government, the Carmelites had obtained a Bull of Prefecture from Rome in 1720. This was not acknowledged by the French Government. As a result, all the Car-

[34] *Prop. Arch. Atti.,* 1722, f. 138, No. 25, in Vogel, p. 23.

[35] Baudier, p. 64.

melites, except Father Maximin at Natchez, had returned to France by 1723. Thus Gallicanism, the great evil in France at this time, strangled the Carmelite mission.[36]

After the withdrawal of the Carmelites from the Mobile mission, the commissioners of the Company were obliged to make a new disposal of that district. Accordingly, on December 19, 1722, they drew up a decree bestowing on the Capuchins the Carmelite district of Mobile.[37]

The division of the territory in accordance with this last decree did not long remain such. In December of 1723 another change was made. Quite unexpectedly on the part of the Capuchins, the Company drew up a decree that fixed the boundary of their mission at Natchez instead of the Ohio River. The upper section between Natchez and the Ohio was added to the territory of the Jesuits. The reason for this division seems to have been the incapacity of the Capuchins to supply sufficient priests for their missions.[38]

As a result of this division, the territory of Mississippi was served by both the Jesuits and Capuchins. However, as might be expected, the Church did not flourish because of civil and religious difficulties.

The Jesuits arrived in New Orleans in 1725. Of their activities in Mississippi little is known in detail. In 1727 Father Mathurin le Petit was chosen to found a mission among the Choctaw Indians who occupied part of what is now southern and southeastern Mississippi. Early in the following year, 1728, Father le Petit took up his post among the Choctaws. Whether he accomplished anything among this tribe during his short sojourn with them is not known. In the latter part of 1729, Father le Petit was recalled and was replaced by Father Michael Baudouin.

For twenty years Father Baudouin spent himself among this tribe. Although he seems to have been highly respected by the natives, the fruit of his labors was small. Just when

[36] Paris Arch., Col. C13A10, f. 296 in Vogel, p. 24; Baudier, p. 52.

[37] Paris Arch., Col. F. 5A3, f. 169 in Vogel, p. 27.

[38] Paris Arch., Col. C, 13A1d, f. 296 in Vogel, pp. 32, 33; Baudier, p. 66.

Father Baudouin was about to see results from his efforts, the disturbances excited by the English in that nation and the danger to which he was manifestly exposed compelled Father Vitry, then superior of the mission, to recall him to New Orleans.

After the troubles subsided, Father Le Fevre, who came to Louisiana in 1748, was sent to the Choctaws. Of the subsequent activity in the mission nothing is known though Shea maintains that the mission continued until 1770.[39]

In addition to the Choctaw mission, the Jesuits also conducted a mission among the Yazoo tribe. Father Souel was appointed to this mission where he was to minister to the French in the district and announce the gospel to the Yazoos, Opagoulas and Corras Indians. However, his stay among them was of short duration. Following the massacre of the French at Natchez by the Natchez tribe in 1729, the Yazoos joined this tribe in their efforts to exterminate the French, and Father Souel was the first victim.[40]

The Jesuit missions were the last effort to convert the Indians in Mississippi until after the establishment of the Diocese of Natchez.

While the Jesuits were engaged with the Indian missions, the Capuchins concentrated their labors on the settlements of the French along the River and Gulf coast, although they did not neglect the surrounding tribes.

Practically from the beginning of the colony, Natchez and the surrounding district attracted many settlers. A fort was established there in 1714 by Bienville and during the following years many colonists settled there. So prosperous and suitable was the region that in 1722 it was spoken of as

[39] Shea, *Catholic Missions*, pp. 450, 651; Delanglez, *The French Jesuits in Lower Louisiana (1700-1763)*, The Catholic University of America Studies in American Church History, Vol. XXI (Washington, D.C.: The Catholic University of America Press, 1935), pp. 476, 477 (hereafter cited Delanglez).

[40] Shea, *Catholic Missions*, pp. 448, 449; Gerow, p. 23; Delanglez, p. 451.

the logical place for the capital of the French possessions in the Mississippi valley.[41]

As previously indicated, Father Maximin, a Carmelite, labored at Natchez while the Carmelites had the spiritual care of the southern part of the colony, and remained there after his brethren returned to France.[42] Father Maximin, however, died shortly after the arrival of the Capuchins in 1722 and Natchez remained without a priest until 1724 when Father Christophe de Chaumont, a French Capuchin, was sent to take charge, accompanied by a lay brother, Eusche de Chaumont.[43] There is no mention of the death of Father de Chaumont, but in 1726, Father Raphael, Superior and Vicar General of the territory, in describing the condition of religion at Natchez during his visitation, spoke of Father Philbert as pastor of the district.[44]

Father Philbert continued at this post at Natchez until 1729 when, providentially, he left for New Orleans before the massacre of the inhabitants by the Natchez Indians. After this tragic event, Natchez was practically abandoned and nothing is heard of a priest in the district until 1783.[45]

Of the activities of the Capuchins in other areas of Mississippi, nothing is known. Father Raphael, in his account of the mission in 1723, mentioned a Father Dorez as pastor of Biloxi. He is the last mentioned resident priest of that area until the founding of the diocese.[46] During the intervening period the Catholics of the area depended for spiritual ad-

[41] Gerow, p. 18; Claiborne, p. 35.

[42] Vogel, p. 45.

[43] Gerow, pp. 22, 23.

[44] Vogel, pp. 43-49.

[45] Cf. *Sketch of the Catholic Church in the City of Natchez, Mississippi, on the Occasion of the Consecration of its Cathedral, September 19, 1886* (Natchez, Miss: The Natchez Democrat Print, 1886), pp. 9, 10 (hereafter cited *Sketch*).

[46] Mereness, *The Journal of Divon d'Artaguette (1722-1723) in Travels in the American Colonies* (London: The Macmillan Co., 1916), p. 17 (hereafter cited Mereness).

ministrations on the occasional visits of missionaries from New Orleans and Mobile.[47]

During the entire period of French domination from 1683 to 1763, the Sacred Congregation of the Propagation of the Faith exercised little power over the great mission area of the French colonies, due to the evils of Gallicanism.[48] For the most part, it was either ignored or merely exercised a passive power. The establishment of the Recollect Vicariate in 1685 by the Sacred Congregation was thwarted by Bishop Saint Vallier of Quebec, who claimed the entire territory as part of his diocese.[49]

Again in 1703, contrary to the wishes of the Sacred Congregation, Bishop Saint Vallier would not acquiesce to the petition of the Jesuits for a permanent division of the Louisiana territory between the different bodies of religious, namely, the Jesuits and the seminary priests of Quebec. As a result, the Jesuits left the southern part of the colony and did not return until twenty years later.[50]

The evils of Gallicanism were particularly manifest in the expulsion of the Carmelites in 1723 by the French Government; an act approved by Bishop Saint Vallier and Bishop Mornay, his auxiliary. The reason for the expulsion is stated by Bishop Mornay himself. In a letter to Abbé Raguet, he states:

> You do not ignore what I have done to have the Carmelites recalled who had gone there and on their own initiative obtained a Brief of Vicar Apostolic,

[47] Gerow, p. 129.

[48] By "Gallicanism" is understood principally the summing up of the so-called "Gallican Liberties," that is, the rights and privileges which the French king and his government had long possessed or had believed they possessed, especially in regard to the filling of ecclesiastical positions and the taxing of ecclesiastical property, as well as the prerogatives of the French clergy, such as the "appeal against abuse" from the spiritual to the secular court.—Cf. Hertling, *A History of the Catholic Church* (Westminster, Maryland: The Newman Press, 1957), p. 433 (hereafter cited Hertling).

[49] Marcellino, *Storia delle Missioni Francescane,* XI, 24-29.

[50] Hughes, pp. 11, 257; Biever, p. 17.

> which, as you know, we do not recognize in France.[51]

Of a similar import was the restriction of the jurisdiction of the Capuchins unknown to Bishop Saint Vallier.[52]

In addition to this unprecedented usurpation of ecclesiastical jurisdiction by the French authorities, and the apparent disregard for the Sacred Congregation of the Propagation of the Faith by the Bishop of Quebec, the ecclesiastical government of the missions was very unsatisfactory. Bishop Saint Vallier and his successors in the See of Quebec exercised control over the missions by the appointment of Vicars General. This arrangement gave rise to many difficulties the powers of the Vicars General were greatly circumscribed, and consequently, necessary faculties and dispensations which had to be obtained from the Bishop of Quebec gave rise to interminable delays in connection with the settlement of ecclesiastical questions. In addition, there was lacking one with proper authority to initiate religious projects or to direct them—someone with episcopal rank to settle on-the-spot difficulties that were bound to arise, and suppress violations and abuses that prevailed. Furthermore, many were left without the sacrament of Confirmation; actually, Confirmation was not administered in the colony until 1785.[53]

Such in general was the status of the Church during the French regime in the territory of Mississippi, and as a consequence, the growth of the Church in the district was to a great extent stymied. It is interesting to note that between the years 1690 and 1700, four diocesan Synods were held in Quebec, the first on November 9, 1690, the second on March 10 and 11, 1694, the third on February 27, 1698, and the fourth on October 8, 1700.[54]

[51] Paris Arch., C13A10, 35, 36 in Vogel, p. 24.

[52] Vogel, p. 35.

[53] Baudier, p. 52.

[54] Desrochers, *Le Premier Concile Plenier de Quebec et le Code de Droit Canonique,* The Catholic University of America Canon Law Studies, n. 152 (Washington, D.C.: The Catholic University of America Press, 1942), p. 2 (hereafter cited Desrochers).

ARTICLE 3. ENGLISH AND SPANISH PERIOD (1763-1798)

In 1763 Great Britain, by virtue of a treaty on February 16 of that year between Great Britain, Spain and France, took possession of Western Florida, including what is now the southern half of Mississippi. At first England claimed only as far north as the thirty-first parallel. Soon, however, she extended her claim northward to a line beginning at the mouth of the Yazoo River and running eastward as far as Georgia.[55]

Under British rule most of the settlers were non-Catholics, so it is not surprising that there exists no record of Catholic activity during this time. However, Great Britain did not proscribe the practice of Catholicism, as can be seen from the following clause of the treaty:

> His Britannic Majesty agrees on his part to allow the inhabitants of the country above ceded, the liberty of the Catholic religion and that in consequence his Britannic Majesty will give the most exact and effectual orders that his new Roman Catholic subjects may profess the worship of their religion according to the rites of the Roman Church, so far as the law of Great Britain permits.[56]

British control over West Florida was of short duration. The peace of 1763 which gave England the Floridas and the right of free navigation on the Mississippi River was a source of uneasiness and alarm for Spain who became the neighbors of the British to the west of the Mississippi River by virtue of the same peace. Nor were the Spanish fears groundless. The British floated by New Orleans with their vessels loaded with British wares which they disposed of on the river without license, to the ruin of the Spanish merchants, and by superior energy their traders monopolized

[55] Claiborne, pp. 89, 90.

[56] Curley, *Church and State in the Spanish Floridas (1783-1822)*, The Catholic University of America Studies in American Church History, Vol. XXX (Washington, D.C.: The Catholic University of America Press, 1940), pp. 20, 21 (hereafter cited Curley).

almost the entire Indian trade.[57] On the other side, the English colonists were angered by the thought that the Spanish were instrumental in stirring up the Indians against them. Moreover, they ardently longed for the possession of the city of New Orleans. Without this outlet to the sea, they knew their river trade was insecure.[58]

In this attitude of mutual suspicion, the colonial rivals had constructed fortifications, strengthened their military forces on the border and watched every significant move of their antagonists. When a crisis arose in their relations in 1771, England planned the capture of New Orleans. However, with the outbreak of the American Revolutionary War and the withdrawal of British troops for service in the East, the attack on New Orleans was suspended.[59]

Peace was not to reign between these old colonial rivals. Spain, taking advantage of the British preoccupation with the Revolution, declared war on England in June of 1779. Galvez, the Spanish governor of Louisiana, captured from the British the forts of Baton Rouge and Natchez, and shortly thereafter the forts on the Gulf also fell into Spanish hands. Thus ended the British rule in Mississippi. Strong Spanish garrisons were stationed at Natchez and Nogales (Vicksburg).

Charles III, elated by the conquest of West Florida, sent out a *cedula* uniting the conquered territory to the Province of Louisiana. The whole territory, now called the Province of Louisiana and West Florida, was placed under Bernardo Galvez with its capital at New Orleans.[60]

In order to understand properly the events relating to the Church during the Spanish control, the following should be kept in mind. The Spanish colonies, though ultimately governed by the Spanish king, depended for their immediate

[57] Claiborne, p. 124.

[58] Philipps, "The West in the Diplomacy of the American Revolution," *The University of Illinois Studies in Social Science*, II (1913), Nos. 2 and 3, pp. 19-21 (hereafter cited Philipps).

[59] *Loc. cit.*

[60] Cf. Claiborne, pp. 125-134.

control on a council appointed by the king. This council, known as the Council of the Indies, was located at Seville and was empowered with supreme legislative and judicial authority.[61] Moreover, in addition to the civil jurisdiction, the council, as representative of the Spanish king, also enjoyed some ecclesiastical jurisdiction in virtue of the *patronato reàl.*[62]

With the arrival of the Spanish in Mississippi, Catholic activity again flourished. However, as a result of the English domination, most of the settlers were non-Catholics, particularly in the Natchez district.[63] This constituted a problem for Governor Miro, the successor of Governor Galvez.[64]

He had received no instructions regarding the religion of these newcomers, though he was certain that if they were obliged to depart on account of their failure to accept Catholicism, as Spanish laws required, trouble would result. Consequently, he wrote to Bernardo Galvez, then Viceroy of Mexico, and suggested the following plan to solve the dilemma.[65] In his opinion it would be better to allow the settlers to remain in the territory and have the King send English-speaking or Irish priests among them to newly erected parishes where they might preach the Catholic religion and endeavor to convert the Anglo-Americans to the faith. While not asking the settlers themselves to change their religious tenets, Miro proposed that the King should oblige them to have their children baptized as Catholics and educated in schools taught by priests. Those not willing to comply with

[61] Chapman, *Colonial Hispanic America* (New York, 1933), p. 11 (hereafter cited Chapman).

[62] Curley, p. 13. *Patronato reàl* was the accumulation of privileges acquired by the Spanish Kings from the Roman Pontiffs. Cf. Bull, *Inter cetera* of Alexander VI (1493), and *Eximiae devotionis* (1501), Julius II, *Universalis ecclesiae* (1508). For texts cf. Hernaez, *Colecciòn de Bulas, Breves, y Otros Documentos Relativos a la Iglesia de America y Filipinas* (2 Vols., Brussels: Vromant, 1879), I, 12, 20, 24 (hereafter cited Hernaez).

[63] Claiborne, pp. 95, 136.

[64] *Ibid.*, p. 150.

[65] Curley, p. 90.

this arrangement would be forced to emigrate. Holding a neutral attitude to the suggestion, Bernardo Galvez cautioned Miro to take no action until the question could be relayed to the Court and settled by higher authority.[66]

The plan of Miro was accepted by the King with one notable modification. By the Royal Order of April 5, 1786, it was decreed that the non-Catholic inhabitants were to be allowed to remain in the Floridas, provided that they took a solemn oath of allegiance and fidelity to the crown and did not leave the districts in which they were settled without the express permission of the governor. Instead of obliging them to have their children baptized in the Catholic religion, as Miro suggested, Charles III declared that parishes should be erected at Natchez and at other suitable places and that Irish priests should be sent from Spain to attempt the conversion of the inhabitants. To achieve this end, Governor Miro was instructed to draw up plans for the erection of parishes and for the methods to be pursued. A report was requested from him concerning the number of priests that would be required.[67]

Accordingly, Governor Miro prepared a plan for West Florida. He proposed that two parishes were needed for the Natchez district, one at St. Catherine's Creek where the services of two priests would be necessary, and the second at Cole's Creek, eighteen miles away.[68]

On the same day that the Royal Order had decreed the erection of new parishes in the Floridas, a command was given to the Bishop of Salamanca to obtain priests for work in the New World.[69] Accordingly, the Bishop of Salamanca wrote to the Royal Irish College of Salamanca for missionaries. However, there were only two priests there at the time, the Rector, Father Patrick Cortes and Father William Savage. The former could not be spared for work overseas; hence, only one priest was obtained at this time. Four months

66 *Loc. cit.*, p. 90.
67 *Ibid.*, p. 91.
68 *Ibid.*, p. 93.
69 *Ibid.*, p. 94.

afterwards, however, the Bishop of Salamanca reported that he had obtained four more volunteers, Fathers Gregory White and Constantine McKenna of the Casa de Venerables in Seville, a Dominican, Father Bernard Lunney of the same city, and Father Michael Lamport from Cadiz.[70]

The King accepted the services of the four secular priests, omitting Father Lunney, and shortly afterwards, the four priests started for Cadiz to embark for New Orleans. After a delay both at Cadiz and Havana, the priests finally arrived in New Orleans in August, 1787.[71]

Having received no direct approbation for his plan for parishes, Governor Miro believed himself justified in proceeding to use the priests as he had planned. Accordingly, he sent Father Lamport to Mobile, where he was to stay until a church could be built on the Tensaw River forty-five miles to the north. The other three were detained in New Orleans until the governor could make provisions for suitable rectories in the Natchez district and at Cole's Creek.[72]

To provide accommodations for the Irish priests at Natchez, Governor Miro, still without sanction from Spain, purchased a plot of ground near the Spanish fort from Stephen Minor on April 11, 1788. Several buildings were on the property which consisted of about 170 acres. Some weeks later, Fathers Savage, McKenna and White took up their residence in a large two-story building on the property. Father Savage was placed in charge with Father McKenna as his assistant. The third occupant, Father White, assigned to work in Cole's Creek, was only temporarily lodged there until arrangements could be made for his work at Cole's Creek.[73]

Shortly after the arrival of the priests, work was begun on a church. After some difficulty in securing laborers, the structure was finally constructed by Stephen Minor and some

[70] *Ibid.*, p. 95.

[71] *Ibid.*, p. 97.

[72] *Ibid.*, p. 97.

[73] *American Catholic Historical Researches*, IV (Philadelphia, 1887), 149-151.

time during the year 1791 was dedicated to the Holy Savior (San Salvador). The Church was situated on what is now Commerce Street.[74]

At Cole's Creek, later called Villa Gayoso, a similar development took place. Although the property of Thomas Calvert was first recommended for purchase by Grand Pré, the Commandant at Natchez, later, the 350 arpent plot of Thomas Elliot seemed a better bargain at $2,000 for, as at Natchez, a house on the property could be readily used for a rectory. There is no record, however, as to what property was purchased, but by February, 1792, a church had been built there with Father Gregory White officially appointed as pastor.[75]

Of the early activity of the fathers in the Natchez district little is known. Father McKenna was the first to record a baptism in August, 1788.[76]

During the following years until the departure of the Spanish from Natchez in 1798, there was a constant shifting of ecclesiastical personnel in the Natchez district, which retarded the growth of the Church there. In 1791 Father McKenna was sent to Tombigbee in the Mobile district, leaving Father Savage alone in Natchez. Father Savage died on April 18, 1793, and Father White was sent to Natchez. Father Lennan, who, on his arrival in 1792, had been sent to Nogales (Vicksburg), was sent to Cole's Creek. Later, Father Lennan was sent to Pensacola, which was in need of an English-speaking priest.[77]

The loss of Father Savage and the removal of Father Lennan left the Natchez district with one priest. The Commandant at the time, Gayoso de Lemos, complained bitterly to Governor Carondolet of New Orleans. As a result, Father Lennan was recalled from Pensacola in July, 1794, and made pastor at Natchez. Father White, suffering from various disabilities which did not allow him much activity, was sent to

[74] Gerow, p. 29.
[75] Curley, p. 153.
[76] Gerow, p. 29.
[77] Curley, pp. 194-244.

Cole's Creek where the few inhabitants, only a handful of them Catholics, would make life easier. Father Lennan was the last pastor at Natchez during the Spanish Regime.

As regards Catholic activity in other parts of Mississippi, nothing is known. Father Lennan, as previously indicated, spent some time at Nogales (Vicksburg), where a colony of Americans had been led by the South Carolina Yazoo Company, and where the Spanish had erected a fort in 1790 to resist their encroachment. There was talk of building a church there for the inhabitants and Spanish soldiers but no proof that it was actually built has been uncovered.[78]

During the Spanish Regime in Mississippi nothing is mentioned of the spiritual care of the Negroes.[79] However, provisions for them were made by a general order from the court in a royal *cedula* in the year 1788. In general, this *cedula* provided that all slaves had to be educated in the principles of the Catholic religion so that they could be baptized within a year after their arrival in the colonies. Masters were not permitted to make them work on Sundays and Holy Days.

Moreover, no effort was made to convert the Indians. Perhaps the blame for this cannot be laid to Spain as most of the Indians lived outside the Floridas, so that Spain's influence over them was very meager.[80]

The spiritual supervision of the Floridas underwent many vicissitudes during this period. As indicated previously, the *patronato reàl* took from the Church authorities some of their jurisdiction; however, the interference of civil authorities in Church affairs was not as obnoxious as it was under the French Regime.

After the capture of the Floridas, Bishop Echevarria of

[78] Cf. Curley, p. 244.

[79] The importation of Negroes to labor in the colonies was first introduced under the French government and was continued during the English reign. It was subsequently forbidden by Spanish law; however, in spite of the prohibition, many Negro slaves were sold in the colony during the Spanish reign by English merchants.—Claiborne, pp. 35, 106.

[80] Curley, pp. 261, 262.

the Diocese of Santiago de Cuba undertook the spiritual supervision of the territory. Actually, during the British occupation he had claimed jurisdiction over the Floridas; however, until its capture he exercised no direct influence over it. In order to regulate the spiritual affairs of the colony more efficiently, he placed Father Cyril de Barcelona, a Capuchin, as Vicar Forane in New Orleans.[81]

Bishop Echevarria, however, was not satisfied with the progress of religion in the province and confessed to Charles III his inability to govern the mainland portion of his diocese. Accordingly, Charles III decided to give him an auxiliary and with the approval of Bishop Echevarria, nominated Father Cyril de Barcelona. Pius VI agreed to the arrangement and appointed the Capuchin, but did not forward the Bulls until 1784. Father Cyril was consecrated in Havana on March 6, 1785.[82]

On his return to New Orleans Bishop Cyril's conduct was far from exemplary. Though requested by Bishop Echevarria to conduct a visitation of the entire mission, Bishop Cyril contented himself with the visitation of the parishes in the vicinity only. At the end of the year, on hearing of the sickness of Bishop Echevarria, he went to Havana contrary to his Ordinary's wishes and left Father Sedella as Vicar in New Orleans. He remained in Havana thirty-two months, incurring during that time the wrath of both the Ordinary and the King.[83]

The year 1787 saw a further change in the ecclesiastical government. Because the amount of administrative work entailed was too great for one bishop, two commissioners, one of them Father Josè de Trespalacios, were engaged in arranging a division. Five years later the matter was settled. By a Consistorial Decree of September 10, 1787, the Diocese of Santiago de Cuba was split into two parts; the old Diocese of Santiago de Cuba was made smaller and the new Diocese

[81] De Castillo, *La Luisiana Española y el Padre Sedella* (San Juan, Puerto Rico, 1929), p. 47 (hereafter cited Castillo).

[82] Castillo, p. 53.

[83] Curley, pp. 101-107.

of St. Christopher with its Episcopal See in Havana was erected. The mainland territories of Louisiana and the Floridas were placed under the jurisdiction of the new See of Havana, for which Father Josè de Trespalacios was chosen bishop on September 10.[84]

Meanwhile, Bishop Cyril, though warned on several occasions by the King to return to his post, did not do so until March, 1788.[85] He still retained his position as Vicar of the territory and prepared to undertake the visitation of the mission. However, before he undertook his visitation he engaged in an unfortunate dispute with Father Sedella, and as a result, in 1790 Bishop Trespalacios deprived him of jurisdiction in the territory, appointing Father Portillo as Vicar. Nevertheless, Bishop Cyril carried out the visitation of the mission but unfortunately he did not visit the parishes in Mississippi.[86]

The appointment of Father Portillo did not prove successful; consequently, within three years two successors were appointed—Father Henrique Henriques and Father Walsh. Finally, Bishop Trespalacios, realizing the unsatisfactory condition of religion on the mainland, appealed to Charles IV to establish a diocese in Louisiana. The King approved of this plan and the Vicar General of Havana, Father Luis Penalver y Cardenas, was nominated and Rome approved. He was consecrated on April 25, 1795, and arrived in New Orleans on July 17, 1795.[87]

Five months after his arrival Bishop Penalver issued an instruction to the pastors of his diocese to act as a guide for them until a diocesan synod could be held.[88] In addition to

[84] Shearer, "Brief of Pius VII: Jan. 21, 1833," *Pontificia Americana: Documentary History of The Catholic Church in The United States (1784-1884)*, The Catholic University of America Studies in American Church History, Vol. XV (Washington, D.C.: The Catholic University of America Press, 1933), p. 133 (hereafter cited Shearer); Curley, p. 99.

[85] Curley, pp. 103-106.

[86] *Ibid.*, pp. 136-147.

[87] *Ibid.*, pp. 251, 252.

[88] *Instrucciòn para el Gobierno de los Parrocos de la Diocese de la*

this instruction, Bishop Penalver undertook an extensive visitation of his diocese. Between April and June of 1796 he visited all the parishes from the "German Coast" to Natchez.[89]

Bishop Penalver's control, however, over the greater portion of Mississippi was short-lived. On March 30, 1798, the Spanish garrison marched out of Natchez. Thus ended the influence of Spain on Catholic activities in Mississippi.[90]

Article 4. The Stars and Stripes (1798-1924)

Section 1. Mississippi as a Territory and State

On March 29, 1798, the Spanish garrison left Natchez for New Orleans and the United States took over control of the northern portion of Mississippi, placing garrisons at Natchez and Fort Nogales (Vicksburg).

With the departure of the Spanish the close cooperation between civil and ecclesiastical authorities came to an end. Subsequent years saw State and Church develop independently of each other. Consequently, to indicate the civil background in which the Church in Mississippi developed in later years, the following summary of the principal historical events is given.

On June 12, 1797, President Adams, in a special message, recommended to Congress the erection of a government in the district of Natchez similar to that established for the territory northwest of the Ohio River, with certain modifications relative to titles, or claims of land, whether of individuals or companies, or to claims of jurisdiction of any individual state. Accordingly, on April 8, 1798, a bill was passed authorizing a government in the Mississippi territory and applying to it the ordinance of July 18, 1787, which introduced the common law and permitted slavery as it

Luisiana, printed with a translation by John G. Shea in the *United States Catholic Historical Magazine,* I (1887), 418-443.

[89] Curley, pp. 262-264.

[90] Gerow, *Cradle Days of St. Mary's at Natchez,* (Natchez, Miss., 1941), p. 3. (hereafter cited Gerow, *Cradle Days*).

existed, but which prohibited the introduction of slaves from foreign parts. Winthrop Sargent was appointed governor and John Steele as secretary of the Territory.[91]

During his term of office Governor Sargent proved very unacceptable to the people, particularly by the arbitrary code of laws which he concocted for the territory. As a result, the people appealed to Congress for relief and secured the annulment of most of the laws enacted by the governor, and in addition the territory was advanced to the second grade of government. This advancement secured for the territory a legislature to be elected by the people and whose advice and consent should be had upon all nominations to office by the governor. Furthermore, it took from the governor the arbitrary power of making laws and gave the legislature that power with the right by a two-thirds vote of overriding the objection of the governor to any law they might choose to enact.

In 1801 Thomas Jefferson was elected President of the United States and shortly thereafter he relieved Governor Sargent of his office, replacing him with Governor William Claiborne. During his term of office Governor Claiborne was to a great extent occupied in determining conflicting land titles, the status of which was in doubt due to the conflicts of claims to portions of the Mississippi Territory by Georgia, Spain and the United States. After the Louisiana Purchase in 1803 and the creation of the Orleans Territory in 1804, Governor Claiborne was appointed governor of the latter and was succeeded in Mississippi by Governor Robert Williams of South Carolina.[92]

In order to understand the territorial boundaries of Missis-

[91] Claiborne, pp. 195-206; Lowry-McCardle, *A History of Mississippi from the Discovery of the Great River to the Death of Jefferson Davis* (Jackson, Miss., 1891), pp. 160-162 (hereafter cited Lowry-McCardle).

[92] Cf. Claiborne, pp. 244-258; *Biographical and Historical Memoirs of Mississippi* (2 Vols,. Chicago: The Goodspeed Publishing Co., 1891), I, 162-164 (hereafter cited *Biographical and Historical Memoirs of Mississippi*).

sippi during this period and its subsequent boundaries as a State, it is necessary to retrogress somewhat. While England was in possession of the Floridas her northern boundary was 32°-28'; however, by virtue of the Treaty of Paris in 1783 England recognized the United States' claim south to the 31st parallel. Spain, by this time ruler in Mississippi by virtue of conquest, refused to recognize this latter boundary. For a period of years, therefore, sovereignty to the land between 31° and 32°-28' was under dispute; Spain claiming it by right of conquest and the United States by right of treaty.

To complicate matters further, the State of Georgia also claimed the region by her charter of 1732, even going so far as to organize it into the County of Bourbon in 1785 and to sell it in the notorious "Yazoo Fraud" of 1795.

By the Treaty of Madrid in 1795 the dispute between the United States and Spain was theoretically settled in favor of the former. But the Spanish took their time in evacuating Natchez. Andrew Ellicott, a Quaker surveyor appointed to run the line of demarcation, was kept waiting a year on this account. Finally, in 1798 the Spanish left the Mississippi Territory.

At this time the Territory of Mississippi had the following boundaries: on the west the Mississippi River, on the south by parallel 31°N. latitude, on the north by a line running east from the mouth of the Yazoo River to the Chattahouchie River and along the latter river on the east. However, in 1802 the State of Georgia ceded to the United States its claim to all territory north of the 31° N. latitude and south of the Tennessee line to the Territory of Mississippi. The boundaries remained such until 1810 when the Spanish relinquished their claim south to the Gulf of Mexico.[93]

On the 7th of July, 1817, a convention met to frame a constitution preparatory to the admission of the Territory

[93] Claiborne, pp. 295-297; *Biographical and Historical Memoirs of Mississippi*, I, 165-167.

into the Union as a state. On the 15th of August it completed its work and on December 10th the Territory of Mississippi, now limited on the east by the formation of the Territory of Alabama, took its place in the Federal Union.[94]

Subsequent years saw a striking increase in the population of the State due to the cotton boom and the opening of Choctaw land to white settlers, secured from the Indians by the Treaty of Doak's Stand in 1820 and the Treaty of Dancing Rabbit Creek in 1830.[95]

In 1832 the Constitution of the State of Mississippi was revised. Under the new Constitution the liberty and power of the people was enlarged through the ballot box by conferring authority on them to elect their own public servants without regard to a property qualification. This Constitution remained in force until 1868 when it again underwent modification.[96]

On January 9, 1861, Mississippi passed an Ordinance of Secession, severing its relations with the Federal Union, and joined the Southern Confederacy immediately upon its establishment. The fact that Jefferson Davis, a resident of Mississippi, was President of the Confederacy, drew the State particularly close to the new government; during the war that followed the State took an active part, supplying 8,000 troops.

Upon the surrender of the Confederacy, the State was placed under military rule. In June, 1865, a provisional government was established by President Johnson with William Sharkey as provisional governor. In October of the same year a civil government was established by the election of the people under the auspices of President Johnson's plan for Reconstruction, with Benjamin G. Humphreys as governor.

A special session of the legislature held in 1866-67 refused to ratify the 13th and 14th Amendments of the United States Constitution. The National Congress retaliated in March, 1867, by placing Mississippi in the Fourth Military District,

[94] Lowry-McCardle, p. 260.

[95] Claiborne, pp. 508-512.

[96] Lowry-McCardle, pp. 271, 272.

under the command of Major General Ord, whose use of Negro troops was especially repugnant to Mississippians. In 1868, General Alva Gillem, commander of the military subdistrict of Mississippi, called a constitutional convention. At that time, 60,167 Negroes and 46,636 white males were registered as voters. This "Black and Tan" convention, as it was called, submitted a constitution to the people in June, but it was defeated and General Humphreys was returned to the governor's chair. However, General Irwin McDowell, who replaced Ord, issued a military order for the removal of Humphreys from the executive offices and began a regime in which all civil government was ended. In 1869 all persons who had associated with the Confederacy were disqualified as officeholders and their places filled with Negroes and the most disreputable element among the native whites, "carpetbaggers and scalawags."

When President Grant ordered the Constitution, with certain objectionable features omitted, to be resubmitted to the people in November, 1869, the faction of the Republican Party headed by James L. Alcorn, rode into power with the ratification of the Constitution. In 1870 the 14th and 15th Amendments to the United States Constitution were ratified and the State was formally readmitted into the Union on the 23rd of February of that year.

Governor Alcorn's troubles with a legislature containing thirty-five Negroes were emphasized when the panic of 1873 caused further distress in the State. In the gubernatorial campaign of that year Adelbert V. Ames, with solid Negro support, defeated Alcorn in an election that marked the climax of Negro rule. Out of 152 seats in the legislature, sixty-four were held by Negroes and twenty-four by "carpetbaggers." The Lieutenant Governor, the Secretaries of State, Immigration, and Agriculture, and the Superintendent of Education, as well as nearly all local officeholders were Negroes. In character with any political movement that suddenly raises a submerged class to power, the Ames administration was marked by extravagance and corruption.

In the exceptionally bitter campaign of 1875, one in which

acts of terrorism were committed by both parties, a coalition party of Democrats and Whigs was formed and defeated the Ames administration in sixty-two out of seventy-four counties. The first act of the new legislature was to investigate the state officials. The impeached Negro Superintendent of Education was first to resign. The Negro Lieutenant Governor was convicted on an impeachment charge in March, 1876, and removed from office. Under fire of impeachment charges, Governor Ames resigned on March 29 and was succeeded in office by the President of the Senate, John M. Stone.

From 1876 to 1890, by various additional legal methods, the white man managed to maintain control of the State. However, the state constitutional convention of 1890 made these methods no longer necessary as the constitution placed limitations on the elective franchise.[97]

SECTION 2. THE CHURCH: STRUGGLE FOR SURVIVAL (1798-1837)

With the withdrawal of the Spanish forces from Natchez, both the priests and many of the Catholic colonists departed. Thus, the little Catholic congregation that remained was left without a priest. Fortunately, however, Father Lennan successfully pleaded that the church there be left to the Catholics who remained in that city.[98] Accordingly, the property was placed in the care of the Spanish consul at Natchez, Josè Vidal, for any Catholics who should continue there as a congregation.[99]

However, as it turned out, much of the property was con-

[97] The facts above narrated are generally accepted as such; nevertheless, verification thereof may be made by reference to: *Biographical and Historical Memoirs of Mississippi*, I, 145-173; Lowry-McCardle, pp. 341-360.

[98] Curley, p. 277.

[99] Baltimore Cathedral Archives, 2F8, Penalver to Bishop Carroll, April 14, 1799; Shea, *Life and Times of Archbishop John Carroll* (New York: John G. Shea, 1888), p. 461 (hereafter cited Shea, *Life and Times of Archbishop John Carroll*).

fiscated by the United States government. The action of the government is described as follows in the "Historical Sketch of the Catholic Church in the City of Natchez on the Occasion of the Dedication of the Cathedral":

> When Mississippi fell under the jurisdiction of the United States, the Church property (300 arpents) was seized by the Federal Government under the pretense that the land was, in reality, a possession of the Spanish Crown, and that the Church not being an incorporated body, was incapable of holding real estate. It is true that the Spanish government held title to the property—no others could be found among the archives, but it was in trust for the Catholic Church which, recognized as the religion of the realm, was by that fact legally incorporated according to Spanish statutes. However, the American government was in actual possession, and by act of Congress proceeded by grants to parcel out the tract to divers parties. The United States government did indeed institute a commission to pass on individual claims, and not until November, 1804, were claims debarred, but as the Church was not a corporate body and had no official head in Natchez, no claim was presented on her behalf and thus passed away property of which she, in equity, had the right of constructive possession.[100]

Subsequently, the Catholic congregation redeemed the property on which the church and cemetery stood.[101] Efforts to

[100] *Sketch,* p. 15.

[101] Gerow, *Cradle Days,* p. 7. This purchase was made from one William Bartland in January 1802. His title to the property, though recognized by the United States government, was in fact without foundation. On May 8, 1786, a grant was issued to William Bartland consisting of 108 acres in the City of Natchez. This grant to Bartland included the property on which the church and cemetery were later located. Afterwards, however, the Spanish government made an agreement with Bartland whereby the land granted to him was to be returned in lieu of another tract of land in Kingston. The property returned by Bartland was granted to the Church. The deeds to the property, however, were not drawn up at this time, and when on the departure of the Spanish in 1798, efforts were made to execute the papers Bartland could not be found. Cf. *ibid.,* p. 7.

recover the rest of the property were made by Bishop Chanche and his successors, but without success.[102]

From the year 1798 until the erection of Natchez as an Episcopal See, Catholic activity in Mississippi centered around Natchez and even there little or no progress was made. For a time after the Territory fell within the jurisdiction of Bishop Carroll of Baltimore, Bishop Penalver kindly volunteered to look after the spiritual interests of the Catholics at Natchez. He gave instructions to Father Lennan, then pastor at Feliciana near Baton Rouge, to visit the people at Natchez from time to time.[103] During the year 1799 a Father Saint Pierre labored at Natchez, probably also at the command of Bishop Penalver. Subsequent years saw various priests at Natchez but none remained for very long.[104]

The ecclesiastical government of Mississippi during this period was far from satisfactory. On January 29, 1791, Bishop Carroll of Baltimore was informed by the Sacred Congregation of the Propagation of the Faith that:

> All the faithful living in communion with the Catholic Church, both Ecclesiastics and lay persons, whether they dwell in the Provinces of Federated America or in the neighboring regions outside of the Provinces, so long as they are subject to the government of the Republic, will be and shall be hereafter under the jurisdiction of the Bishop of Baltimore.[105]

Consequently, in 1798, with the withdrawal of the Spanish, Archbishop Carroll became the Ordinary of the greater portion of Mississippi, excluding the coastal area which still remained in Spanish control until 1810.

As previously indicated, Bishop Penalver promised to provide for the spiritual welfare of the people of Natchez until Bishop Carroll was in a position to do so. However,

[102] Cf. Gerow, *Cradle Days*, pp. 88, 89, 123-126.

[103] Curley, p. 320.

[104] For a detailed account of these priests and the activities of the congregation, cf. Gerow, pp. 3-34.

[105] Shea, *Life and Times of Archbishop Carroll*, p. 382.

Bishop Penalver resigned his See in 1801 and was shortly afterwards appointed to the See of Guatemala.[106]

The difficulty which Bishop Carroll had in obtaining priests for Mississippi during the following years can be seen in the frequent petitions of the Catholics of Natchez.[107] However, in 1815 when Bishop Du Bourg was appointed Bishop of Louisiana and the two Floridas, the Archbishop of Baltimore confided the jurisdiction of Mississippi to him as his Vicar.[108]

The situation remained thus until 1820 when Archbishop Marechal, then Archbishop of Baltimore, petitioned the Holy See to again divide the southern portion of his Archdiocese. In compliance with his request, the Sacred Congregation of the Propagation of the Faith authorized the erection of the See of Richmond, which included the territory of Virginia, and the See of Charleston, which embraced North and South Carolina and Georgia.[109]

This action greatly complicated the situation because Alabama and Mississippi still belonged to the Archdiocese of Baltimore. Accordingly, Archbishop Marechal explained the situation to the Holy See and to correct it the Holy See erected the Territories of Mississippi and Alabama into a Vicariate Apostolic and appointed Father Joseph Rosati on August 13, 1822, as the Vicar with the title of Bishop of Tenegra *in partibus infidelium.*[110] Father Rosati, however, declined the offer and, as a result, the Vicariate was suppressed on July 14, 1823.[111]

[106] Gams, *Series Episcopum Ecclesiae Catholicae* (Ratisbon, 1873), p. 151 (hereafter cited Gams).

[107] Gerow, pp. 6, 11, 13.

[108] Shearer, p. 124.

[109] Shearer, *loc. cit.*

[110] *Bullarium Sacrae Congregationis de Propaganda Fide* (7 Vols., Romae: Typis Collegii Urbani, 1839-1841), IV, 399, 400 (hereafter cited *Bullarium Sacrae Congregationis de Propaganda Fide*).

[111] Easterly, *The Life of Rt. Rev. Joseph Rosati, First Bishop of St. Louis (1789-1843)*, The Catholic University of America Studies in American Church History, Vol. XXXIII, (Washington, D.C.: The Catholic University of America Press, 1942), pp. 64-69 (hereafter cited Easterly).

In a letter to Cardinal Consalvi of the Sacred Congregation, Father Rosati gave the following account of Mississippi which gives an interesting insight to the condition of religion there at this time.

> At Natchez, Mississippi, the number of Catholic families does not go beyond thirty, and they are incapable of supporting the pastor, so that Rev. Constantin Maenhant, who had been put in charge of that parish, is soon to leave it; finally at Bay St. Louis, there are about twenty Catholic families, naturally likewise unable to support a priest.[112]

After the suppression of the Vicariate Apostolic, Mississippi was again subject to the Archbishop of Baltimore, who once again entrusted it to the care of Bishop Du Bourg.[113] Finally, in 1825 the Congregation of the Propaganda, in an effort to bring order out of chaos, erected the Vicariate Apostolic of Florida and Alabama and placed Mississippi under the jurisdiction of the Diocese of New Orleans with Bishop Du Bourg as Vicar Apostolic.[114] This arrangement continued until the erection of the Diocese of Natchez in 1837.

SECTION 3. NATCHEZ: EPISCOPAL SEE (1837-1852)

On the 28th of July, 1837, His Holiness, Pope Gregory XVI, at the instance of the Provincial Council of Baltimore, erected an Episcopal See at Natchez with the State of Mississippi as the diocese dependent on it.[115] The clergyman first

[112] *St. Louis Catholic Historical Review*, III (1921), n. 313, "Rosati to Consalvi," April 2, 1823.

[113] Shearer, p. 143.

[114] *Bullarium Sacrae Congregationis de Propaganda Fide*, V, 14; Cf. Shearer, pp. 193-244.

[115] ". . . Itaque rebus omnibus mature examine perpensis, motu proprio et ex certa scientia, deque nostra apostolicae potestatis plentitudine hisce litteris in civitate Natchetensi novam episcopalem sedem erigimus atque instituimus, cui totam provinciam Mississipiensem subiicimus, quam provinciam ex iurisdictione Episcopi Novae Aureliae omnino subtractam in proprium Episcopum pariter constituimus. Ipsi autem Episcopo ab hac sede adlegendo omnes et singulas facultates solitas eadem auctoritate nostra concedimus atque impertimur . . ." *Bullarium Sacrae Congregationis de Propaganda Fide*, V, 161, 162.

proposed for the new See, Rev. Thomas Heyden, after some hesitation, finally declined the mitre and it was not until December 15, 1840, that the Rev. John J. Chanche, president of St. Mary's College, Baltimore, was selected and accepted the Bulls.[116]

After receiving Episcopal consecration at the hands of Archbishop Eccleston of Baltimore on March 14, 1841, Bishop Chanche proceeded to his new See, arriving there on April 18, 1841. The task which faced him was formidable indeed. His entire diocese embraced the whole State of Mississippi, more than 46,000 square miles, with a population of approximately 400,000. There was not one church in the entire diocese; the church at Natchez had been destroyed by fire on December 28, 1832.[117]

Two priests were exercising the ministry in the State—one at Natchez and the other at Vicksburg. How many Catholics were in his jurisdiction he did not know. There were groups at Natchez, at Vicksburg, and at certain places along the Gulf Coast, and throughout the entire state were scattered Catholic families, some of whom had not seen a priest for many years.[118]

Probably the only property in the possession of the Catholic Church in Mississippi at this time was the property at Natchez. During the Spanish regime, the Church had some property at Vicksburg and Cole's Creek, but this was probably lost like most of the property at Natchez after the withdrawal of the Spanish garrison.[119]

The property at Natchez was in the hands of a board of trustees. This group had become incorporated by an act of the legislature of the State of Mississippi on February 18, 1815, under the title of the "Roman Catholic Society of

[116] Shea, *A History of the Catholic Church Within the Limits of the United States from the First Attempted Colonization to the Present Time* (New York: John G. Shea, 1890), p. 660 (hereafter cited Shea).

[117] Gerow, *Cradle Days*, p. 32.

[118] Gerow, *Catholicity in Mississippi*, p. 39.

[119] Cf. Shea, *Life and Times of Archbishop Carroll*, p. 461.

Christians, in the city of Natchez and its vicinity."[120] Bishop Chanche, however, probably well aware of the evils of trusteeism, took steps to secure the property in his own name and that of his successors.[121] Accordingly, on May 20, one month after his arrival, Bishop Chanche informed his congregation of his intention. Shortly thereafter the property was transferred to Bishop Chanche and his successors forever in the Roman Catholic Episcopal See of Natchez. Subsequently, however, it would seem that Bishop Chanche decided to use the board of trustees and was himself elected president of the board.[122]

Having thus settled the question of property, Bishop Chanche made plans for the construction of a cathedral. In 1842 he laid the cornerstone for the new structure and on Christmas Day, 1843, the structure, though not completed, was blessed. In addition to the cathedral, Bishop Chanche endeavored to provide a Catholic education for the children of Natchez. His efforts to provide a school for boys did not succeed; however, with the help of his nieces he opened an academy for girls, but this institution had closed before the death of the Bishop. Perhaps the Bishop's greatest contribution to education was the opening in 1847 of an orphanage for girls and a day school under the direction of the Sisters of Charity.

The Bishop's activities were not confined to Natchez; he made frequent visits to the Catholic communities scattered throughout the State. At the time of his death in 1852 there were thirteen priests ministering to the spiritual needs of the people in Mississippi, and churches had been built in Natchez, Jackson, Sulphur Springs, Vicksburg, Yazoo City, Port Gibson, Bay St. Louis, Pass Christian, Biloxi and Paulding; while preparations had been made for the erection

[120] Gerow, *Cradle Days*, p. 16.

[121] "Les mêmes difficultes se presentirent dans l'evèche de Natchez, crée en 1843 (sic) et confie a Mgr. Chance, prêtre de Saint Sulpice;" —André, *Une page d'Histoire sur les Associations Cultuelles*, (Paris), p. 20.

[122] Gerow, p. 109.

of churches at Canton, Columbus, Pascagoula and Woodville.[123]

It is interesting to note that Bishop Chanche made efforts to recover the Church property confiscated by the United States Government after the withdrawal of the Spanish. For this purpose he went to Havana to consult the old Spanish records and to obtain first hand information and bring back authentic copies of the documents relating to the original Spanish grant. Having obtained the necessary documents, he returned to Natchez and subsequently petitioned Congress to make good the $2,000 originally expended by the King of Spain, or to grant other lands of extent or value equal to those formerly and virtually belonging to the Church. However, his efforts were in vain.

In addition to petitioning Congress, Bishop Chanche instituted action to obtain possession of the lots surrounding the church as constituting part of the Spanish grant. He was successful in this action; however, as will be seen, this judgment was later reversed in a higher court.[124]

In 1852 Bishop Chanche left Natchez to attend the Plenary Council of Baltimore where, as chief Promotor of the Council, he took an active part in its deliberations. Unfortunately, he did not return from the Council. On his return journey he became ill and died at Fredericksburg, Maryland. After the death of Bishop Chanche, Archbishop Blanc of New Orleans became administrator.[125]

SECTION 4. THE GROWTH OF THE CHURCH AND SUCCEEDING BISHOPS (1853-1924)

A whole year passed before Bishop Chanche's successor was appointed. Finally, on July 29, 1853, Pope Pius IX issued a brief transferring Bishop James Oliver Van de Velde, S.J., from the See of Chicago to the See of Natchez.[126]

[123] Gerow, *Catholicity in Mississippi,* pp. 40, 41.

[124] Gerow, *Gradle Days,* pp. 87, 89.

[125] Gerow, pp. 108, 109.

[126] Clark, *Lives of the Deceased Bishops of the Catholic Church in*

Bishop Van de Velde arrived in Natchez on November 23, 1853, and was immediately faced with the problem of repairing the cathedral which had not been completed by his predecessor due to lack of funds. In an effort to obtain the necessary funds, Bishop Van de Velde went on a lecturing tour and thereby obtained sufficient funds to put a new roof on the cathedral.

In the interests of Catholic education, Bishop Van de Velde was exceedingly desirous of establishing a college at Natchez to be conducted by the Jesuit fathers. Accordingly, he purchased a large piece of property known as Rose Hill, formerly the site of the girls' academy opened by Bishop Chanche. He then attempted to obtain the Jesuit fathers to open the college but his efforts were unsuccessful. However, he had the pleasure of seeing the Sisters of St. Joseph of Bourg open a new school at Bay St. Louis.[127]

The property acquired by Bishop Chanche in virtue of the action brought by him in the state court was again in dispute during the administration of Bishop Van de Velde. He had scarcely completed the necessary fencing of the property when the City of Natchez brought an action for its recovery. In the litigation which followed, the Church lost the property and was even deprived of the expenses incurred in its improvement.[128]

Bishop Van de Velde's administration was of short duration. On October 23, 1855, he fell on the steps of the rectory and fractured his leg in two places. Shortly afterwards he developed yellow fever and died on November 13, 1855. Upon his death, the administration of the diocese once again reverted to the Archbishop of New Orleans, Archbishop Blanc.[129]

For well over a year the See of Natchez remained vacant. Finally, on January 9, 1857, the Holy See named as its third

the United States (New York, 1872), pp. 372-390 (hereafter cited Clarke).

[127] Gerow, *Catholicity in Mississippi*, p. 46.

[128] *Sketch*, p. 16.

[129] Gerow, p. 46.

Bishop, Father William Henry Elder, who was at this time a member of the faculty of Mount St. Mary's College, Emmitsburg, Maryland.

Although the Bulls appointing Father Elder were signed by Pius IX on January 9, 1857, nevertheless, they were not received by him until April 4 of that year.

After being consecrated by Archbishop Kenrick, Archbishop of Baltimore, Bishop Elder set out for Natchez and arrived there on May 30, the eve of Pentecost. Much work lay before him as the diocese was yet in its infancy.[130]

In a report to the Propagation of the Faith, Bishop Elder gives the following account of the status of his diocese:

> The population (of the state) in 1850 was 606,000 of whom 309,000 were negro slaves. There are no large cities, Natchez being the largest with less than 5,000 inhabitants.... There are few places large enough to support a resident priest. Hitherto, unhappily our priests have been still fewer, so that all do not reside in fixed congregations. Their support is small and they are exercised pretty well in the spirit of the Apostle....
>
> The number of Catholics was stated in the Almanac several years ago to be about ten thousand.... It is necessary for you to understand that more than half our population consists of Negro slaves who number 309,000, besides free Negroes to the number of 930. These poor Negroes form in some respects my chief anxiety.... Commonly, their masters are well disposed to allow them religious instructions, and sometimes they pay ministers to come and preach on the plantation.... The Negroes must be attended in great measure on the plantation, because ... in our case there are so few churches, and even where there is a church, the Negroes of four or five plantations would fill it up and leave no room for the whites.... The priests then must go to the plantations, and these are scattered through the country.... They are not ill disposed toward religion.

[130] Meline and McSweeney, *Story of the Mountain* (Emmitsburg, 1911), p. 522 (hereafter cited Meline and McSweeney).

> Indeed they often have a craving for its ministrations. . . .
> The number of our priests at present is thirteen, of whom two are quite infirm. One will be obliged to spend some months yet in learning the English language. . . . I hope to ordain one more in a few weeks. Eleven of these priests are residing at churches where there are regular congregations, needing Mass every Sunday. Of all our clergy, I myself am the only native of the United States. . . .
> We have at present eleven churches built, one more is in the process of erection and in another place a small building serves now as a chapel which afterwards will be made the pastor's house. Five of these churches are of brick, the rest of wood.
> There are nine young men preparing for the missions of the diocese, but they are studying in various places according as I was able to make arrangements with the least expense. We have one college conducted by the Brothers of the Christian Schools at Bay St. Louis. Some of the pastors have established parochial schools and others are trying to do so as soon as they can. I urge them all to be very diligent in this regard.
> There is one orphan asylum for girls and also a day-school kept by the Daughters of Saint Vincent of Paul. It is at Natchez and contains seventy orphans and forty day scholars. The sisters are nine. There is an academy for young ladies—a boarding school —kept at Sulphur Springs, in the interior of the country about 150 miles from Natchez, by the Sisters of St. Joseph. It has about twenty-five boarders and twenty day scholars. The same sisters have a day school for small boys. The sisters are seven. There is another house of the Sisters of St. Joseph from Bourg, at Bay St. Louis. They are four in number and have a day school of fifty girls.[131]

Having thus become acquainted with his diocese, Bishop Elder outlined plans for its future development. To help him in his work he appointed Father Grignon, a priest at Natchez, as his Vicar General. However, the Bishop's plans were to a great extent stymied by the advent of the war

[131] Gerow, *Catholicity in Mississippi*, pp. 51-54.

between the states. The war years were trying for the Bishop. Many of his priests were scattered ministering to the soldiers, while he himself was a frequent visitor to the battlefields. After the occupation of the State by Federal troops, he came into conflict with the authorities at Natchez. In fact, for a time he was imprisoned.[132]

From the termination of the war until his transfer to Cincinnati, Bishop Elder labored zealously for the interests of his diocese. During this time an orphanage for boys and a cathedral school were opened at Natchez, both conducted by the Brothers of the Sacred Heart.[133]

But Bishop Elder had yet another cross to carry before leaving the diocese. In 1878 yellow fever raged furiously in the State. Priests, sisters and brothers labored zealously among the victims, as did the Bishop himself. But the toll was heavy. Within a short time six priests had succumbed to the disease. The Bishop himself was afflicted but God spared him for future labors.

In 1878 Rome appointed Bishop Elder Coadjutor Archbishop of San Francisco. However, at his request the Holy See permitted him to remain at Natchez until his successor should be appointed. This respite was not of long duration. On January 30, 1880, the Holy See officially appointed Bishop Elder as Coadjutor Archbishop of Cincinnati. Consequently, on April 14, 1880, he left Natchez for his new See.

Perhaps the most significant event of Bishop Elder's administration from a canonical point of view was his convocation of the First Synod of the diocese in 1858.[134] This synod was subsequently followed by synods held in 1862 and 1874.[135] Bishop Elder was likewise the first Bishop to govern

[132] Gerow, *Cradle Days*, pp. 145-184; *Catholicity in Mississippi*, pp. 59-62.

[133] Gerow, *Catholicity in Mississippi*, p. 56.

[134] *Synodus dioecesana Natchetensis prima, habita a Gulielmo Henrico Elder* (New Orleans, 1858).

[135] *Acta Synodi dioecesanae Natchetensis anno 1862 celebratae; Synodus dioecesana Natchetensis habita diebus 19, 20, 21 mensis Januarii, 1874, a Gulielmo Henrico Elder, in monasterio cui nomen*

the diocese under the decrees of the recent Provincial Council of New Orleans, convened on January 20, 1856.[136] Moreover, Bishop Elder attended the Second Provincial Council of New Orleans in 1864.[137]

After the departure of Bishop Elder, Father Janssens, then administrator of the Diocese of Richmond, was appointed to the See of Natchez. On May 1, 1881, he was consecrated in St. Peter's Cathedral, Richmond, by Archbishop James Gibbons of Baltimore and on May 7 he arrived at Natchez.[138]

Shortly after his arrival Bishop Janssens set out to get acquainted with his diocese. On his visitation, passing through the counties in the central part of the State inhabited by the Choctaw Indians, he saw their spiritual desolation. Consequently, when in May, 1882, he returned to his native country, Holland, he sought for a priest to minister to these people. He was successful and in September, 1882, he returned to the diocese accompanied by Father Bekkers. Subsequently, Father Bekkers settled among the Indians, and started a mission—perhaps the first since the departure of the Jesuits in 1763, and the foundation of what is today the Holy Rosary Mission at Tucker.

Like his predecessors, Bishop Janssens took a great interest in improving the cathedral and to him was reserved the pleasure and privilege of seeing the structure finally solemnly consecrated on September 9, 1886.[139]

The growth of the Church during the administration of

"St. Theresa's Retreat" patrum congregationis SS. Redemptoris apud Chatawa. (There are no extant records of the second Synod; the above are the third and fourth respectively).

136 In compliance with the request of the Seventh Provincial Council of Baltimore, the Holy See in 1850 established the Province of New Orleans with the following suffragans: Mobile, Natchez, Little Rock and Galveston.—Shearer, pp. 256, 257.

137 *Concilium Neo-Aurelianense Provinciale Primum, habitum anno 1856* (New Orleans, 1857) *Concilium Neo-Aurelianense Provinciale Secundum* (New Orleans, 1864).

138 Gerow, *Catholicity in Mississippi*, p. 64.

139 Gerow, *Catholicity in Mississippi*, pp. 65, 66; *Sketch*, pp. 50-52.

Bishop Janssens is shown by comparing the statistics of the diocese in the Catholic Directories of 1881 and 1889. The Catholic population increased from 12,500 to 15,174 and secular priests from nineteen to thirty. Churches and schools likewise showed an increase.

Two years before his departure, Bishop Janssens convoked the Fifth Synod of the diocese, September 17 and 18, 1886.[140]

On August 7, 1888, Natchez was again deprived of its chief shepherd. The Holy See appointed Bishop Janssens to the See of New Orleans as its Archbishop. Following his departure on September 13, the diocese was administered by Father Theophile Meerschaert whom Bishop Janssens had appointed as administrator.

The next incumbent of the See of Natchez was Bishop Heslin, formerly pastor of St. Michael's Church in New Orleans. Following his consecration in New Orleans on June 18, by Archbishop Janssens, he arrived at Natchez on June 23 of that year and took canonical possession of his See.

Bishop Heslin felt that his first duty was to get acquainted with his diocese. Accordingly, after a delay of ten days in Natchez, he set out on his visitation tour. Before the end of the year he had visited the principal churches of the diocese and had administered Confirmation in many of these churches.[141]

In 1891 he left the diocese to make his *ad limina* visit and on his way visited his native home in Ireland. During his travels he succeeded in enlisting the services of some twelve young seminarians who volunteered to devote their lives as priests to the missions in Mississippi.

On his return from Europe, Bishop Heslin took steps to provide more effective spiritual care for the Negroes of the state. Up to this time there was not one church in the diocese giving its entire service to the colored. There were small

[140] *Synodus dioecesana Natchetensis quinta habita, diebus 16, 17 mensis Septembris, A.D. 1886, Francis Janssens.*

[141] Gerow, *Catholicity in Mississippi*, pp. 69-71.

groups of colored Catholics here and there attending the general church, and six small schools for colored, but no significant effort had been made to provide for their spiritual welfare due to the lack of priests. In 1899 Bishop Heslin invited the Society of St. Joseph—the Josephites—to send missionaries into the diocese to work among the Negroes. The invitation was accepted and within a few years resident priests were established at Holy Family Parish, Natchez, St. Peter's, Pascagoula, and Pass Christian.

In addition to the Josephites, the Bishop also succeeded in obtaining the services of the Society of the Divine Word. He assigned the northern half of the diocese, including Vicksburg, Jackson and Meridian, to the Society. By 1910 the Divine Word Fathers had established missions in Jackson, Vicksburg and Meridian.[142]

During the administration of Bishop Heslin, two diocesan synods were convened, the sixth in 1892 and the seventh in 1897.[143] In addition to these synods, the Bishop issued many pastoral letters for the guidance of his clergy and people.

On February 11, 1911, Bishop Heslin, worn out by his arduous labors, passed to his eternal reward.

Bishop Heslin was succeeded by Bishop Gunn, a Marist father, who at the time of his appointment by the Holy See, was laboring at Atlanta. On August 29 he was consecrated by Archbishop Blanc of New Orleans and on September 14 he arrived at Natchez and took canonical possession.

Like that of his predecessors, Bishop Gunn's first year in the diocese was a period of reconnaissance as it were. He visited everywhere, the poorest and most distant missions. He became acquainted with the pastors and their struggles with the people and their needs.

Having seen that many of his flock, scattered over the vast area of the state, had to content themselves with occasional

[142] Gerow, *Catholicity in Mississippi*, pp. 73, 74.

[143] *Synodus dioecesana Natchetensis sexta habita, mense Aprilis, A.D. 1892, a Thoma Heslin; Synodus dioecesana Natchetensis septima habita fine Aprilis principioque mensis Maii, 1897, a Thoma Heslin.*

visits from a priest, and thus were often deprived of the Mass and the sacraments for long periods at a time, he determined to build small churches in the midst of each little group of the faithful. In this endeavor he was generously assisted by the Catholic Church Extension Society. Each year two, three, or four new chapels arose in the missions so that by the end of his administration it could be said that practically every group of Catholics in the diocese was within reach of a chapel and of Mass at least once a month. In addition to these chapels, eight other parishes with resident pastors were established.

In January, 1915, Bishop Gunn left Natchez for Pass Christian because of his ill health and remained there until his death on February 22, 1924.[144]

During the thirteen years of Bishop Gunn's administration, the condition of the Church in the state of Mississippi greatly improved. The Catholic population increased from 17,355 to 31,387 and was ministered to by sixty priests including religious and secular. The Eighth Diocesan Synod was held during the administration of Bishop Gunn and constituted the most comprehensive treatment of the rules and discipline affecting the diocese that had been issued up to this time.[145]

[144] Gerow, *Catholicity in Mississippi*, pp. 79-82.

[145] *Constitutiones Dioecesios Natchetensis quae in Synodo Dioecesana Octava Die 14 Julii, 1922, habita in Ecclesia Parochiali Bay St. Louis, a Revmo. Ioanne Edwardo Gunn.* (Jackson, Mississippi, 1922).

CHAPTER II

CANONICAL AND CIVIL LEGISLATION GOVERNING THE TENURE OF CHURCH PROPERTY IN MISSISSIPPI

In accordance with its divine commission to teach the gospel to every creature, the Church knows no territorial limits, but establishes itself in every nation to bring to its citizens the teaching of Christ. Being an external visible society of men, it is evident that the Church must have temporal possessions for the fulfillment of its mission. The exercise of external worship, the support of its ministers, as well as the care of orphans, of the sick and the aged, the education of youth, all involve the need of temporal possessions. Hence, the Church has always asserted its native right to acquire, hold and administer temporal goods, free and independent of the civil authority, for the attainment of the purpose for which it was founded. In the course of history, temporal society has accepted this claim of the Church only in varying degrees. In the United States, and in Mississippi in particular, the right of the Church to acquire, hold and administer temporal goods is completely subject to the civil authority.

Article 1. Canonical Legislation

Section 1. The Law of the Code

A. The Concept of Moral Personality

Fundamental to an understanding of the tenure of Church property in Canon Law is the concept of moral personality. A personality in the juridical order is a subject of rights.[1]

[1] Vermeersch-Cruesen, *Epitome Iuris Canonici* (3 vols., 7. ed., Mechliniae-Romae: H. Dessain, 1949), I, n. 206, p. 185 (hereafter cited Vermeersch-Cruesen).

Every man is a subject of rights in the natural order. Through membership in society positive rights are added to those which are man's by nature.[2] For example through baptism a man becomes a member of the Church and acquires all the rights and duties proper to a christian.[3]

In every human society, however, there are certain aims which only indirectly affect physical persons or exceed the limited capacity of the latter as to resources or as to duration, but which provide a necessary or highly useful contribution to the attainment or preservation of the society's interests. To promote these aims the law recognizes determined entities (institutions, corporate bodies) as capable of having rights and obligations. These entities, existing in contemplation of law, are variously termed in legal systems as moral or juridic persons or as in Anglo-American law, which recognizes juridic capacity in corporate bodies only, corporations.[4]

It must be noted, however, that this concept of a juridic entity with which we are so familiar today is not a self-evident and natural idea. Actually, in the course of history different forms were developed to give expression to this concept,[5] but it is to Roman Law more than any other legal system that the origin of the concept is due.[6]

B. *The Origin of the Concept of Moral Personality*

The concept of juristic or moral person, as an entity

[2] *Loc. cit.*

[3] Can. 87: Baptismate homo constituitur in Ecclesia Christi persona cum omnibus christianorum iuribus et officiis, nisi ad iura quod pertinet, obstet obex, ecclesiasticae communionis vinculum impediens, vel lata ab Ecclesia censura.

[4] Abbo-Hannan, *The Sacred Canons* (2 vols., St. Louis: B. Herder Book Co., 1952), I, 144 (hereafter cited Abbo-Hannan). Beste, *Introductio In Codicem* (4 ed., Neapoli: M. D'Auria, 1956), p. 156 (hereafter cited Beste).

[5] Sohm-Leddie, *The Institutes—A Textbook of the History and System of Roman Private Law* (3. ed., Oxford: At the Clarendon Press, 1907), p. 186 (hereafter cited Sohm-Leddie).

[6] Michiels, *Principia Generalia de Personis in Ecclesia* (2. ed., Parisiis-Tornaci-Romae: Desclée, 1955), p. 348 (hereafter cited Michiels).

juridically distinct from physical persons and endowed with its own proper and distinct rights, was entirely unknown to earlier Roman Law. The old *ius privatum* (the *ius civile*) was throughout a law for the individual (*civis*) only, and hence, as far as the ancient private law of Rome was concerned there could be no subject of rights and duties other than a natural person, i.e., an individual.[7] It is true that these could unite to form societies, for example, clubs and trade guilds (*collegia, sodalitates*), but these were without proprietary capacity. The property designed for the purposes of the society had to be formally vested in the individual members and treated as their separate property. Hence, the idea that a society as such could have property of its own was unknown to the ancient private law of Rome, at least as far as private societies were concerned.[8]

In the field of the *ius publicum* and *ius sacrum*, the *civitas romana,* that is, the totality of the Roman people and the national gods, possessed juridic capacity but were not moral or juridic persons in the strict sense of the word.[9] The property of both the gods and the state was considered as *res extra commercium,* that is, as things standing outside the range of ordinary dealings. It was considered as *res publicae* as opposed to *res privatae.* It was not in fact owned by any private individual nor could it in law be so owned.[10] The state and the national gods, therefore, were not juridic persons in the strict sense. Whatever they possessed was *extra commercium*; it could neither be owned nor in any way disposed of by private persons. In other words they

[7] Michiels, p. 349; Sohm-Leddie, p. 187.

[8] Sohm-Leddie, p. 187.

[9] Michiels, p. 349.

[10] "Quae publicae sunt, nullius in bonis esse, ipsius enim universitatis esse creduntur; privatae autem sunt, quae singulorum sunt."—*Corpus Iuris Civilis* (Ed. stereotypa quinta decima, Vol. I, *Institutiones,* recognivit Paulus Krueger, *Digesta,* recognovit Theodorus Mommsen, retractavit Paulus Krueger, Berolina: apud Weidmannos, 1928), Digesta (1, 8), 1, #1 (hereafter cited D.).

were considered something transcendent as far as private law was concerned.[11]

The concept of juristic or moral person was not introduced into the private law of Rome until the Empire. Its appearance was due, to a great extent, to the development of the system of municipal government which took place towards the close of the Republic.[12] The property of the *municipium,* or town community, was brought within the rules of private law, the *municipium* being thus allowed to rank as a person capable of private rights and duties.[13] After the example of these municipalities, lawful societies (*collegia, sodalitates, universitates*) were also acknowledged to have proprietary capacity for the purposes of private law.[14] Finally, when the property of the Emperor, the *fiscus Caesaris,* came to be more and more avowedly identified with the property of the state, the Roman State too, in the form of the *fiscus* came to be regarded as a person in private law.[15]

Thus was born the "collegiate moral person"; a new entity, existing in contemplation of law, capable of rights and duties and entirely distinct from the individuals which composed it.[16] Nevertheless, it must be remembered that nowhere in Roman Law will the distinction between physical and moral person be found. Yet the sources indicate sufficiently the principal elements of the concept.

So far reference has been made to what would now be

[11] Cf. Brown, *The Canonical Juristic Personality with Special Reference to Its Status in the United States,* The Catholic University of America Canon Law Studies, n. 39 (Washington, D.C.: The Catholic University of America, 1927), pp. 9, 10 (hereafter cited Brown).

[12] Michiels, p. 350.

[13] Sohm-Leddie, p. 189.

[14] Sohm-Leddie, pp. 189, 190. "Quibus autem permissum est corpus habere collegii societatis sine eiusque alterius eorum nomine proprium est ad exemplum rei publicae habere res communes, arcam communem et actorem sive syndicum, per quam tamquam in republica quod communiter agi fieri oporteat fiat."—D. (3, 4), 7, #1.

[15] Sohm-Leddie, *loc. cit.*

[16] "Si quid universitati debetur, singulis non debetur, nec quod debet universitas, singuli debent."—D. (3, 4), 7, #1.

called "collegiate moral personalities" or "corporations." There remains to be discussed the origin of the non-collegiate moral personality of the Code of Canon Law, often referred to by authors by the term *universitas bonorum.*[17]

It seems certain that this entity was unknown not only in the ancient but also in classical Roman Law. Some traces of the institute may be seen in the foundation of charitable institutions by the emperors to care for the material needs of the poor children of Italy. However, these institutions did not enjoy a distinct juridic personality but were merely state undertakings, functioning by the grace of the emperor.[18]

At the time of Justinian the institute appeared in three forms:

(1) The institute was thought of as a fund administered by an individual person. Here the connection between the individual and the fund was necessary.

(2) The institute could have its *persona* in a corporation. Property was left to a corporation which administered it, but the property itself was not thought of as capable of standing alone.

(3) The institute could stand alone as an independent personality. It is this notion of the institute at the time of Justinian which is not clear and certain. However, the sources indicate a trend in the legal doctrine of the period to endow this institute with a distinct personality.

As a matter of fact, however, it was actually Canon Law which developed the theory of the *universitas bonorum* (the non-collegiate moral person), personifying the common ideal end to which masses of property, money and land had been dedicated.[19]

C. The Concept of Moral Personality in the Code of Canon Law

It was under Roman Law that the Church began to func-

[17] Brown, p. 19.

[18] Sohm-Leddie, pp. 196, 197; Brown, p. 19.

[19] Brown, pp. 19-21.

tion; hence, it is not surprising that it accepted the Roman concept of moral personality to give legal expression to its rights.[20] Moreover, after the period of persecutions Roman Law recognized the Church as a perfect, sovereign society, that is, as a perfect juridic society in itself and possessing the right to utilize inferior moral persons in the attainment of its end.[21] Wherefore, the concept of moral personality as it exists in the Code is merely the Roman concept, developed and refined by the canonical jurisprudence of past centuries.

The Code does not define moral person; however, the various canons which deal with the concept express its essential elements. A moral person in the Church may be defined as a juridic entity, constituted by an act of a competent authority for a charitable or religious purpose, existing independently of other persons and endowed with the capacity of acquiring rights as well as of contracting obligations by means of and to the extent determined by competent authority.[22]

D. Creation of Moral Persons in the Church

Before determining the title and conditions on which the juridic personality of moral persons existing within the Church is founded, the Code recalls the fundamental constitutive principle of the Church itself. Juridic personality, granted by the Church to determined groups of persons or things, presupposes as a necessary foundation that the Church itself by divine institution is a juridically perfect society endowed with perfect juridic personality, by virtue of which it enjoys the power of using all the means necessary to attain the end determined by its divine founder.[23] Canon 100 states that the Catholic Church and the Apostolic See have the *ratio* or character of a moral person by divine

[20] Wernz-Vidal, *Ius Canonicum ad Normam Codicis Exactum* (7 vols. in 8, Romae: Apud Aedes Universitatis Gregorianae, Vol. II, 3. ed., 1943; Vol. IV, Pars II, 1935), II, n. 25 (hereafter cited Wernz-Vidal).

[21] Brown, p. 27.

[22] Beste, p. 156; Abbo-Hannan, I, 144; cf. canons 99, 100 #1, 87.

[23] Michiels, p. 371.

ordination.[24] The proof of this statement pertains to theology and public ecclesiastical law. It is sufficient to state here that the Church is a perfect juridic society and has the right to use all the means conducive to the attainment of its end and in particular the creation of inferior moral persons. The term Apostolic See as used in this canon signifies the primacy of the Roman Pontiff, that is, the office of the Roman Pontiff inclusive of its respective organs as they exist in the concrete, constituted for the benefit of all christians to preserve the unity of faith through which the faithful may the more easily reach their eternal destiny.[25]

The creation of inferior moral persons in the Church is dependent entirely on ecclesiastical authority. This logically follows from the nature of the Church as a supernatural society, destined to a supernatural end. Wherefore, to exercise rights in the Church an ecclesiastical moral person must have a relation to the supernatural end of the Church, that is, to the public religious good, the care of which is entrusted to ecclesiastical authority alone.[26] There is thus implied the incompetency of the civil power in the creation of any ecclesiastical moral person.

Moral persons in the Church are of two kinds, collegiate and non-collegiate according as they result either from an association of physical persons,[27] enjoying in this case a personality distinct from that of the members (v.g., a religious congregation, chapter), or from an aggregation of specified things or goods (v.g., seminaries, hospitals, churches).[28] These elements, the plurality of persons or the aggregation of specified things or goods, constitute the material element of the respective moral person. The formal element, the sanction of public authority, may be granted either by provision of law or by a special decree emanating from a com-

[24] Can. 100, #1.

[25] Abbo-Hannan, I, 145; Wernz-Vidal, II, n. 29.

[26] Wernz-Vidal, II, n. 27.

[27] Can. 100, #2: "Persona moralis collegialis constitui non potest nisi ex tribus saltem personis physicis."

[28] Can. 99.

petent ecclesiastical authority.[29] In both cases the attribution may be effected either implicitly or explicitly, in so far as there is an explicit statement to that effect, or the law or the decree attributes to the entity some capacity which can exist only in a moral person, v.g., the capacity for ownership of property, or the capacity to sue and be sued, etc.[30]

It should be noted that this twofold method of obtaining moral personality in the Church is not to be understood in a conjunctive sense, viz., in the sense that one and the same entity can achieve moral personality in the Church in either of these ways. Accordingly, this twofold method is to be understood disjunctively, so that certain entities always can be classified as moral personalities created by the law itself, while others can obtain their juridic personality only from the proper ecclesiastical authority by means of special formal decree to that effect.[31]

The reason for the distinction is based on the nature and finality of the different entities. Those ecclesiastical moral personalities which are brought into being by the very operation of law itself are those entities which are either absolutely or relatively necessary to the social-public life of the Church for its well ordered operation and existence. On the other hand, those moral personalities which are brought into being by a special decree of a competent ecclesiastical superior are not necessary but useful for the Church in the pursuit of its ultimate end.[32]

E. The Juridical Capacity of Moral Persons in the Church

Whatever may be the juridic capacity of moral persons in civil law, in ecclesiastical law the general principle is that the juridic capacity of moral persons is the same as that of any member of the faithful. Hence, they can acquire and possess all the rights proper to physical persons ex-

[29] Can. 100, #1; cf. Abbo-Hannan, I, p. 144.
[30] Michiels, p. 400.
[31] Michiels, pp. 398, 399.
[32] Michiels, pp. 399, 340.

cepting those which from the nature of the matter or from the positive provisions of law are proper to physical persons alone, v.g., the right to marry. Accordingly, a moral person has a right to a name, seal, honorary titles, etc.[33]

Moral persons, however, enjoy the favor of the law for they enjoy the same protection under the law as minors.[34] The reason for this provision is obvious. For just as a minor can easily suffer detriment from the negligence of his tutor or guardian, so also a moral person, which can act only through an administrator or rector in the administration of its goods and in the defense of its rights,[35] needs the protection of the law. Hence, a moral person, like a minor can maintain an action for a *restitutio in integrum*.[36]

The fundamental principle with regard to the property rights of moral persons is enunciated in canon 1495. The canon states that the Catholic Church and the Apostolic See have an inherent right, without restriction and independent of the civil authority, to acquire, own and administer temporal property in the prosecution of the ends for which they were established. In the second paragraph of the canon this right is vindicated for individual churches[37] and other

[33] Michiels, p. 456.

[34] Can. 100, #3: "Personae morales sive collegiales sive non-collegiales minoribus aequiparantur."

[35] Cf. cans. 512, 535, 536, 1491, 1519-1523, 1525-1528, 1530-1536, 1653, 1682, 1676. The norms governing the actions of moral persons is beyond the scope of this treatment. Suffice it to indicate that a collegiate moral person may act *per se* (can. 101), but this manner of acting is less suitable for certain juridic acts, as the administration of its goods or defense of its rights; hence, the necessity of acting through an administrator. Non-collegiate moral persons cannot act *per se* as is obvious, but only through administrators. The norms governing the actions of the latter are determined by both the common law and particular statutes (Can. 101, 2°, #2.).

[36] Can. 1687, #2.

[37] In 1953, the Code Commission gave an affirmative reply to the following question: Whether the words of canon 1495, #2, of the Code of Canon Law, *ecclesiis singularibus* are to be understood also, and perhaps primarily, of dioceses? Code Comm., 23 June, 1953—Bouscaren, *The Canon Law Digest* (4 vols., Milwaukee: Bruce

moral persons which have been established as juridic persons by ecclesiastical authority.[38]

Prior to the promulgation of the Code there were various theories as to the precise subject of the ownership of ecclesiastical property. Some canonists contended that ecclesiastical property was owned by God, Christ, or the saints; others maintained that it was owned by the Roman Pontiff, or the Universal Church; still others maintained that the poor formed the subject of dominion.[39] While these theories may indicate their ultimate purpose and sacred character, they do not designate their legal owner. Wherefore, the Code explicitly states, as the best canonists had taught for some time, that the title to ecclesiastical property is vested in the particular moral person that has legitimately acquired it, under supreme authority of the Holy See.[40] The Holy See therefore enjoys not the right of ownership, but the right of control or as it is technically called, the right of eminent domain, whereby it can for a sufficient reason, limit the property rights of ecclesiastical entities.[41]

F. The Extinction of Moral Personalities in the Church

An ecclesiastical moral person is of its nature perpetual. It becomes juridically extinct, however, on suppression by competent authority or where it has been out of factual existence

Publishing Co., Vol. I, 1934; Vol. II, 1943; Vol. III, 1954, edited by T. Lincoln Bouscaren; Vol. IV, 1958, edited by T. Lincoln Bouscaren and James I. O'Connor), IV, 391.

[38] Can. 1495, #1: "Ecclesia Catholica et Apostolica Sedes nativum ius habent libere et independenter a civili potestate acquirendi, retinendi et administrandi bona temporalia ad fines sibi proprios prosequendos. #2: Etiam ecclesiis singularibus aliisque personis moralibus quae ab ecclesiastica auctoritate in iuridicam personam erectae sint, ius est, ad normam sacrorum canonum, bona temporalia acquirendi, retinendi et administrandi."

[39] Cf. Wernz-Vidal, IV, Pars II, nn. 739-741.

[40] Can. 1499, #2: "Dominium bonorum, sub suprema auctoritate Sedis Apostolicae, ad eam pertinet moralem personam, quae eadem bona legitime acquisiverit."

[41] Vermeersh-Cruesen, II, n. 821, p. 574.

for a period of one hundred years.[42]

With regard to the first method of suppression, the competent authority generally would be the authority by which it was established or the successors or superiors of that authority.[43] However, there are exceptions to this general rule, where it is provided otherwise by general or particular law.[44] In either case, non-ecclesiastical power would be entirely incompetent to effect a dissolution.[45]

The second method by which an ecclesiastical moral person becomes *de iure* extinct occurs when the moral person has ceased to be active for one hundred years.[46] This principle applies equally to both collegiate and non-collegiate moral persons. It is verified in the latter case when the substratum of goods is entirely destroyed or irrevocably removed from its possession,[47] and in the case of collegiate moral persons, upon the resignation or death of every member of the group, when at the same time there is no replacement of membership, or upon the voluntary act of the group dissolving itself. It must be noted, however, that if but a single member of a collegiate moral personality survives, all its rights and powers become centered in that one survivor.[48]

In addition to the above mentioned modes of extinction equivalent extinction occurs when there is a merger or con-

[42] Can. 102, #1: "Persona moralis, natura sua, perpetua est; extinguitur tamen si a legitima auctoritate supprimatur, vel si per centum annorum spatium esse desierit."

[43] Abbo-Hannan, I, 149.

[44] Cans. 493, 1494, 1422.

[45] Beste, p. 160.

[46] Can. 102, #1: "Persona moralis ... extinguitur ... si per centum annorum spatium esse desierit."

[47] Cf. Michiels, pp. 542, 543, where he gives the following examples: when a church is totally destroyed, or has deteriorated in such a way that divine services can no longer be conducted there; when the endowment of a benefice or the payment which is due to it ceases to exist; or when the patrimony, in virtue of which a charitable institute was established, ceases to exist.

[48] Can. 102, #2: "Si vel unum ex personae moralis collegialis membris supersit, ius omnium in illud recidit."

solidation of moral persons.[49] Likewise, equivalent extinction occurs when a moral person dissolves its union with the Church, either through heresy or schism. In this case its moral personality together with its consequent rights automatically ceases. It is of interest to note that the civil law follows the same principle in determining property rights of schismatic churches.[50]

G. Destination of the Property of an Extinct Moral Personality in the Church

One further question remains to be treated: what is to to be done with the property of a moral personality in the Church which has become extinct? The law of the Church provides for this eventuality in canon 1501. The canon states that if a moral personality in the Church becomes extinct, its goods are to belong to the moral personality immediately superior to it, subject always to the will and the intentions of the founders and benefactors, to the legally vested rights, and to the special laws which governed the extinct moral person.

SECTION 2. PONTIFICAL AND CONCILIAR DECREES REGARDING TENURE OF CHURCH PROPERTY IN THE UNITED STATES

The principles enunciated in the foregoing section, namely, that the Catholic Church is a perfect juridical society with the inherent right to establish inferior moral persons, have not been recognized by the laws of the United States with the exception of its territorial possessions.[51]

This lack of recognition may be traced to the fact that under the Common Law of England the so called Concession Theory of Corporations is followed. "The corporation is,

[49] Can. 1419, 1°: "Unio beneficiorum est: Exstinctiva, cum aut ex suppressis duobus vel pluribus beneficiis novum atque unicum beneficium efficitur, aut unum vel plura ita alii uniuntur ut esse desinant."

[50] Vromant, *De Bonis Ecclesiae Temporalibus* (3. ed., Bruges-Paris: Desclée de Brouwer, 1953), p. 23 (hereafter cited Vromant).

[51] Santos v. Holy Roman Catholic Church, 212 U.S. 463, 29 S. Ct. 338, 53 L. Ed. 599 (1909).

and must be, the creature of the state. Into its nostrils the state must breathe the breath of fictitious life, for otherwise it would be no animated body, but individualistic dust."[52] Consequently, the Common Law of England hesitated to concede moral personality to the Church *per se.* By a long and devious process of legal reasoning and development it finally compromised on the theory of the corporation sole, whereby the bishop, pastor or other ecclesiastical dignity was recognized as a corporation sole.[53]

The American legal theory of corporations is fundamentally the same as that of the English Law. There can be no corporation which is not the creation of the civil law, and all tenure of property requires civil authority. Hence, this concept precludes legal recognition of the Church as a moral person. However, unlike the Common Law, courts in the United States in general have refused to accept the device of the corporation sole in the absence of enabling legislation.[54]

As a religious society, however, the Catholic Church enjoys the same rights and the same protection as that granted to other religious sects. The First Amendment to the Constitution of the United States provides "Congress shall make no law respecting an establishment of religion or prohibiting the free exercise thereof." The object of this amendment was explained as follows by the Supreme Court in 1889:

> To allow everyone under the jurisdiction of the United States to entertain such notions respecting his relations to his maker and the duties they im-

[52] Gierke-Maitland, *Political Theories of the Middle Ages* (Cambridge, 1900), Translator's Introduction, p. xxx; Blackstone, *Commentaries on the Laws of England* (4 vols., New York, 1852), I, 472.

[53] *Mode of Tenure: Roman Catholic Church Property in the United States,* A Survey by the Legal Department, *National Catholic Welfare Conference* (Washington, D.C.: National Catholic Welfare Conference, 1941, Supplement, 1954), Supplement, p. 5 (hereafter cited as *Mode of Tenure, Survey,* or *Mode of Tenure, Supplement*).

[54] *Mode of Tenure, Supplement,* p. 5; Kain v. Gibboney, I O I. U.S. 362, 25 L. Ed. 813 (1879). The courts of Florida and Georgia have adopted the Common Law concept, recognizing bishops as corporations sole. Cf. *Mode of Tenure, Survey,* pp. 33-37, 39, 40.

> pose, as may be approved by his judgment and conscience, and to exhibit his sentiments in such form of worship as he may think proper, not injurious to the equal rights of others, and to prohibit legislation for the support of any religious tenets or the modes of worship of any sect.[55]

The provisions of this amendment, when first enacted were binding on the Federal Government alone.[56] Hence, any action taken by an individual state establishing some religion and prohibiting the free exercise of all other religions would not be in contravention of it.[57] However, by an elliptic judicial interpretation it is now applicable to all of the states through the "due process" clause of the Fourteenth Amendment.[58]

The individual states, however, adopted the same view as the Federal Government towards religion. Article 1, sects. 3 and 4 of the Constitution adopted by the people of Mississippi in 1817, for example, provided:

> The exercise and enjoyment of religious profession and worship without discrimination shall ever be free to all persons in this state; no preference shall ever be given by law to any religious sect or mode of worship.[59]

These provisions were incorporated into the subsequent constitutions of the State adopted in 1832 and 1869.[60] The pertinent provisions of the present Constitution, adopted on November 1, 1890, are no less specific in their exclusion of a

[55] Davis v. Beason, 133 U.S. 333, 342, 10 S. Ct. 299, 33 L. Ed. 637 (1889).

[56] By the Tenth Amendment to the Constitution the individual states retained "all the powers not delegated to the United States by the Constitution and not prohibited by it to the States."

[57] Cf. Zollman, *American Church Law* (St. Paul, Minn.: West Publishing Co., 1933), p. 8, #6, 7 (hereafter cited Zollman, *American Church Law*).

[58] Cantwell v. Conn., 310 U.S. 296 (1940); Murdock v. Penn., 319 U.S. 105 (1943); Everson v. Board of Education, 330 U.S. 1 (1947); Zorach v. Clauson, 343 U.S. 306 (1952).

[59] Mississippi Constitution of 1817, Art. 1, sects. 3, 4.

[60] Mississippi Constitution of 1832, Art. 1, sects. 3, 4; Mississippi Constitution of 1869, Art. 1, sect. 23.

state-church and in securing for all freedom of conscience in the worship of God. Art. 111, sect. 18 provides:

> No religious test as a qualification for office shall be required; and no preference shall be given by law to any religious sect or mode of worship, but the free enjoyment of all religious sentiments and the different modes of worship shall be held sacred.

The religious freedom, without preference for any sect, thus granted by Congress and the several states was scarcely realized in the legal enactments concerning church property tenure, particularly in the period preceding the Civil War.[61] State legislatures consistently favored the congregational type of church organization in which control of church property was vested in lay-trustees or held by corporations dominated by laymen. While acceptable to the belief and practice of Protestants, it forced the Catholic Church to conform to a system of laws inconsistent with its constitution and as a result various devices had to be resorted to, to secure legal protection for church property, which on occasion led to the detriment of the Church.

After the Civil War, however, several states departed from the old idea of merely providing for the congregational type of religious society and legislation was secured either specifically providing for the holding of Catholic Church property, or providing a system which, while available to all denominations, was more in conformity with Catholic practice. This trend has continued to the present time, so that practically all states now have some system of legal tenure suitable to the constitution of the Catholic Church.[62] Unfortunately, however, Mississippi laws still favor the congregational type of religious society.

In the light of the foregoing, it is not surprising that the

[61] Dignan, *A History of the Legal Incorporation of Catholic Church Property in the United States, (1784-1932)* (New York: P. J. Kenedy and Sons, 1935), pp. 44, 45 (hereafter cited Dignan).

[62] *Mode of Tenure, Supplement,* p. 6.

problem of the tenure of church property was a perennial subject for discussion and legislation in the Provincial and Plenary Councils of Baltimore. Likewise, the Holy See, cognizant of the difficulties involved, issued opportune instructions and decrees to guide the American Hierarchy.

When the Catholic Church was organized in the United States as a distinct body in 1784 under the jurisdiction of Bishop Carroll, ecclesiastical property, as such, did not exist. In his report to the Sacred Congregation for the Propagation of the Faith dated February 27, 1785, Bishop Carroll stated:

> Priests here (Maryland) are maintained chiefly from the proceeds of the (Jesuit) estates; elsewhere by the liberality of Catholics. There is properly no ecclesiastical property here; for the property by which the priests are supported is held in the names of individuals and transferred by will to devisees. This course was rendered necessary when the Catholic Religion was cramped by adverse civil laws.[63]

Following the Revolution and the founding of the American Republic, Bishop Carroll, in view of the missionary character of his territory, in which many congregations were without a resident priest, authorized and instituted the system of lay-trustees to provide for the tenure of ecclesiastical property.[64] Moreover, he wished, in view of the minority status of Catholics and the precarious position of religious freedom, to assimilate as far as possible the outward administration of Catholic Church property in a way that would harmonize with the democratic principles on which the new government was founded.[65] Subsequently, to secure the stability of church property, the various Catholic congregations either petitioned the respective legislatures for charters of incorporation or became incorporated under the gen-

[63] Cited in Baart, *The Tenure of Catholic Church Property in the United States of America* (Authorized Copy, 1900), pp. 18, 19 (hereafter cited Baart).

[64] Brown, p. 149.

[65] Baart, p. 21.

eral incorporation statutes where such existed.[66]

Whether Bishop Carroll did or did not foresee that this system of lay-control of ecclesiastical property could give rise to many difficulties, in later years he had reason to regret admitting such a system.[67] The lay-trustees, influenced perhaps by the democratic spirit of the age,[68] undertook not only to control ecclesiastical property, but to usurp episcopal jurisdiction in the appointment and dismissal of pastors. Consequently, numerous conflicts arose between ecclesiastical authorities and the lay-trustees to the great detriment of religion.[69]

As a result of these conflicts, Pius VII issued a brief to Archbishop Marechal and his suffragans, in which he condemned the abuses of the trustee system. To help remedy these abuses he entrusted to the Sacred Congregation for the Propagation of the Faith the duty of drawing up certain regulations and instructions concerning the choice and direction of trustees.[70]

In this instruction the Sacred Congregation distinguished between churches already built and those to be built in the future. With regard to the former the instruction provided that congregations be urged: (1) to choose only men of proven piety as trustees; (2) in the election, to lay down definite limits so that the trustees cannot in any way dismiss

[66] Dignan, pp. 52-66. The defects of tenure by trustees without incorporation were recognized early in American Legal History. For upon the death of a trustee, if he were a tenant in common, his interest passed to his heirs; if he had a life estate, it reverted to the original owner, and if he was a joint tenant, it went to the surviving trustees; but in any event, the legal title might be lost or pass into the hands of incompetents. Hence, the enactment of corporation statutes or the grant of charters by special acts of the legislatures.—Brown, pp. 154, 155.

[67] Dignan, p. 93.

[68] Dignan, p. 72.

[69] Cf. Dignan, pp. 67-93.

[70] Brief of Pius VII, *Non sine Magno,* August 24, 1822,—De Martinis, *Iuris Pontificii de Propaganda Fide* (5 vols., Roma: Typographia Polyglotta S.C. de Propaganda Fide, 1892), IV, 620-622 (hereafter cited De Martinis).

at their pleasure pastors approved by the bishop, or exclude them from the church, or deny them the revenues which are necessary for their sustenance; (3) they should by no means admit priests deprived of faculties, and above all under censure; (4) that pastors should be entirely independent of the trustees in the exercise of their sacred ministry; finally (5) that the trustees should concur with the bishop in everything pertaining to sacred things, and that the bishops should have at all times the power to keep the trustees within proper limits.[71]

With regard to churches to be constructed in the future, the Sacred Congregation advised that the bishop should hold them in trust for the congregation and secure their transmission to their successors by a will made in duplicate, one copy of which was to be retained in his own possession, the other copy in the possession of a trustworthy layman. Should, however, the congregation prefer to commit the administration to laymen, the bishop should take care by civil contract, that neither they, nor their successors, be able to abuse it to the detriment of the Church.[72]

Though the Pope did not condemn the trustee system itself, nevertheless, in the First Provincial Council of Baltimore, held seven years after the brief was issued, the basis for its disappearance as a mode of tenure was enunciated in the fifth decree. It provided:

> Since lay trustees have frequently abused the right given them by the civil power to the great detriment of religion, and not without scandal to the faithful, we most earnestly desire that no church be erected or consecrated in the future unless it is assigned by a written document to the bishop in whose diocese it is to be erected, for divine worship and the utility of the faithful, whenever that can be done. . . .[73]

[71] *Instr. de S.C. Cong. de Propaganda Fide,* Julii 27, 1822—cited in footnote (1) De Martinis, IV, 621, 622.

[72] *Loc. cit.*

[73] *Concilia Provincialia Baltimori habita 1829-1849 (Editio Altera,* Baltimori: Apud Ioannem Murphy et Socium, 1851), p. 74 (hereafter cited *Concilia Provincialia*).

The period subsequent to the Council witnessed a drastic change in the tenure of ecclesiastical property. Up to this time ecclesiastical property had been held almost exclusively by trustees, there being a few places where the property was vested in the priest in charge or in the name of the bishop.[74] From this time forward the system of tenure through lay-trustees disappeared with the exception of particular localities, and was replaced by tenure in fee simple.[75]

The Second Provincial Council held on October 20, 1833, did not discuss the question of property tenure. However, the Third Provincial Council which was convoked on April 16, 1837, manifested the growing dissatisfaction with the fee simple tenure which since the First Provincial Council had been spreading at the expense of the old lay-trustee system. The fourth decree warned bishops, priests and all others to whom goods were entrusted for ecclesiastical uses to take care that they secure such goods as soon as possible according to the manner deemed best in each of the states, so that, protected by the civil laws, they may be preserved for the uses designated by the donors.[76]

The Fourth Provincial Council held on May 14, 1840, was again occupied with the problems incident to fee simple tenure and the necessity of obtaining a more satisfactory system. The eighth decree admonished bishops to provide for the security of ecclesiastical property to the best of their ability by seeking the protection of the laws or of the civil authority, without however, prejudicing their own rights. If such protection could not be obtained they should at least, by a will made in duplicate and skillfully drawn up according to the dispositions of the civil law, secure the safe transmission of ecclesiastical property to their successors. Finally, bishops were urged not to permit priests to hold ecclesiastical property in their own names.[77]

In answer to a letter of this Council the Sacred Congrega-

[74] Baart, p. 53.

[75] Cf. Dignan, pp. 148-157.

[76] *Concilia Provincialia*, n. 4, p. 142.

[77] *Concilia Provincialia*, n. 8, p. 172.

tion for the Propagation of the Faith sent an instruction concerning the safeguarding of ecclesiastical goods. The congregation adverted to the fact that ecclesiastical succession was not admitted by the laws of the United States, and that consequently no right was given to bishops or priests to transmit ecclesiastical property to their successors. To provide for its safe transmission, therefore, the Sacred Congregation prescribed the observance of various formalities in the drawing up of wills.[78] The Fathers of the Fifth Provincial Council (1843), realizing that the execution of the instruction would impose grave hardships in view of the special laws of the individual states, and the local circumstances, asked the Holy See to mitigate the instruction. The mitigated form of the instruction as formulated by the Council provided that each bishop was obliged in conscience to make a will in duplicate and deposit one copy with the archbishop, the latter with the senior suffragan, within three months after his consecration. The obligation of seeing that this decree was executed rested with the archbishop.[79]

Neither the Sixth Provincial Council of Baltimore (1846) nor the Seventh (1849) made any advance on the conciliar legislation with respect to the tenure of ecclesiastical property as developed by the preceding councils. That of 1846 made no reference to the problem either in the decrees or in the pastoral letter. The Council of 1849 supposes tenure by the bishop as the normal practice. The Fathers decreed that all churches and other ecclesiastical goods, acquired either by gift or by the offerings of the faithful, belong to the ordinary, unless it appears from a written instrument that

[78] *Decretum Sacrae Congregationis de Propaganda Fide circa Ecclesiastica bona tuto servanda,* Dec. 15, 1840—*Bullarium Pontificium Sacrae Congregationis de Propaganda Fide* (7 vols., Romae: Typis Collegii Urbani, 1839-1841), V, 81-84 (hereafter cited *Bullarium Pontificium de Propaganda Fide*); *Concilia Provincialia,* pp. 198-203.

[79] *Concilia Provincialia,* n. 1, p. 216. The decrees of this Council, inclusive of the amended instruction were approved by the Holy See on September 30, 1843—*Concilia Provincialia,* pp. 228, 229.

they were given to some order of regulars or congregation of priests for their use.[80]

The fact that the Sixth and Seventh Provincial Councils passed no legislation on the subject of church property tenure showed that troubles arising from trusteeism were decreasing in number. However, the problem of tenure was by no means settled as is evidenced by the extensive treatment of the subject in the Plenary Councils, particularly that of the Second and Third.[81]

The legislation of the First Plenary Council (1852) on the subject of tenure was little more than a restatement of what had come to be fixed law from preceding councils. The sixteenth decree forbade laymen to assume the administration of Church property without the free consent of the bishop, while the seventeenth commanded priests not to appoint trustees without the authority of the bishop, nor to allow the faithful to elect trustees or impede the administration of Church property.[82]

The Second Plenary Council of Baltimore which commenced on October 7, 1866, gave the question of the legal tenure of Church property a forthright and thorough treatment. Though no new system of tenure was provided, the legislation of former councils was arranged in systematical order and the rules laid down by the Third Provincial Council of New York determining the powers of lay-trustees were quoted. These rules were similar to those drawn up by the Sacred Congregation for the Propagation of the Faith in 1822, previously referred to. Finally, the Fathers of the Council indicated that since religious liberty is guaranteed by the law of the land there is no reason why the laws of the Church, which were passed up to the present by Councils and Pontiffs for properly acquiring and safely protecting ecclesiastical goods, should not be observed. Moreover, they stated that this full liberty guaranteed by the law can only

[80] *Concilia Provincialia,* n. 4, p. 278.

[81] Cf. Dignan, p. 180.

[82] *Concilium Plenarium Totius Americae Septentrionalis Foederatae* (Baltimori: Apud Ioannem Murphy et Socios, 1852), nn. 16, 17.

be said to exist if the laws and provisions made by the Church itself be also admitted in this respect by the civil forum, and thus given civil force.[83]

In the period preceding the Third Plenary Council of Baltimore there were two developments which to a great extent formulated the legislative enactments on Church property tenure of that council. The liberal attitude adopted by some states resulted, as previously indicated, in legislation either specifically providing for the holding of Catholic Church property, or providing a system which, while available to all denominations, was more in conformity with Catholic practice.[84] This liberal attitude was manifested in the State of New York by a satisfactory incorporation statute, which was subsequently adopted by some other states, and in other jurisdictions by the recognition of the bishop as a corporation sole.[85]

Though these systems of tenure existed prior to the Second Plenary Council, their lack of recognition by this Council was probably due to the fact that the merits of the respective systems had not as yet been tested.

The second development which helped to formulate the legislation of the Council centered around the danger inherent in fee simple tenure as manifested in the cases of Bishop Baraga and Bishop Purcell. Bishop Frederick Baraga, who was born at Treffen Castle in Camiola, Austria, had been transferred from the Vicariate Apostolic of Upper Michigan to the diocese of Sault Sainte Marie, as its first bishop, on January 9, 1857. Following his death in 1868, his will was contested by relatives in Europe. As the property of the diocese was vested in the Bishop in fee simple, it was thought advisable to pay to the relatives a considerable sum of money, rather than to permit the case to enter the

[83] Cf. *Concilii Plenarii Baltimoriensis II in Ecclesia Metropolitana Baltimoriensi habiti, Acta et Decreta* (Baltimorae: Ioannes Murphy, 1868), nn. 182-204.

[84] Dignan, p. 214.

[85] Dignan, pp. 206, 207, 210.

courts, where a judgment for the relatives was not an unlikely possibility.[86]

A somewhat similar case occurred in Ohio. Archbishop Purcell of Cincinnati had agreed, as a private individual, to guarantee the indebtedness of his brother who had undertaken to act as a banker for Cincinnati Catholics. His brother having become bankrupt, creditors sought to recover about two and a half million dollars from Archbishop Purcell by levying on diocesan property, the fee simple of which was vested in him. Fortunately, the Supreme Court of Ohio ruled that Archbishop Purcell did not hold diocesan property as absolute owner, but in trust. The final decision, however, was not handed down until four years after the Council.[87]

On November 6, 1884, the Third Plenary Council convened in Baltimore. As in former councils the question of the tenure of Church property was a subject for legislation, resulting in a detailed analysis of the subject in title IX.

In addition to the reaffirmation of the decrees of the Second Plenary Council, the Fathers stated the right of the Church as a perfect society on the basis of the natural law itself, to possess property for the prosecution of its mission.[88] As in the Second Plenary Council the Fathers lamented the fact that the laws of many states were based upon principles opposed to the discipline of the Church. The methods of tenure then in existence were given in the order of desirability.

> In the states in which a civil legal incorporation of parishes or of ecclesiastical congregations, in harmony with ecclesiastical laws does not exist, the bishop himself, by a law to be passed in the assemblies may become a corporation sole to hold and administer the goods of the entire diocese; or the property of the diocese can possibly be committed to the bishop in trust, so that, he may hold it in the

[86] Cf. Baart, p. 68.

[87] Mannix v. Purcell, 46 Ohio 102 (1888).

[88] Cf. *Acta et Decreta Concilii Plenarii Baltimorensis Tertii,* A.D. 1884 (Baltimorae: Typis Ioannis Murphy et Sociorum, 1886), Tit. IX, Cap. ii, n. 265 (hereafter cited *Acta et Decreta Concilii Plenarii III*).

> name of the diocese and administer it for the benefit of the diocese in accordance with the mind of the Church; or as a last resort, the bishop may hold and administer the temporal goods of the diocese in his own name, by that absolute and full title of right, which in English is termed in fee simple, in which case the bishop is by all means to be mindful, that no matter how complete dominion of ecclesiastical goods is given him by the secular power, according to the admonition of the sacred canons he has not dominion of them but is merely their administrator.[89]

In decree 268, the bishops were commanded, lest the goods dedicated to divine worship or pious works be diverted to other uses, to draw up a double inventory; one containing an accurate description of the ecclesiastical goods which the bishop held in fee simple, or in trust, or as a corporation sole; the other describing his personal possessions. In the subsequent decree, the bishops were again warned that they were obliged in conscience to draw up a will, or other legal document in duplicate to secure the transmission of Church property to their successors, where this property was held in their own names. One copy was to be retained in the diocesan archives, the other in archives of the metropolitan. The metropolitan was obliged to deposit a copy of his will with the senior suffragan. In this regard the Council urged that the civil laws of the respective states be observed and the entire matter complied with within three months from their consecration.[90]

In 1911 the Sacred Congregation of the Council, while recommending the provisions of the Third Plenary Council, issued the following instruction to be used as a uniform norm in the matter of tenure in the entire American Republic. It provided:

> (1). Among the methods which are now in use in the United States for holding and administering Church property, the one known as Parish Corpora-

[89] *Acta et Decreta Concilii Plenarii III,* n. 267.

[90] *Acta et Decreta Concilii Plenarii III,* nn. 268, 269.

> tion is preferable to the others, but with the conditions and safeguards which are now in use in the State of New York. The Bishops therefore should immediately take steps to introduce this method for the handling of property in their dioceses, if the civil law allows it. If the civil law does not allow it they should exert their influence with the civil authorities that it may be made legal as soon as possible.
> (2). Only in those places where the civil law does not recognize Parish Corporations, and until such recognition is obtained, the method commonly called Corporation Sole is allowed, but with the understanding that in the administration of ecclesiastical property the Bishop is to act with the advice and in more important matters with the consent of those who have an interest in the premises and of the diocesan consultors, this being a conscientious obligation for the Bishop in person.
> (3). The method called in fee simple is to be entirely abandoned.[91]

As the New York Corporation Plan, with the conditions and safeguards now in use, has been approved by the Sacred Congregation as the mode of tenure most preferable in the United States, it is necessary to consider this plan in some detail.

The New York Plan provides that the archbishop or bishop, the vicar general, the pastor of the parish being incorporated and two laymen selected by these three, may incorporate the parish by filing articles of incorporation with the Secretary of State.[92] The New York courts have interpreted this statute as having the effect of incorporating all the members of the parish, not just the five trustees who file the incorporating document with the Secretary of State.[93]

[91] S.C. Conc., 29 July, 1911 (Private)—*The Canon Law Digest*, II, 444.

[92] Murphy, *The Laws of the State of New York Affecting Church Property*, The Catholic University of America Canon Law Studies, n. 388 (Washington, D.C.: The Catholic University of America Press, 1957), p. 55 (hereafter cited Murphy).

[93] People's Bank v. St. Anthony's Roman Catholic Church, 109 N.Y. 512, 17 N.E. 408 (1888).

The special conditions and safeguards referred to by the Sacred Congregation concern the manner of selecting the five trustees, the filling of their offices when they become vacant, the requirements for the validity of the acts of these trustees, and the rules for the disposition of property in the event of the division of a parish. By virtue of the provisions governing these matters, ecclesiastical control of parish property is insured.

With regard to the naming of the five trustees, the filling of vacancies in their offices, and the validity of their acts, the New York statute decrees as follows:

> The Archbishop or Bishop, and the Vicar General of the diocese to which any incorporated Roman Catholic Church belongs, the rector of such Church, and their successors in office, shall, by virtue of their office, be trustees of such Church. Two laymen, members of such incorporated Church, selected by such officers or a majority of them, shall also be trustees of such incorporated Church, and such officers and such laymen shall together constitute the board of trustees thereof. The two laymen signing the certificate of incorporation of an incorporated Roman Catholic Church shall be the two laymen trustees thereof during the first year of its corporate existence. The term of office of the two laymen trustees of an incorporated Roman Catholic Church shall be one year. Whenever the office of any such layman trustee shall become vacant by expiration of term of office or otherwise, his successor shall be appointed from members of the Church by such officers or a majority of them. No act or proceeding of the trustees of any such incorporated Church shall be valid without the sanction of the Archbishop or Bishop of the diocese to which such Church belongs, or in case of their absence or inability to act, without the sanction of the Vicar General or of the administrator of such diocese.[94]

With regard to the division of parishes, the New York

[94] *McKinney's Consolidated Laws of New York Annotated* (68 vols., Brooklyn, N.Y.: Edward Thompson Company), Vol. 50, *Religious Corporations Law, 1952, with 1956 Cumulative Annual Pocket Part,* sect. 90 (hereafter cited *New York Religious Corporations Law*).

statute gives the archbishop or bishop powers to act which are quite consonant with the powers granted him in the Code of Canon Law.[95] In brief the statute provides that the bishop has the right to divide parishes independently of any action or consent of the trustees. He must, however, act in accordance with the New York Code of Civil Procedure in the same manner in which the trustees of any religious corporation are compelled to do, before making a transfer of Church property.[96]

Article 2. Civil Legislation

Section 1. Past and Present Status of Tenure in Mississippi

The period between the departure of the Spanish from the Mississippi Territory in 1798 and the arrival of the first bishop in 1841 to the newly erected See of Natchez, was one of stagnation as far as the activity of the Church was concerned. The Catholics, few in number, were scattered over the vast expanse of the state with groups concentrated at Natchez, Vicksburg and certain places along the Gulf Coast, especially at Biloxi, Pass Christian, Bay St. Louis and Pascagoula.[97] Exclusive of Natchez and Bay St. Louis, there are no records as to the property holdings of these congregations.

The property granted by the Spanish King to the Catholics of Natchez was, as already indicated, seized by the Federal Government when the Mississippi Territory fell under the jurisdiction of the United States. Subsequently, however, the Catholic Congregation purchased the property on which the church and cemetery were situated and in order to secure its title to the property, obtained from the Territorial Legislature a charter of incorporation in the year 1807.[98]

When the Mississippi Territory was admitted into the Union as a state in 1817 the trustees petitioned the state

[95] Cf. can. 1427.

[96] *New York Religious Corporations Law*, sect. 92.

[97] Gerow, *Cradle Days*, p. 63.

[98] Gerow, *Cradle Days*, p. 29.

legislature and obtained a new charter of incorporation. This charter was amended in 1821 and finally, in 1837, was surrendered and a new charter obtained.[99] A similar charter of incorporation was obtained by the Catholic Congregation of Shieldsborough (Bay St. Louis) on November 26, 1821.[100]

With the arrival of Bishop Chanche, the first bishop of the See, a change in the tenure of Church property occurred. Mindful of the evils of trusteeism and the fifth decree of the First Provincial Council of Baltimore he took steps to secure the property of the diocese in his own name.[101] That Bishop Chanche was successful in this venture is indicated by a letter of Bishop Elder, the third bishop of the See, to Cardinal Barnabo in which he stated:

> Formerly, all so-called church property was vested not in the bishop but in the trustees. Through the zeal and prudence of the venerable founder of this See, Rt. Rev. Dr. Chanche, the title to the greater part was transferred to the bishop.[102]

The same method of vesting church property was continued under the successors of Bishop Chanche, as is evi-

[99] Summary of Private and Local Acts: An Act to incorporate the President and Trustees of the Roman Catholic Society of Christians in the city of Natchez and its vicinity—passed Feb. 6, 1818; An Act supplemental to an Act entitled An Act to incorporate the President and Trustees of the Roman Catholic Society of Christians in the city of Natchez and vicinity—passed Febr. 12, 1821—*The Revised Code of the Laws of Mississippi in which are comprised all such acts of the General Assembly of a public nature, as were in force at the end of the year* 1823 (Natchez, Miss.: Francis Baker, 1824), pp. 597-599; *Code of Mississippi:—Being an Analytical Compilation of the Public and General Statutes of the Territory and State, with Tabular References to the Local and Private Acts from 1798-1848* (Jackson, Miss, 1848 Ch. 15, art. 27 "Churches Incorporated—1798-1848" (hereafter cited *Mississippi Code of 1848*).

[100] *Loc. cit.*

[101] Gerow, *Cradle Days,* p. 64.

[102] *Natchez-Jackson Diocesan Archives,* Elder to Cardinal Barnabo, 1858. Elder, Bishops Letter Book, n. 3, p. 257 (hereafter cited N.J.D.A.).

denced by the decrees of the successive synods.[103] However, the deeds transferring property to later bishops express a trust for a particular parish or mission.

In 1905, the Catholic Diocese of Natchez was incorporated under the general incorporation statute of Mississippi, passed by the legislature in 1892. The officers of this corporation are the Bishop, the Vicar General and the diocesan consultors. Its purpose is to hold title to all the real and personal property belonging to the several Catholic congregations, parishes and missions in the State of Mississippi. Pursuant to this end, it is empowered to receive, hold, lease, mortgage, sell and convey, and to deal with the said property in the manner and upon the conditions prescribed by the regulations of the Catholic Diocese of Natchez in Mississippi, relating to and governing the power and authority of the Bishop of Natchez, in respect to conveyances by him, by lease, by mortgage or sale of said property.[104]

Subsequent to this act of incorporation all property formerly held by the bishop either in his own name or in trust

[103] Nulla Ecclesia nec aliud aedificium, in quo impenda est pecunia Ecclesiae, aut a fidelibus collecta incipi debet, nisi terra in qua erigenda est, fuerit legali forma tradita sive Episcopo sive iis qui iuxta leges dioecesios eam tenere debent. Instrumentum autem traditionis (deed of conveyance) non debet in libris tribunalis scribi (be recorded) antequam Episcopo subiiciatur.—*Acta Synodi dioecesana Natchetensis anno 1862 celebratae*, n. 17; *Synodus Dioecesana Natchetensis quarta habita diebus 19, 20, et 21 Mensis Ianuarii A.D. 1874* a Rev. mo. Gulielmo Henrico Elder, n. 15; *Synodus Dioecesana Natchetensis Quinta, habita diebus 16, 17 Mensis Septembris, A.D. 1886*, a Rev. mo. Francisco Janssens, n. 16. The Sixth and Seventh Synods provided in the first decree respectively that all former decrees retained their force unless expressly revoked. The instant decree was not revoked by these synods, hence it retained its binding force.—*Synodus Dioecesana Natchetensis Sexta, habita Mense Aprilis A.D. 1892*, a Rev. mo. Thoma Heslin in Civitate Natchez, Mississippi; *Synodus Dioecesana Natchetensis Septima, habita fine Aprilis principioque mensis Maii, 1879*, a Rev. mo. Thoma Heslin in Civitate Natchez, Mississippi.

[104] Cf. Charter—*State of Mississippi to the Catholic Diocese of Natchez*, 1905, *Book of Incorporations*, Office of the Secretary of State, Book 13, p. 546.

was deeded to the corporation.[105] Succeeding bishops, however, not particularly satisfied with the corporation, thought it best to vest the property in their own names in trust for the individual parishes, congregations or missions. Consequently, at the present time some property is vested in the bishop as trustee for the use and benefit of the members of particular parishes, congregations or missions, while the rest is vested in the corporation.[106]

In addition to the diocesan property which is vested in the corporation or held by the bishop in trust, both orphanages of the diocese are separately incorporated, so that the property of each is vested in the respective corporation.[107] Moreover, religious communities are separately incorporated, and hence all their property is vested in the respective corporations.

SECTION 2. THE INCORPORATION OF RELIGIOUS SOCIETIES UNDER MISSISSIPPI LAW

A. The Religious Corporation Statute

In the early history of the state there were no general incorporation acts of any kind. Hence, religious societies desiring corporate powers had to petition the legislature for a special charter to that effect. Many charters of this nature were acquired, including as we have seen the Catholic Congregation of Natchez in 1818 and the Catholic Congregation of Shieldsborough (Bay St. Louis) in 1821. However, as early as 1838 an act was passed granting certain powers and privileges to the officers of organized religious societies

[105] Cf. Charter.

[106] N.J.D.A. "Title to Church Property," File 10, No. T. 1, Correspondence of Mr. J. Brunini, Attorney at Law, with Bishop Gunn; *Mode of Tenure, Survey,* p. 85.

[107] An Act to incorporate the St. Mary's Orphan Asylum, a charitable and educational Institution in the City of Natchez, Approved Feb. 18, 1854, *Book of Incorporations,* Office of the Secretary of State, Jackson, Mississippi; Charter of the D'Evereux Hall Orphan Asylum, Approved Jan. 25, 1858, *Book of Incorporations,* Office of the Secretary of State, Jackson, Mississippi.

within the state. By virtue of this act the officers of organized religious societies enjoyed the power to transact all the legal business touching the interests of the society in as full and ample a manner as if they had been incorporated by law respectively.[108]

The provisions of this act, though rather general, set the stage for the subsequent legislation on the corporate capacity of religious societies. The provisions of the Code of 1857 were more specific, and indicated the requirements whereby the society would be recognized in law as an organized society. It decreed:

> Any religious society consisting of the members of any particular denomination or congregation, desiring to act as an organized body, may do so by associating together and electing or appointing from its membership any number of officers, trustees or managers, by whatever name known for the purpose of managing the affairs of the society and such society or association shall keep a record of its proceedings, which shall show the name of the society, its organization and the election of the officers, trustees or managers but the society so organized at each particular locality shall be a distinct and independent society. . . .[109]

The provisions of the Code of 1857 are substantially incorporated in section 5350 of the Mississippi Code of 1942,[110] and in paragraph 1, section 5350, of the recompiled edition of 1956.[111] However, the present statute specifies further

[108] *Mississippi Code of 1848*, Ch. 15, art. 8, p. 324.

[109] *The Revised Code of the Statute Laws of the State of Mississippi* (Jackson, Mississippi: E. Barksdale, 1857), Ch. 35, sect. X, art. 52 (hereafter cited *Revised Code of 1857*).

[110] *Mississippi Code of 1942 Annotated—Containing Permanent Public Statutes of Mississippi to the End of the Legislative Session 1942* (8 vols., Atlanta, Ga.: The Harrison Co.; Rochester, N.Y.: The Lawyers Co-operative Publishing Co., 1942), Vol. IV, Ch. 4, sect. 5350 (hereafter cited *Mississippi Code of 1942 Annotated*).

[111] *Mississippi Code of 1942 Annotated—Containing Permanent Public Statutes of Mississippi to the End of the Legislative Session 1956*

that upon the completion of the organization of any such society the title to the real property theretofore owned by it shall thereupon vest in the society, and shall not be divested out of the same, or encumbered except by a deed, deed of trust, or mortgage duly executed under the authority of a resolution adopted by a majority vote of the members present at a meeting duly called for that purpose, at which meeting at least twenty percent (20%) of the members in good standing of such organized society must be present. The aforesaid resolution shall also designate which officers, trustees or managers are to execute the deed, deed of trust or mortgage.[112]

In interpreting this statute the Supreme Court of Mississippi indicated that it was not the purpose of the legislature in enacting the statute to bring the churches of the State under the provisions thereof, and constitute them corporate bodies or legal entities, without some affirmative action on their part to avail themselves of the provisions of the statute. Hence, it stated:

> Whether any particular society or congregation shall become an organized body and act as such is purely voluntary upon its part; and for any such society or congregation to become an organized body under this statute, it must not only elect from its membership officers, trustees or managers for the purpose of managing its affairs, but it must keep a record of its proceedings, which must show among other things, its organization—that is, the affirmative action of the society, congregation or association showing its purpose so to organize and the completion of its organization.[113]

(15 vols., Atlanta, Ga.: The Harrison Co.; Rochester, N.Y.: The Lawyers Co-operative Publishing Co., 1956), Recompiled Vol. 4A, Ch. 4, sect. 5350 (hereafter cited *Mississippi Code of 1942 Annotated, Recompiled*).

[112] *Mississippi Code of 1942 Annotated, Recompiled,* Vol. 4A, Ch.4 sect. 5350, #1.

[113] Gullett v. First Christian Church of Meridian, 154 Miss. 516, 122 So. 732 (1929).

As is obvious, this statute is particularly adapted to the congregational and assembly form of religious societies and is not consistent with the laws of the Catholic Church as outlined in the previous article. Wherefore, the Catholic Church in Mississippi has not at any time attempted to avail of its provisions. In the absence of more suitable legislation, it might be possible to incorporate the parishes, congregations or missions of the diocese under the terms of the statute in a manner somewhat similar to the system of incorporating parishes in the State of New York but without the safeguards proper to that system. The latter portion of the statute however, would render administration rather cumbersome.

It is evident that the diocese as such could not be incorporated under the statute as heretofore outlined. In 1956, however, the Mississippi Legislature amended section 5350, so as to provide that an association composed of churches or religious societies, by whatever name called, may likewise act as an organized body, as now provided for separate churches, societies or congregations. The amendment reads:

> Whenever any number of religious societies or organized bodies or congregations formed under section 1 of this act (section 5350 of the Mississippi Code of 1942) shall decide to act together as an organized body they may do so in the manner provided in section 1 by and through representatives elected or appointed for that purpose, and when so organized shall likewise be a distinct and independent society or group, by whatever name called, and subject to sue and be sued and be served with process in the same manner.[114]

In the absence of more suitable legislation the incorporation of the diocese under this section likewise appears feasible. The diocesan consultors could be appointed as representatives of the parishes, congregations or missions, but provision would have to be made to secure for the bishop

[114] *Laws of the State of Mississippi*, ch. 177, Senate Bill, n. 1715—paragragh II (section II), of sect. 5350 *Mississippi Code of 1942 Annotated, Recompiled, Vol.* 4A.

the office of presidency of the corporation. The entire statute is, however, completely unsatisfactory from the Catholic point of view, for it is based on the premise that all religious societies are democratic in government, whereas the government of the Catholic Church is hierarchical.

Religious communities within the diocese could probably avail themselves of this statute because of their peculiar organizational status.

B. The Non-Profit Corporation Statute

Mississippi law regarding non-profit corporations has undergone many changes. Previous to the Constitution of 1890, which provided that corporations shall be formed under general laws only,[115] the Mississippi legislature, in the various acts relating to corporations, provided for the incorporation of religious and charitable societies among other non-profit corporations.[116]

Following the Constitution of 1890, the legislature enacted a general statute providing for the creation of corporations for every lawful purpose and of every kind except for the construction and the operation of a railroad, other than street railroads and the carrying on of an insurance business.[117] It was under the provisions of this statute that the Catholic Diocese of Natchez was incorporated in 1905. However, since that time the statute has been amended and specific enactments incorporated relative to the creation, duration and termination of non-profit corporations.

[115] Mississippi Constitution of 1890, Art. VII, sect. 178.

[116] *The Revised Code of the Statute Laws of the State of Mississippi, as Adopted at the January Session A.D. 1871 and Published by the Authority of the Legislature* (Jackson, Miss.: Alcorn and Fisher, 1871), Ch. 55, art. 1, sect. 239 (hereafter cited *Revised Code of 1871*); *The Revised Code of the Statute Laws of the State of Mississippi, Prepared by J. A. Campbell and Reported to the Amended, and Adopted by the Legislature at its Biennial Session in 1880* (Jackson, Miss.: J. L. Power, 1880), Ch. 38, sect. 1027 (hereafter cited *Revised Code of 1880*).

[117] *The Annotated Code of the General Statute Laws of the State of Mississippi* (Nashville, Tenn., 1892), Ch. 25, sect. 832 (hereafter cited *Annotated Code of 1892*).

a. The Creation of Non-Profit Corporations

Under the terms of the General Corporation Statute of the Mississippi Code of 1942 as amended by the Mississippi Legislature in 1958 in regard to non-profit corporations provision is made for the incorporation of the following:—The local lodges, chapters or councils, by whatever name known, of the Masons, Odd Fellows, Knights of Pythias, Elks, Woodmen of the World, and other fraternal organizations together with temperance societies and charitable associations, schools, churches, literary institutions, lyceum associations, religious societies, fire companies, mechanics associations, fair associations, agricultural societies, civic improvement societies, cemeteries and for medical and surgical purposes or for establishing, maintaining and operating local clinical, pathological, medical or surgical research laboratories, hospitals, institutions of learning, and gymnasiums and organizations otherwise for improving the physical, mental and moral education of mankind.[118]

Incorporation of any of the above organizations may be achieved on application of any three members, all of whom must be adult resident citizens of the State of Mississippi, and authorized by any of the said organizations in its minutes to apply for the charter. The three persons thus authorized must prepare an instrument to be styled "The charter of incorporation of (naming corporation)," and containing in appropriate paragraphs the following information:

(1) The corporate title of said company;[119]

(2) The names and post office addresses of the incorporators;

(3) The domicile of the corporation in this state;[120]

[118] *Mississippi Code of 1942 Annotated, Recompiled,* Vol. 4A, *Cumulative Supplement,* 1958, Ch. 4, sect. 5310.

[119] No corporation shall be created under the laws of this state with the name of any existing corporation of this state. . . . *Mississippi Code of 1942 Annotated, Recompiled,* Vol. 4A, Ch. 4, sect. 5322.

[120] Change of corporation's domicile from place stated in its charter, by stockholders resolution, as authorized by charter, was held matter of internal management not requiring charter amendment, in the ab-

(4) A statement that the corporation is non-profit and that no shares of stock are to be issued;

(5) The period of existence shall be stated as perpetual;

(6) The purposes for which the corporation is created, not contrary to law, including a statement that the rights and powers that may be exercised by said corporation in addition thereto are those conferred by the provisions of Chapter 4, Mississippi Code of 1942 Recompiled, sections 5309 *et seq.*[121]

Having drawn up the instrument in accordance with the above requirements it must be signed by each of the incorporators and acknowledged by each before a notary public or other officer authorized by law to take acknowledgements. Thereafter, it may be filed with the Secretary of State, together with the requisite fee, at any time within six months of the date of the last acknowledgement.

Subsequently, the charter is submitted to the Attorney General who, either *per se* or through his assistants, makes such investigation as he may deem necessary to determine in his opinion whether the issuance of the charter to the corporation, as applied for, is contrary to the best interests of the State of Mississippi. Should the Attorney General be of the opinion that the charter, as applied for, is not to the best interest of the state, though not violative of the Constitution or laws of the state, he submits his written opinion to that effect to the Governor together with the charter. The Governor then approves or rejects the charter, returning it to the Secretary of State with his action endorsed thereon. In the event of approval by the Governor, the Secretary of State shall record the charter, certify to the same under the great seal of the state and transmit it to the applicants. Thereupon, the powers specified in the charter shall be vested in the corporation and it shall go into operation.

sence of statutory prohibition.—Estes v. Bank of Walnut Grove, 172 Miss. 499, 159 So. 104 (1935).

[121] *Mississippi Code of 1942 Annotated, Recompiled,* Vol. 4A, *Cumulative Supplement,* Ch. 4, sect. 5310.

If the Governor disapproves of the charter, the Secretary of State shall notify the applicants, who within thirty days must amend the charter so as to meet the approval of the Governor. Should the applicants fail to amend the charter, the Secretary of State shall refund them the fee less three dollars which shall be paid into the state treasury for charters examined, disallowed and filed.[122]

Finally, the statute provides that non-profit corporations shall not be required to make publication of their charters; shall issue no shares of stock; shall divide no dividends or profits among their members; shall make expulsion the only remedy for non-payment of dues; shall vest in each member the right to one vote in the election of all officers; shall make the loss of membership by death or otherwise, the termination of all interest in the corporate assets; and shall not hold individual members liable for corporate debts but that the entire corporate property shall be liable for the claims of creditors.[123]

In evaluating the non-profit corporation statute in the light of the instruction of the Sacred Congregation of the Council and the legislation of the Councils of Baltimore, as outlined in the foregoing article, it is evident that this statute does not measure up to the requirements therein contained. The provision in the latter section of the statute, viz., that all members shall have a right to one vote in the election of all officers, might, if completely enforced in the incorporation of a Catholic parish or diocese, result in the lay-control of ecclesiastical property and hence the possible recurrence of

[122] *Mississippi Code of 1942 Annotated, Recompiled*, Vol. 4A, *Cumulative Supplement*, sect. 5310.

[123] *Loc. cit.* It is to be noted that it shall not be a defense to any suit against a corporation, that there was a defect or informality in its organization.—*Mississippi Code of 1942 Annotated, Recompiled*, Vol. 4A, sect. 5333. Moreover, it has been held that where there was a *bona fide* attempt to form a valid corporation and everyone acted in good faith and received the benefit of their efforts to form the corporation, there was a *de facto* corporation, so that, those dealing with it are as fully protected as if it had been a corporation *de iure*.—In re Vicksburg Bridge and Terminal Co., 22 F. Suppl. 490 (1937).

the evils which characterized the lay-trustee system adopted by the Catholic Church in its formative years in the United States. This provision was not incorporated in the general statute of 1892 relative to non-profit corporations under which the Diocese of Natchez was incorporated in 1905.[124]

Moreover, under that charter, the bishop and his consultors were themselves constituted the corporation and hence the Catholics of the diocese were not members of the corporation as such. Whether a similar arrangement could be accomplished under the present statute is a matter of speculation. Likewise the incorporation of parishes or congregations with the bishop, vicar general, the pastor of the parish being incorporated and two lay-trustees appointed by these being the duly constituted officers of the corporation, is a matter of speculation. It would appear, however, that incorporation as contemplated above would require enabling legislation.

Catholic schools, hospitals, etc., desiring corporate existence could more easily avail themselves of this statute. Likewise, religious communities could avail themselves of this statute without the possibility of running afoul of the law, either ecclesiastical or civil.

b. Duration and Termination of Non-Profit Corporations

(1) Duration.

Prior to 1950 the period of existence of non-profit corporations was fifty years. However, in 1950 the legislature by an amendment to section 5310 of the Mississippi Code of 1942 extended the period of existence of all non-profit

[124] Under the corporation statute of 1892 only the following provisions had to be complied with to obtain corporate existence. The persons desiring to be incorporated were required to prepare a charter containing the following information: (a) the title of the corporation; (b) a clear and definite statement as to the purpose of the corporation; (c) the names of the persons desiring to form the corporation; (d) the power to be exercised; (e) the period for which said corporation is to exist; and (f) whatever else may be proper to be stated.—*Annotated Code of 1892*, sect. 833.

corporations whether heretofore or hereafter granted to perpetual, with the proviso that these charters shall be subject at all times to alteration, amendment or repeal by the legislature.[125]

As regards charter amendments, the present statute provides that every corporation heretofore or hereafter created with the exception of railroads and insurance companies desiring an amendment to its charter, shall prepare and present to the Secretary of State the proposed amendment in writing, acknowledged by its president or secretary before a notary public or other officer authorized to take acknowledgements, together with a certified copy of a resolution of the stockholders (members) adopting and approving the proposed amendment. Upon receipt of the amendment by the Secretary of State, it shall be dealt with in the same manner and shall be subject to the same laws and regulations governing the filing, approval and recordation of original charters of incorporation.[126]

(2) Termination

Blackstone regarded the capacity of perpetual succession or continuity as an essential attribute of a corporation.[127] He indicated, however, four ways in which a corporation may be dissolved: (1) by an act of Parliament which is boundless in its operations; (2) by the natural death of all its members, in the case of an aggregate corporation; (3) by surrender of its franchises, into the hands of the King, which is a kind of suicide; (4) by forfeiture of its charter, through negligence or abuse of its franchise, in which case the law judges that the body politic has broken the condition

[125] *Mississippi Code of 1942 Annotated, Recompiled,* Vol. 4A, ch. 4, sect. 5310.

[126] *Mississippi Code of 1942 Annotated, Recompiled,* Vol. 4A, ch. 4 sect. 5323. Pursuant to the provisions of the above, an amendment was obtained in 1957 changing the name of the corporation from "The Catholic Diocese of Natchez" to "The Catholic Diocese of Natchez-Jackson."—*Tenth Diocesan Synod of the Diocese of Natchez—Jackson, 1957, Appendix XVIII,* p. 101.

[127] Blackstone, *Commentaries,* I, 475.

upon which it was incorporated, and thereupon the incorporation is void.[128] This enumeration has received the approval of the courts in the United States; however, under Anglo-American law dissolution may also occur by the expiration of the charter through the lapse of time and the happening of a condition subsequent upon which by the terms of the charter the corporate existence is *ipso facto* to terminate.[129]

Dissolution by the expiration of charter through the lapse of time is no longer applicable to non-profit corporations under Mississippi law. For as previously indicated the Mississippi legislature in 1950 extended the period of existence of all non-profit corporations to perpetual. However, it is possible that dissolution may occur in either of the other enumerated ways, though not all have been applied by the Supreme Court of Mississippi.

With regard to the first way in which a corporation may be dissolved as outlined by Blackstone, dissolution may occur under Mississippi law in a similar manner. In sect. 178 of Art. 7 of the Mississippi Constitution, it is provided that the legislature shall have power to alter, amend or repeal any charter of incorporation now existing and revocable, and any that may hereafter be created, whenever in its opinion, it may be for the public interest to do so, provided, however, that no injustice shall be done to the stockholders (members).

In this regard it is to be noted that the power of the state to destroy its corporations is not greater than its power to repeal legislation, and the latter power is clearly subject to the constitutional guaranty against the impairment of the obligation of contracts.[130] In other words, since the grant of a corporate charter is contractual in its nature, such a grant is entitled to the protection of the provision of the

[128] Blackstone, *Commentaries*, I, 485.

[129] 13 *Am. Jur. Corporations*, 1286.

[130] Graham v. Folsom, 200 U.S. 248, 26 S. Ct. 245, 50 L.Ed. 464 (1905).

Federal Constitution prohibiting any state from enacting any law impairing the obligation of contracts,[131]

The surrender of corporate franchise is governed by statute in Mississippi.[132] However, in this regard, the Supreme Court of Mississippi stated as follows in a case involving the assets of a dissolved non-profit corporation:

> Although it is a general rule that there is no legal dissolution or surrender of the charter of a non-profit corporation until so decreed pursuant to this section (5352), a court of equity may in a proper case treat the corporation as dissolved, even though in a legal sense no dissolution has occurred, and a dissolution may be implied as by the consent of all the members when the meetings are voluntarily discontinued and the activity of the members of such comes to an end.[133]

A corporation may be dissolved under Mississippi law through misuser or nonuser of its franchises. In such an eventuality the state (and only the state) can sue to terminate its existence in an action of *quo warranto*.[134] Finally, it is of interest to note that just as in Canon Law, equivalent dissolution may also occur under Mississippi law through the consolidation or merger of corporations.[135]

131 13 *Am. Jur. Corporations,* 1287.

132 Cf. *Mississippi Code of 1942 Annotated, Recompiled,* Vol. 4A, sect. 5352. A corporation cannot surrender its franchise with the freedom of an individual.—Southern Electric Securities Co., v. State, 91 Miss. 195, 44 So. 785, 124 Am. St. Rep. 638 (1907).

133 Woodville Lodge G.U.O.O.F. v. Poole, 19 Miss. 798, 1 So.2nd 780 (1941).

134 A private corporation created by the legislature may lose its franchises by a misuser or nonuser of them, and they may be resumed by the government under a judicial judgment, upon a *quo warranto* to ascertain and enforce the forfeiture. This is the common law of the land, and is a tacit condition annexed to the creation of every such corporation.—State v. Commercial Bank, 13 Smedes and Marshall (Miss.) 569, 53 Am. Dec. 106 (1850).

135 A consolidation of the stock of two corporations necessarily results in the creation of a new corporation, rather than in a mere merger of the two corporations.—Adams v. Yazoo & M. V. R. Co. 317 Miss. 194, 24 So. 200, 60 A.L.R. 33 (1901); Yazoo & M. V. R. Co.

SECTION 3. THE BISHOP AS TRUSTEE

An unincorporated religious society under Mississippi law cannot own title to property; hence, the title must be vested either in some person or in some corporation.[136] Consequently, the property of the Catholic Church in Mississippi which is not vested in the corporation, is held in trust by the bishop for the use and benefit of the members of the particular congregation, parish or mission.[137]

The nature of this trust relationship has not been construed by the courts of Mississippi; it seems certain, however, that the courts would recognize the bishop as an active trustee, empowered to deal with the trust *res*, within the limitations of the trust instrument, according to the rules and discipline of the Catholic Church. For it is generally admitted that where property is acquired by churches, it is to be presumed that it was the intention of the donor that the property is to be devoted to religious purposes and in such a manner and in such a way as the governing body, whatever it may be, shall under its constitution and rules determine.[138] Where, however, a particular trust instrument specifies the manner and use of the trust *res* this presumption would cede to the terms of the trust, and hence, the

v. Adams 21 S. Ct. 240, 180 U.S. 1, 45 L. Ed. 395 (1898); Yazoo & M. V. R. Co. v. Adams, 77 Miss. 194, 28 So. 956, 60 L.R.A. 33 (1901); 21 S.Ct. 240, 180 U.S. 1, 45 L.Ed. 395 (1899).

[136] West v. State, 169 Miss. 302, 152 So. 888 (1934).

[137] *Tenth Diocesan Synod of the Diocese of Natchez-Jackson, 1957*, Form of Church deed, Appendix XIX.: "Most Reverend (name of Bishop) Bishop of the Catholic Diocese of Natchez-Jackson, and his successors in office forever, Trustee, for the use and benefit of the members of the __________ Catholic Congregation, or Parish, in the City of __________, Mississippi."
And further provided:
"Should at any time __________ Catholic Parish or Congregation, pass into or be placed in another Catholic Diocese, or any other Catholic Diocese in succession thereto, then the Catholic Bishop of such new Catholic Diocese, or succession of Catholic Dioceses thereto, and his, or their, successors in office forever, shall, without further action, in turn succeed to said trust."

[138] 45 *Am. Jur.* 764, sect. 53.

bishop, just as the trustee of any charitable trust, would be obliged to fulfill the intentions of the donor as expressed in the instrument.

The case of Kilpatrick v. Graves, decided by the Supreme Court of Mississippi in 1875, though involving the construction of a trust instrument which specified that the trust *res* was subject to be dealt with according to the rules and discipline of the Methodist Episcopal Church South, nevertheless, set a precedent as to the extent to which trusts executed in that manner will be recognized by the courts of Mississippi.[139] The facts of the case were as follows: In 1860, Kilpatrick conveyed by deed to the trustees of the Methodist Episcopal Church South, at Hazelhurst, a lot of ground in said town on which to build a house of worship, for the use of the members of the M. E. Church South according to the rules of the discipline which may from time to time be agreed upon and adopted by the ministers of said church at their general conferences. A church was erected on said lot, and was used as a house of worship by the members until some time in the year 1871. In that year, the church authorities sold the lot, tore down the church and rebuilt it on another lot in the same town. The sale of the lot was contested by the donor as a breach of trust and he demanded a reconveyance to him.[140]

The court held that the primary inducement of the donation was a site for the Methodist Episcopal Church in Hazelhurst, the gift subject to be dealt with according to the rules and discipline of the church. The grant, therefore, adopted the discipline of the church as affording the rules and regulations for the use of the grant as fully as if the donor had embodied them in his deed of conveyance. Hence, the changing of the site to a more eligible place was not a breach of trust but rather rendering it more useful for the purposes intended.[141]

It is to be noted, however, that though the members of

[139] Kilpatrick v. Graves, 51 Miss. 432 (1875).

[140] Kilpatrick v. Graves, 51 Miss. 432 (1875).

[141] Kilpatrick v. Graves, 51 Miss. 432, 436 (1875).

the Methodist Episcopal Church South were named as beneficiaries in the trust instrument,[142] the donation was for the use of specified members, viz., those of the town of Hazelhurst. It is clear from the language used by the court[143] that any diversion of the trust estate to members of the Methodist Episcopal Church South in another district would not be upheld by the court. Consequently, the bishop under the present trust instrument could not subject the property held by him in trust for one parish to the debt or obligation of another parish.

Moreover, the case of Kilpatrick v. Graves likewise indicates that where the details of the use of the trust estate are spelled out in the trust instrument such must be observed by the trustee. The court stated:

> . . . the trust ought to be carried out on the terms prescribed by the founder. If the particular purpose is clearly defined that must be pursued by the trustee. As where the estate is given for the repair of a chapel, it would be a diversion to use any of the funds for general parish purposes. If it be to establish a hospital, it would be improper to apply it to paving a street of the town . . . if donated for the benefit of the inhabitants of one town or parish, it could not be used for those of another town or parish.[144]

What if the trust instrument makes no provision for the rules and discipline of the Church but simply provides that the property is held in trust by the bishop, his successors and assigns forever, for the use of a particular parish, con-

[142] Kilpatrick v. Graves, 51 Miss. 432, 436 (1875).

[143] ". . . the donor donated his gift to the members of the Methodist Episcopal Church South, to be used in accordance with their discipline. The acts which he complains of are no diversion of the state to some other denomination of Christians, nor to a Methodist Church in some other town, or for the benefit of some other congregation; nor that it has not been used in aid of a house of worship for the same people in the pale of the same church organization. The acts done have been in furtherance of the charity."—Kilpatrick v. Graves, 51 Miss. 432, 441 (1875).

[144] Kilpatrick v. Graves, 51 Miss. 432, 439 (1875).

gregation or mission? In this eventuality also it appears certain that the courts would recognize the bishop as an active trustee, empowered to deal with the trust *res* within the limitations of the trust instrument according to the rules and discipline of the Church.

There are no Mississippi cases in point. The cases of other jurisdictions, however, involving the construction of an instrument of this kind, even when no trust is expressed, support the above contention. In the case of Alemany v. Wensinger, cited in Kilpatrick v. Graves, the Supreme Court of California upheld the right of the Archbishop of San Francisco as against the parishioners to sell the property of a certain St. Boniface parish. The facts of the case indicate that the Archbishop held the property of St. Boniface's parish in trust for the use of the Roman Catholic German Congregation. The property of the parish, with the change of neighborhood, became surrounded with business establishments, hotels, etc. The Archbishop thought it advisable to sell the property and apply the proceeds after paying off the indebtedness of the parish to the purchase of another and more suitable lot and the erection thereon of a suitable church edifice and other necessary buildings to be held by him subject to the same trust.[145]

Similarly, in a case decided by the Supreme Court of Michigan, the court in upholding the right of the bishop to enjoin the parishioners of a certain St. Mary's parish at North Dorr from building a church on church property without the permission of the bishop, stated:

> We think it unnecessary to decide whether any trust is shown to exist in this case. If there is a trust, it is altogether clear that it was a trust to hold the property according to the rules and tenets of the Roman Catholic Church, which gave the bishop control of the property, and which prohibit the erection of church edifices without his express assent and appoval.[146]

[145] Alemany v. Wensinger, 40 Cal. 288 (1860).

[146] Foley v. Kleibusch, 123 Mich. 416, 82 N.W. 225 (1900).

In a Kansas case, though the right of the bishop to sell a portion of the property of a particular parish, and to use it for other diocesan purposes, was not upheld as against the parishioners, on the basis that the property was given to the bishop for the purpose of the particular parish and no other, nevertheless, the concurring opinion stated:

> If, however, it had been established upon the trial that the title to the property was conveyed with the understanding between the parties that, by the usages and customs of the Catholic Church, it was vested in the bishop in trust, to be used for church purposes generally, as his own judgment might determine, the judgement of the trial court could not be sustained.[147]

The most significant cases involving the nature of this trust relationship are that of Blanc v. Asbury and Olcott v. Gabert, decided by the Supreme Court of Texas in 1885 and 1893 respectively. The case of Blanc v. Asbury concerned property that had been conveyed to the Bishop for the use of the church in Hempstead.[148] The Bishop had the church built and gave certain lots to the builders to pay for the construction of the church. This conveyance was challenged by the parishioners. In upholding the right of the Bishop, the court stated:

> In securing that object (building a church in Hempstead), much was left to the discretion of the bishop, who, as head of the church in the diocese, had the necessary power as supplemented by the conveyance, to manage the property in such a manner as his judgment might approve as the best in securing the object intended, and in promoting the

[147] Fink v. Umscheid, 40 Kan. 271, 19 Pac. 623 (1888).

[148] Blanc v. Asbury, 63 Tex. 489, 51 Am. Rep. 666 (Com. App., 1885); the conveyance stated:

> To have and to hold unto him the said Claudius M. Dubuis, for the use aforesaid, and his successors and his or their assigns, forever. It is hereby declared that the premises herein described are granted the said Claude M. Dubuis for the purpose of erecting thereon a Roman Catholic Church, and other buildings pertaining thereto, or to be exchanged or used in the purchase of other property in the town of Hempstead for said purpose.

> welfare of the church at Hempstead . . . it is a matter of historical and common knowledge, that the form of government in the Roman Catholic Church is an episcopacy, and in which the diocesan bishops possess enlarged powers, respecting the temporal as well as the spiritual affairs of the church, in their respective dioceses.[149]

The case of Olcott v. Gabert involved a reconveyance of property donated to the Catholic Church. The Houston and Texas Central Railway Company donated land to Claude M. Dubuis, Bishop of Galveston, and his successors in office, for the Catholic Church. The company went bankrupt in 1889 and the land was returned by Bishop Gallagher, the administrator of the diocese at the time. Olcott, the receiver of the property, entered a trespass to try title suit. The court held:

> It is a matter of historical and common knowledge that the form of government of the Roman Catholic Church is an episcopacy in which the diocesan bishops possess enlarged powers respecting the temporal as well as the spiritual affairs of the church in their respective dioceses. It could not be lightly assumed that the Bishop acted without authority. The presumption is that public officers do as the law and their duty require. The members of the Roman Catholic Church are found in every part of the world, and their interests, temporal and spiritual, are looked after by a well-disciplined hierarchy consisting of functionaries of successive grades, whose respective powers are accurately defined, and among themselves well understood. In such a case, in the absence of proof to the contrary, the presumption that everything has been rightfully done ought to apply with peculiar force.[150]

In the light of the above cases, it seems certain that the bishop would be recognized by the Mississippi courts as an active trustee, but only within the terms of the trust in-

149 Blanc v. Asbury, 63 Tex. 489, 51 Am. Rep. 666 (Com. App., 1885).

150 Olcott v. Gabert, 23 S. W. 985 (1893).

strument. The problem, therefore, is to determine whether the trust instrument should be so formulated that the bishop may use the property for any purpose beneficial to the diocese as a whole, or whether merely for the particular parish or congregation. With regard to the former method of holding the property, the observation has been made that this general practice may have certain difficulties. When the bishop raises money, he may use the entire trust, that is, all the property of the diocese, in order to secure the loan. Therefore, all the property could be reached in equity in satisfaction of a judgment recovered against the bishop as trustee. Further, the debts of one parish or group of parishes would be the debts of every parish and the inefficient operation of one parish would be visited upon the whole diocese. This situation would be true even if the bishop did not pledge the whole of the trust as security for a debt. The reason is that as long as the trust fund is for the same purpose, that is, the Roman Catholic Church, all the property is automatically joined.[151]

With regard to the latter method, the disabilities mentioned above are avoided. Moreover, it seems to be more in conformity with the law of the Church, as will be indicated when the question of the administration of Church property is discussed. It should be noted, however, that in either case much depends on the construction of the trust instrument; hence, its terms should be spelled out with precise exactness. Thus, the incorporation of the phrase "according to the rules and discipline of the Catholic Church" in the trust instrument would almost certainly place the status of the bishop as trustee beyond controversy.

[151] *Mode of Tenure, Survey*, p. 160.

CHAPTER III

ACQUISITION OF PROPERTY

ARTICLE 1. CHURCH LAW ON ACQUISITION

In the subsequent discussion of the law of the Church regarding the acquisition of temporal goods, the terminology employed must be understood in accordance with the explanations indicated as follows, unless expressly stated otherwise.

The term "Church" includes not only the Church Universal, and the Apostolic See, but also all moral persons in the Church unless the contrary is evident from the context or from the nature of the matter treated.[1]

The term "ecclesiastical goods" or "church property" includes all temporal goods whether corporeal or incorporeal, movable or immovable, which belong either to the Church Universal and the Apostolic See, or to some other moral person in the Church.[2] Corporeal property is that property which is preceivable to the senses in some manner, whereas, incorporeal property is that property which is not perceivable by the senses but by the mind only, such as legal rights and obligations regarding property. Immovable property is that which cannot be moved from place to place either naturally or legally, while movable property can be so moved.[3]

Ecclesiastical property may be either sacred or precious. Sacred things are those which are destined for divine worship by reason of their consecration or blessing.[4] Precious property includes all church property which has a special value by reason of its artistic, historical, or material content.[5]

[1] Can. 1498.
[2] Can. 1497, #1.
[3] Bouscaren-Ellis, p. 799.
[4] Can. 1497, #2.
[5] Can. 1497, #2.

SECTION 1. THE RIGHT OF THE CHURCH TO ACQUIRE PROPERTY

The Catholic Church, as previously indicated, is a perfect juridical society, founded by God Himself; hence, it is independent of any human power both in its origin and in the exercise of its prerogatives. Since the Church is a visible society composed of human beings with bodies as well as souls, it is evident that the Church must have temporal possessions for the fulfillment of its mission. The exercise of external worship, the support of its ministers, as well as the care of orphans, the sick, and the aged, the education of youth—all involve the need of temporal goods.

In canon 1495, the Church vindicates for itself the right to acquire temporal goods. The canon states that the Catholic Church and the Apostolic See have an inherent right, without restriction and independent of the civil authority, to acquire, own, and administer temporal property in the prosecution of the ends for which they were established. In the second paragraph of the same canon, this right is also vindicated for individual churches and other moral persons, which have been duly established by ecclesiastical authority as juridical persons, but subject to the norms established by the sacred canons.[6]

In laying claim to its native right regarding temporal possessions, the Church merely repeats what it has stated from the time of its institution by Christ. Thus the Church vindicated its native right to acquire property against the errors of Arnold of Brescia, the Waldenses, Marsilius of Padua, Jean de Jandun and Wycliffe who taught that the Church's acquisition of temporal goods was forbidden by Christ; likewise against the Gallicans and Regalists who held that the Church had not an inherent right to tempo-

[6] Can. 1495, #1, 2: #1, "Ecclesia Catholica et Apostolica Sedes nativum ius habent libere et independenter a civili potestate acquirendi, retinendi et administrandi bona temporalia ad fines sibi proprios prosequendos." #2, "Etiam ecclesiis singularibus aliisque personis moralibus quae ab ecclesiastica auctoritate in iuridicam personam erectae sint, ius est, ad normam sacrorum canonum, bona temporalia acquirendi et administrandi."

ralities but acquired it by the arbitrary concession of civil authorities. The Council of Constance and Pope Martin V condemned several Wycliffean propositions which impugned the Church's right to temporal goods. Finally, Pius IX in his Syllabus of condemned propositions and his Consistorial Allocution, *Quibus Luctuosissimis*, virtually formulated the language employed by the Code.[7]

Through the centuries, however, the exercise of this right of the Church has been effectively challenged by the civil power. In England this encroachment of the civil power took the form of mortmain statutes. The remnants of these statutes are now evidenced in the United States by the various statutes limiting the proprietary capacity of religious societies, as well as the denial or at least the partial denial of the capacity of religious societies to acquire property by devise.

SECTION 2. MODES OF ACQUISITION

The Church claims the right to acquire property in the same manner as any other society or private person by all just means which natural and positive law sanction.[8] Wherefore, the Church can acquire property by occupation, accession, prescription, contracts, etc., just as any private person. The Code, however, does not consider all the possible modes of acquisition, but only those by which the Church, at the present time, generally acquires temporal goods.[9]

A. Taxation

From the fact that the Church has a native right, freely and independently of the civil power to acquire property, it follows as a corollary that the Church has also the right,

[7] Cf. Doheny, *Church Property: Modes of Acquisition*, The Catholic University of America Canon and Roman Law Studies, n. 41 (Washington, D.C.: The Catholic University of America, 1927), p. 25 (hereafter cited Doheny).

[8] Can. 1499, #1: "Ecclesia acquirere bona temporalia potest omnibus iustis modis iuris sive naturalis sive positivi, quibus id aliis licet."

[9] Vermeersch-Cruesen, II, n. 821, p. 574.

independent of the civil power, to demand from the faithful whatever is necessary for the attainment of its proper ends.[10]

For many centuries, the Church exercised this right through the exaction of tithes and first fruits. This system of levying support was borrowed from the Mosaic law,[11] in virtue of which, the Jews had the obligation of giving tithes, or the tenth part of the produce of the land, as well as its first fruits, as an offering to God and His ministers. The obligation of offering the first fruits, however, never became general law, but it was introduced in some places by particular law or custom. Tithing, on the other hand, became general law after the ninth century and for several centuries afterwards formed one of the principal sources of income for Church and clergy.[12] However, as a tax imposed by general law, the system of tithing has long since fallen into desuetude, with the exception of a few regions which have retained the system through local statutes or custom.[13]

The present law of the Church does not impose any tax on the faithful, as such, for the support of the Church. However, it does require that the special statutes and the laudable customs of individual regions should be observed in regard to the payment of tithes and first fruits.[14] The fact that the general law does not impose a tax is not an indication that the faithful are absolved from the obligation of supporting the Church. It simply means that the Code allows each region and country great latitude as to the determination of the means of acquiring church support. Fortunately, the voluntary offerings of the faithful are generally sufficient to take care of the needs of the Church in the United States, at least, to the extent that strictly defined laws have been unnecessary.[15]

[10] Cf. can. 1496.

[11] Deut., 14:22; Num. 18:19.

[12] Ayrinhac, pp. 391, 392.

[13] Can. 1502; Doheny, p. 47.

[14] Can. 1502.

[15] In the diocese of Natchez-Jackson: Each one should support his own parish according to his means, and even though he attend another

The general precept of contributing to the support of the Church and its ministers is binding on all the faithful according to their means. While this precept binds gravely, it is difficult to hold any individual delinquent guilty of grave sin unless his neglect to contribute his just share should place the ecclesiastical ministers in dire need or impose an undue burden upon the other faithful.[16]

Taxes for the performance of various ecclesiastical functions are permitted, but only within the limitations prescribed by law. Canon 1507 prescribes that without prejudice to the prescriptions of canons 1056 and 1234, it belongs to a provincial council or meeting of the bishops of a province to specify the taxes payable throughout the entire ecclesiastical province for the various acts of voluntary jurisdiction, for the execution of rescripts of the Holy See, and on the occasion of the administration of the sacraments or sacramentals.[17] Such a schedule, however, is of no effect unless it is previously approved by the Holy See. Canon 1056 provides that in granting marriage dispensations, except with permission from the Holy See, local ordinaries or their officials can exact no other compensation than a small offering for chancery expenses and even this they should not demand from the poor. All customs contrary to this provision are abrogated and the obligation of restitution imposed on those who violate it. And in accordance with the norms of canon 1234, local ordinaries are authorized, each one for his own territory, with the advice of the diocesan consultors and if opportune the co-operation of rural deans and pastors of the episcopal city, to draw up a list of funeral fees, if none such exists already.

The provincial council or meeting of the bishops must

church this does not relieve him of the obligation of supporting his own parish.—*Tenth Diocesan Synod, Diocese of Natchez-Jackson,* n. 87.

16 Doheny, p. 49.

17 In all these cases in which it is permitted to impose a tax every danger of simony of the divine or ecclesiastical law is to be avoided (can. 730), and the truly poor must never be discriminated against (can. 463, #4).

likewise establish the charges for judicial acts connected with ecclesiastical trials.[18] In this case the schedule of judicial taxes need not be submitted to the Holy See for approval.[19]

Within the Church itself, there is a system of taxation, which in general provides revenue for projects beneficial to the diocese. As this system of taxation, however, from the point of view of this work, is a mode of distribution rather than a mode of acquisition, the various taxes will merely be referred to. Each year, the cathedratic tax, that is, a moderate tax determined in accordance with the norm of canon 1507, #1, unless it has already been determined by ancient custom, must be paid to the bishop as a sign of subjection, by all churches and benefices subject to his jurisdiction.[20] For the establishment of a seminary and the support of its students, if it lacks its own income, the bishop can direct pastors or other rectors of even exempt churches to take up a collection for this purpose, in church, at given times; levy a contribution or tax in his diocese, and if these means prove inadequate, assign and attach certain simple benefices to the seminary.[21] The bishop may likewise impose pensions on benefices, both parochial and non-parochial but only in accordance with the provisions of canon 1429.[22]

[18] Can. 1507, #2.

[19] Can. 1909, #1.

[20] Can. 1504. The cathedratic tax need not be paid to the vicar capitular or to the administrator of the diocese during the vacancy of the episcopal see.— S. C. Conc., Aug. 20, 1917—*A.A.S.*, IX (1917), 479; Bouscaren, *The Canon Law Digest*, I, 719.

[21] Can. 1355, 1°-3°; cf. can. 1356.

[22] Can. 1429, #1: "Beneficiis quibuslibet nequeunt Ordinarii locorum pensiones perpetuas aut temporarias imponere quae ad vitam pensio-narii durent, sed possunt, dum beneficium conferunt, ex iusta causa in ipso collationis actu exprimenda, eisdem imponere pensiones temporarias, quae durent ad vitam beneficiarii salva huic congrua portione. #2: Beneficiis autem paroecialibus non possunt, nisi in commodum parochi vel vicarii eiusdem paroeciae a munere abeuntis, imponere pensiones, quae tamen ne excedant tertiam partem reditus paroeciae, quibusvis deductis expensis et incertis reditibus.

#3: Pensiones beneficiis sive a Romano Pontifice sive ab aliis colla-

Finally, to meet a special pressing diocesan need, the local ordinary can impose a moderate extraordinary tax on all incumbents of benefices, religious as well as secular.[23]

Other taxes for the benefit of the diocese or in favor of a patron may not be imposed by the bishop on churches, benefices and other ecclesiastical institutions subject to him, except on the occasion of their foundation or consecration; and in no case can a tax be imposed on manual or founded Mass stipends.[24]

B. Alms Gathering

The Code distinguishes between the free-will offerings of the faithful and the offerings given in response to requests. With regard to the latter, ecclesiastical law forbids private persons, whether clerics or laymen, to collect funds for any pious or ecclesiastical institute or purpose without the written permission of the Holy See or of both their own ordinary and the local ordinary.[25] However, the privileges of strictly

toribus, impositae, cessant morte pensionarii, qui tamen nequit eas alienare, nisi id expresse concessum sit."

[23] Can. 1505. Exempt religious are not bound by this obligation.—Doheny, p. 59.

[24] Can. 1506. The tax, mistakenly called the cathedratic tax, which is imposed on all parishes of the dioceses of the United States for the support of the respective bishops and to defray the expenses of their chancery offices, cannot be reconciled with the prescriptions of canons 1505 and 1506. Abbo-Hannan maintain that such a tax is now forbidden.—Abbo-Hannan, II, 713, footnote 16. Bouscaren-Ellis, on the other hand, maintain that since the same needs are present today as were present at the time when the tax was introduced (*Concilii Plenarii Baltimorensis II, Acta et Decreta*, n. 100) and approved by the Holy See, it may be continued as long as necessary, unless the Holy See prohibits it.—Bouscaren-Ellis, p. 808. This opinion is strengthened by the fact that in 1929 the Sacred Congregation for the Oriental Church approved this same method of parish assessment for the Greek Ruthenian dioceses of the United States.—S.C.Or., Jan. 4, 1929—*A.A.S.*, XXI (1929), 152; Bouscaren, *The Canon Law Digest*, I, 9.

[25] Can. 1503. Oriental clerics, even of the highest rank, whenever they are outside their own territory cannot obtain such permission from local ordinaries but they must approach the local ordinary through the Sacred Congregation for the Oriental Church or through

mendicant orders, when they collect within the dioceses in which their monasteries are located in accordance with the prescriptions of canons 621-624, are not affected by this provision.[26]

Pastors are not private persons within their parishes and hence are not subject to the restriction of this canon,[27] but they cannot give the permission required by this canon unless delegated to do so by the local ordinary. On the other hand, the local ordinary can command a pastor, even one who is an exempt religious, to take up a collection inside or outside the parochial church for some determined end or pious work and, moreover, if the local ordinary gives the required permission to any private person, the consent of the pastor is not necessary, but courtesy would suggest and sometimes diocesan statutes demand that an understanding be reached with him.[28]

Though the law makes no distinction as regards the modes of soliciting and is clearly intended to protect the faithful against indiscreet and, at times, dishonest solicitors, nevertheless, it is probable that appeals through letters would not fall under the prohibition of the canon.[29] Moreover, the canon employs the phrase *stipem cogere* which implies soliciting from a fairly large number hence, asking a donation from two or three wealthy friends would not be soliciting help in violation of this canon.[30]

C. Gifts to Pious Causes

The term "pious cause" as used in the Code of Canon Law, has a meaning akin to but is not as broad as the Anglo-

the Apostolic Delegate.—S.C.Or., Jan. 7, 1930—*A.A.S.*, XXII (1930)—108; Bouscaren, *The Canon Law Digest*, I, 719.

[26] Can. 1503.

[27] Cans. 415, #2, 5°; 630, #4.

[28] Coronata, *Institutiones Iuris Canonici* (5 vols., Vol. II, 4. ed., Taurini-Romae: Marietti, 1951), II, n. 1042, p. 457 (hereafter cited Coronata).

[29] Bouscaren-Ellis, p. 805.

[30] Vermeersch-Cruesen, II, n. 823, p. 577; Doheny, p. 51.

American term "charity." It may be defined as anything that is done principally in consideration of God and for a supernatural end, either to merit grace or glory with God or in satisfaction for one's own or another's sins.[31] The term therefore, includes works, which, either by reason of their direct purpose (*ex fine operis*) or by reason of the intention of the donor (*ex fine operantis*) are destined for a supernatural end. This supernatural end may be the worship of God, the honor of the saints, or the spiritual and temporal welfare of one's neighbor.[32]

Ordinarily, there is no difficulty in determining whether the object of a person's benevolence constitutes a pious cause, when the gift is directed to a work which is pious of its nature (*ex fine operis*). Thus gifts made for the celebration of Masses, for the performance of acts of religion, or for the purposes of any moral person or association in the Church are gifts made to pious causes. However, there are other works which in their internal character are indifferent as regards piety. Such works would be recreation centers, schools, hospitals, etc. These works and also gifts in aid of them cannot be established as pious through any application of the standard of intrinsic piety. Whether such works therefore constitute pious causes must be derived from the intention of the donor; if undertaken and promoted from a supernatural motive, v.g., the promotion and preservation of purity of faith and integrity of morals, then such works are pious causes.[33]

a. Acts by Which Goods are Dedicated to Pious Causes

Canon 1513, #1, provides that any person who is capable both in accordance with the natural and ecclesiastical law, of disposing of his property may give it to pious causes

[31] Vromant, p. 158.

[32] Bouscaren-Ellis, p. 813; Beste, p. 787.

[33] Cf. Visser, "De Solemnitatibus Piarum Voluntatum in Iure Canonico," *Appolinaris* XX (1947), pp. 65, 66 (hereafter cited Visser); Beste, p. 787.

either by acts *inter vivos* or by acts *mortis causa*.[34] By virtue of this principle, the Church asserts the capacity of each individual, who is capable both by natural and ecclesiastical law of disposing of his goods, to dispose of them in favor of pious causes without restriction from the civil power.[35]

Every man is capable by natural law of disposing of his goods as long as he has the ownership of the same and is endowed with the free use of reason. Therefore, infants, insane persons, and persons under the influence of unjust fear are barred by the natural law. Similarly, under Canon Law, anyone endowed with the sufficient use of reason can dispose of his goods, except minors without the previous consent of their parents,[36] novices during the time of novitiate,[37] and professed religious in congregations during their lifetime.[38]

The terms *per actum inter vivos* and *per actum mortis causa* as used in this canon must be understood in the broad sense to include all acts by which a person may dispose of his property. Hence, the term *actus inter vivos* includes any donation or contract by which ownership of property is transferred irrevocably to another without any consideration of the death of the donor entering into the act.[39] The term *actus mortis causa* is used synonymously with the term *ultima voluntas*,[40] and includes every provision made for the transfer of property to take place after the death of the donor, whether by gifts *mortis causa*, wills, codicils or legacies.[41]

Whether the disposition of property to a pious cause is

[34] Can. 1513, #1: "Qui ex iure naturae et ecclesiastico libere valet de suis bonis statuere, potest ad causas pias, sive per actum inter vivos sive per actum mortis causa, bona relinquere."

[35] Beste, p. 806.

[36] Beste, p. 806.

[37] Can. 568.

[38] Can. 583, #1.

[39] Bouscaren-Ellis, p. 814.

[40] Wernz-Vidal, Vol. IV, Pars. II, n. 800; Beste, p. 806.

[41] Beste, p. 806; Bouscaren-Ellis, p. 814.

effected by an act *inter vivos* or by act *mortis causa,* it may take the form of a direct gift, with or without a use imposed,[42] or it may take the form of a canonical trust (*fiducia*), whereby the donor gives the property to some person, lay, clerical or religious, to hold in trust for the pious cause.[43]

The canonical *fiducia* or trust is very similar in effect to the charitable trust of Anglo-American law, but is not an exact counterpart. The principal difference appears to lie in the fact that the Roman or Canonical notion of a trust is concerned with an obligation to transfer to another the title to the property involved or to spend it for some pious cause, while the Anglo-American concept of trust involves the trustee's continued holding of the title to the trust property while conferring the benefit of that property upon another or for the accomplishment of some charitable purpose. Thus the Anglo-American concept of a trust is a specific mode of holding property which does not have a canonical counterpart.[44]

b. The Solemnities of the Civil Law in Regard to Gifts to Pious Causes

The Code, while asserting the right of each individual, competent in accordance with both the natural and ecclesiastical law to donate his property to pious causes,[45] never-

[42] Thus a person may donate his property for the purpose of establishing a pious foundation. By a pious foundation is meant any kind of property given to a moral person in the Church in any manner whatsoever with the obligation of using the annual income either for the celebration of masses, or for carrying out certain defined ecclesiastical functions, or for the performance of some works of piety and charity. These obligations may be imposed *in perpetuum* or for a long time.—Can. 1544, #1. Cf. cans. 1544-1551 for the law concerning pious foundations. Likewise a person may donate his property for the purpose of establishing a hospital, orphanage and other like institutions.—Cf. cans. 1489-1494.

[43] Cf. can. 1516.

[44] Byrne, *Investment of Church Funds,* The Catholic University of America Canon Law Studies, n. 309 (Washington, D.C.: The Catholic University of America Press, 1951), p. 92 (hereafter cited Byrne).

[45] Can. 1513, #1

theless, prescribes that where last wills and testaments are made in favor of the Church, the solemnities of the civil law should be observed in so far as this is possible.[46] The omission of the civil solemnities, however, does not affect the validity of the bequest or devise, as this provision is rather a precautionary measure to facilitate and expedite the probating and filing of testamentary dispositions as well as to provide for their security.

The text of the canon as well as the traditional teaching of the Church vindicate this conclusion. For while the canon states that the civil formalities should be observed in so far as this is possible, it provides further, without any distinction as to their observance or non-observance, that if the civil formalities are omitted the heirs should be admonished (*moneantur*) to fulfill the will of the testator. It is evident, therefore, that the Church, while it exhorts benefactors to observe the solemnities of the civil law for convenience and security, in no way relinquishes its right to testamentary benefactions merely because the solemnities were not observed.[47]

Moreover, this has been the traditional teaching of the Church particularly since the time of Alexander III (1159-1181).[48] In 1901, the Sacred Penitentiary declared that pious bequests are generally valid in the eyes of the Church and considered binding in conscience even if they are held as invalid in civil law on account of the omission of formalities.[49] Likewise, the recent decision of the Code Commission interpreting the word *moneantur* of the canon as containing a precept rather than an exhortation confirms this teaching.[50]

[46] Can. 1513, #2: "In ultimis voluntatibus in bonum Ecclesiae serventur, si fieri possit, solemnitates iuris civilis; hae si omissae fuerint, heredes moneantur ut testatoris voluntatem adimpleant."

[47] Doheny, p. 89.

[48] c. 11, X, *de testamentis et ultimis voluntatibus*, III, 26.

[49] S. Penit., 10 Jan., 1901.—*Collectanea Sacrae Congregationis de Propaganda Fide* (2 vols., Romae: Typographia Polyglotta S.C. de Propaganda Fide, 1907), II, n. 2099 (hereafter cited Collectanea).

[50] Code Comm., 17 Feb., 1930—*A.A.S.*, XXII (1930), 196; Bouscaren, *The Canon Law Digest*, I, 725.

The phrase *in bonum Ecclesiae,* as used in the second paragraph of canon 1513, has been interpreted by some canonists in a restrictive sense in accordance with canon 1498,[51] and hence they limit the significance of the canon to legacies made to an ecclesiastical moral person, that is, one duly established by ecclesiastical authority. However, neither the context, nor the traditional teaching of the Church warrant such a restrictive interpretation.

The argument from the context refers to both canon 1513, ♯1, and canon 1514. In canon 1513, ♯1, pious causes in general are named as being entitled to receive gifts made to them by persons not incapacitated by the natural or ecclesiastical law. It is almost inconceivable that the legislator, being aware that he had so recently referred to pious causes in general would have unobtrusively made a restriction in the very next paragraph of the same canon without a more explicit indication of his intention to do so. In canon 1514 the legislator immediately speaks of pious causes in general as if this had been the subject matter of the intervening legislation.[52] Besides, the traditional teaching of the Church has made no such distinction.[53]

The fact that donations *inter vivos* were not mentioned in this canon indicates that the solemnities of the civil law should be observed in their regard in accordance with the provisions of canon 1529.[54]

[51] "In canonibus qui sequuntur, nomine Ecclesiae significatur non solum Ecclesia Universa aut Sedes Apostolica sed etiam quaelibet persona moralis in Ecclesia, nisi ex contextu sermonis vel ex natura rei aliud appareat." Cf. Noldin-Schmitt, *Summa Theologiae Moralis* (3 vols.: 30. ed., Oeneponte: Typis et Sumptibus Feliciani Rauch, 1954), II, n. 550; Vromant, p. 168; Coronata, II, n. 1054, p. 476.

[52] Cf. Hannan, *The Canon Law of Wills*, The Catholic University of America Canon Law Studies, n. 86 (Washington, D.C.: The Catholic University of America Press, 1934), p. 287; Beste, p. 807.

[53] Cf. Beste, p. 807; Dec. of the Sacred Penitentiary, Jan. 10, 1901. —*Collectanea*, II, n. 2099.

[54] Can. 1529: "Quae ius civile in territorio statuit de contractibus tam in genere, quam in specie, sive nominatis sive innominatis, et de solutionibus, eadem iure canonico in materia ecclesiastica iisdem cum effectibus serventur, nisi iuri divino contraria sint aut aliud iure

c. Fulfillment and Execution of Gifts to Pious Causes

The guiding principle with regard to the execution and fulfillment of gifts to pious causes is the strict adherence to the intentions of the donors in all their details, in regard to both the administration and distribution of the property, as long as nothing is demanded which is contrary to natural and ecclesiastical law.[55] To insure the fulfillment of this principle the Code appoints ordinaries as the executors of all pious wills whether effected by an act *inter vivos* or by an act *mortis causa*.[56] Therefore, the ordinary is referred to as an *exsecutor natus* to distinguish him from the *exsecutor delegatus*, that is, the executor appointed by the testator or donor, or by the civil law, or in defect of either of these by the ordinary himself.[57]

The ordinary as *exsecutor natus* does not supersede the *exsecutor delegatus*,[58] but the latter is subject to the vigilance and to the visitation of the ordinary and is obliged to render an account to him on the completion of his duties.[59] Moreover, the Code provides that any clauses contrary to

canonico caveatur." Coronata, II, n. 1054, p. 476, footnote 4 states: "hic agi solummodo de ultimis voluntatibus, quam ob rem si formalitates civilis legis servatae non sint in aliis donationibus inter vivos hic canon non urget." Cf. also Vromant, p. 176; Vermeersch-Cruesen, II, n. 850, p. 597. Noldin and Visser hold the opposite opinion and maintain that all such donations are valid irrespective of the requirements of the civil law.—Noldin, II, n. 55; Visser, pp. 135, 136.

[55] Can. 1514: "Voluntates fidelium facultates suas in pias causas donantium vel relinquentium, sive per actum inter vivos, sive per actum mortis causa, diligentissime impleantur etiam circa modum administrationis et erogationis bonorum, salvo praescripto can. 1515, #3."

[56] Can. 1515, #1: "Ordinarii omnium piarum voluntatum tam mortis causa quam inter vivos exsecutores sunt."

[57] Bouscaren-Ellis, p. 760.

[58] Beste, p. 809.

[59] Can. 1515, #2: "Hoc ex iure Ordinarii vigilare possunt, ac debent, etiam per visitationem, ut piae voluntates impleantur, et alii exsecutores delegati debent, perfuncti munere, illis reddere rationem."

this right of ordinaries are to be considered as non-existent.[60]

Regarding the execution and fulfillment of canonical trusts, canon 1516, #1, provides that as soon as a cleric or religious has received property in trust[61] for a pious cause, whether by donation *inter vivos* or by a last will and testament, he must inform his ordinary of his trust and indicate to him the nature and extent of the property involved, whether movable or immovable and the burdens thereto attached. Should the donor or testator expressly and absolutely forbid any reference to the ordinary in this regard the trusteeship cannot be accepted.[62] The ordinary must demand that the trust *res* be safely invested, and he must carefully see to it that the trust is carried out according to the norm laid down in canon 1515.[63] It is to be noted that the provisions of this canon (can. 1516), are not imposed on lay trustees. Hence, they have no other obligation than that prescribed in canon 1515, #2, that is, of submitting to the visitation of the ordinary and of rendering an account to him on the completion of their duties.[64]

The term ordinary as used in reference to the execution and fulfillment of gifts to pious causes whether absolutely or in trust, has reference to the local ordinary, when the property is destined for the benefit of pious causes in places subject to his jurisdiction. Where, however, property is destined for the benefit of pious causes subject to the jurisdiction of a religious ordinary, then the religious ordinary

60 Can. 1515, #3: "Clausulae huic Ordinariorum iuri contrariae, ultimis voluntatibus adiectae, tamquam non appositae habeantur."

61 Canonists generally agree that a gift of a definite sum of money to be used for a determined end, when no administration is required does not come under the provisions of this canon.—Cf. Coronata, II, n. 1056, p. 480; Wernz-Vidal, IV, Pars II, p. 277, note 9.

62 Can. 1516, #1.

63 Can. 1516, #2.

64 Vermeersch-Cruesen, II, n. 836, p. 588; Vromant, p. 174.

is the competent ordinary in regard to the execution and fulfillment of the pious will.[65]

d. The Modification of Gifts to Pious Causes

Consistent with the principle stated in canon 1514, that the wishes of the faithful who donate their property to pious causes must be diligently fulfilled, the Code restricts any modification of last wills and testaments to very narrow limits. The modification of gifts *inter vivos* is not mentioned for the simple reason that the donor in such cases is still living and hence, any readjustment necessary can be made with his consent.[66]

In general, the Code reserves to the Holy See any reduction,[67] restriction,[68] or commutation[69] of last wills and testaments. Local ordinaries may exercise this power only if such was expressly granted by the person who made the will.[70] In either case, however, a just and necessary cause is required not only for licitness but also for validity.[71]

Should it occur that the obligations imposed by last wills and testaments become impossible of fulfillment because of decreased revenues or other reasons, due to no fault of the administrators, the ordinary may diminish the burdens equitably after consulting all interested parties.[72] In exercising this power the ordinary may diminish the obligations (*reductio*) or specify their conditions (*moderatio*) but he

[65] Cf. cans. 1516, #3; 535, #3, 2°; 630, #3, 4; 631, #3; 1425; 1525; 1550.

[66] Vermeersch-Cruesen, II, n. 836, p. 589; Beste, pp. 809, 810.

[67] By reduction is meant any diminution of the obligations imposed by a last will, as for instance in the number of masses to be said, or the number of free scholarships.

[68] By restriction is meant a more specific determination regarding secondary and accessory conditions, such as a sung mass or a mass to be said in a particular church.

[69] By commutation is meant a substitution of one obligation for another, as when money given to decorate a church is used for the support of the poor.

[70] Can. 1517, #1.

[71] Can. 1517, #1; cf. Coronata, II, n. 1057, p. 481.

[72] Can. 1517, #2.

may not substitute works of a different kind or works in aid of different beneficiaries (*commutatio*) unless the performance of the type of work intended had become truly impossible, or unless works of the specified kind can no longer aid the beneficiaries indicated.[73] Whatever action he should take, he is obliged to conform as closely as possible to the will of the donor.[74] Moreover, even in the situation envisioned above, the reduction of Mass stipends is always reserved to the Holy See, unless the testator stipulated otherwise in his will.[75]

Finally, it is to be noted that interpretation is not the same as the commutation of a last will. Since the ordinary is the executor of all pious wills,[76] he has the right to interpret them if necessary. This he is to do by determining the exact wishes of the donor expressed in his last will and testament, even though it be invalid at civil law, or as determined by the testimony of trustworthy witnesses, etc.[77]

D. Prescription

Prescription at Canon Law may be defined as a method introduced by positive law for acquiring ownership or of ridding oneself of burdens, by prolonged possession or nonfulfillment of obligations, under certain conditions.[78] Thus prescription at Canon Law can be acquisitive or liberative and includes the three Anglo-American institutes of adverse possession, prescription, and limitation of actions. As this latter institute, both in Canon[79] and civil law, is primarily

[73] Cappello, *Summa Iuris Canonici* (3 vols., Vol. II, 4. ed., Romae: Apud Aedes Universitatis Gregorianae, 1945), II, n. 600, 2 (hereafter cited Cappello).

[74] Can. 1517, #2.

[75] Can. 1517, #2; cf. can. 1551, #1; Code Comm., 14 July 1922—*A.A.S.*, XIV (1922), 529; Bouscaren, *The Canon Law Digest*, I, 726.

[76] Can. 1515, #1.

[77] Bouscaren-Ellis, p. 820.

[78] Can. 1508; Ayrinhac, *Administrative Legislation in The New Code of Canon Law* (London-New York-Toronto: Longmans, Green and Co., 1930), p. 407 (hereafter cited Ayrinhac).

[79] The canonical *praescriptio* as affecting the limitation of actions, is treated in canons 1701-1705.

a matter of procedural law affecting one's right to sue, it is not entirely germane to the topic and will not be considered *ex professo.*

The Code of Canon Law provides, with regard to prescription that, with certain specified exceptions, the Church accepts for the prescription of ecclesiastical property what is provided in the civil legislation of the respective nation, whether it be considered as a mode of acquiring property or rights, or as a mode of freeing oneself from an obligation.[80] By virtue of this principle, therefore, in the absence of canonical provisions to the contrary, the norms relating to prescription must be taken from the civil law of the nation where the prescription is to be applied.[81]

In general the following five conditions are required to establish prescription: (1) a thing that is prescriptible, (2) good faith, (3) some kind of title, (4) possession, and (5) the time required by law.[82]

With regard to the first condition, the Code excludes the following goods and rights from the scope of prescription: (a) whatever pertains to the divine law, whether natural or positive;[83] (b) things which can be obtained by Apostolic privilege only;[84] (c) spiritual rights which lay persons are not capable of receiving, that is, when there is question of prescription in favor of lay persons;[85] (d) the certain and undisputed boundary lines of ecclesiastical provinces, dioceses, parishes, vicariates, and prefectures apostolic, abbacies

[80] Canon 1508.

[81] Vromant, p. 139.

[82] Beste, p. 803; Bouscaren-Ellis, p. 810.

[83] Canon 1509, 1°. The reason for this is evident as no human law can annul the divine law. Thus property seized by theft or violence can never be acquired by prescription.

[84] Canon 1509, 2°. However, possession for one hundred years is equivalent to an Apostolic privilege.—Cf. can. 63, #2. An example of such a privilege would be the privilege sometimes granted to priests to administer confirmation or minor orders.

[85] Can. 1509, 3°. Thus a lay person is incapable of receiving jurisdiction or a benefice in the Church.—Can. 118.

and prelacies *nullius*;[86] (e) Mass stipends and their obligations;[87] (f) an ecclesiastical benefice in the absence of title;[88] (g) the right of visitation and of obedience, if the consequence would be that subjects can be visited by no prelate and are no longer subject to any prelate;[89] (h) payment of the cathedratic tax.[90]

In addition to the above, the Code imposes the following limitations regarding the prescription of sacred objects.[91] Sacred objects which are owned by private persons can be acquired by private persons through prescription, but they cannot devote them to uses that are not sacred; if, however, they have lost their consecration or blessing[92] they may be acquired even for such purposes without restriction, but not for sordid uses.[93] Sacred objects which are not owned by private persons cannot through the agency of prescription be acquired by a private person, but they may be prescribed by one ecclesiastical moral person against another.[94]

With regard to the second condition, namely that of good faith, the Code prescribes that prescription will not avail unless it is radicated on good faith which must be verified not only at the moment of entering into possession but also

[86] Can. 1509, 4°. If the boundaries are uncertain or disputed, prescription is admitted since it will solve the doubt.—Vermeersch-Cruesen, II, n. 831, p. 584.

[87] Can. 1509, 5°. The prohibition applies to manual as well as to founded masses and applies both to the person who is obliged to give a stipend and to the person who is obliged to say the mass by reason of the stipend received.—Bouscaren-Ellis, p. 811.

[88] Canon 1509, 6°. Prescription is operative if color of title exists.—Can. 1446.

[89] Canon 1509, 7°.

[90] Canon 1509, 8°.

[91] Sacred objects are such as have been destined for divine worship by consecration or benediction.—Can. 1497, #2.

[92] Sacred objects lose their consecration or blessing when they are so badly damaged or so much changed as to lose their original form and thus become useless for their purpose, or if they are used for unbecoming purposes or offered for sale publicly or at auction.—Can. 1305.

[93] Can. 1510, #1.

[94] Can. 1510, #2.

during the whole period of possession required for prescription.[95] Since this principle is merely a declaration of the natural law it must be observed not only in regard to church property but also in regard to all other things as well, even though it may not be required by the civil law.[96] Hence, in the absence of good faith Canon Law will never recognize a right acquired by prescription even though externally bad faith is not proven.

Good faith at Canon Law, if there is question of acquisitive prescription, may be described as a judgment by which a person prudently judges that the thing which he possesses is his own, or at least does not belong to anyone else. In the case of liberative prescription, good faith is a prudent judgment of the person prescribing, that he is free from every burden, either because he erroneously believes that the debt was paid, or condoned, or because he honestly believes that he is under no obligation to make payment until demand has been made on him by the creditor.[97] In the case of moral persons, this good faith must be verified in the majority of the members of a collegiate moral person, and in the responsible administrator where a non-collegiate moral person is involved. And since moral persons always retain the same identity, the good faith of subsequent members or administrators does not counteract the bad faith of their predecessors.[98]

This good faith is required not only at the beginning of possession, but throughout the entire time required for prescription. Nevertheless, if a person takes possession of a thing in good faith but later begins to doubt whether the thing belongs to another or not, he remains in good faith and may use prescription even though the doubt still remains; provided, however, that he made diligent inquiry to resolve the doubt. The reason for this is that *in dubio*

[95] Can. 1512.

[96] Bouscaren-Ellis, p. 812.

[97] Beste, p. 805.

[98] Abbo-Hannan, II, 720.

melior est conditio possidentis.[99] The Code says nothing about good faith after the required time has run. Consequently, knowledge subsequently induced that the property had in fact belonged to another, or a serious doubt regarding its ownership, will not destroy title passed by operation of law.[100]

The element of good faith constitutes the principal dividing point between Canon and civil law regarding prescription. The basis for this is traceable to the objective of each society; for whereas the canonical legislator seeks the salvation of souls, the civil legislator seeks the common good and tranquility of society. Thus, while the civil legislator may require less in the external forum and allow the individual to follow his own conscience in the matter, the canonical legislator, no matter what appears externally, cannot grant any right through prescription unless good faith exists in the internal forum also, for otherwise the law would reward the violation of rights.[101]

The Code is silent regarding the third and fourth conditions, hence the provisions of the civil law must be applied. Similarly, with regard to the fifth condition, that of time, the Code accepts the norms of the civil law with the following exceptions. A period of one hundred years is required for the operation of prescription against the immovable property of the Holy See, precious movable property belonging to it, as well as against rights and claims at law, whether personal or real, pertaining thereto.[102] A period of thirty years is required in the case of other ecclesiastical moral persons.[103]

[99] Bouscaren-Ellis, p. 813.

[100] Martin, *Adverse Possession, Prescription and Limitations of Actions. The Canonical "Praescriptio,"* The Catholic University of America Canon Law Studies, n. 202 (Washington, D.C.: The Catholic University of America Press, 1944), p. 54 (hereafter cited Martin).

[101] Cf. Bouscaren-Ellis, p. 812.

[102] Can. 1511, #1.

[103] Can. 1511, #2. Since the provisions of Canon 1511, #1, 2, contain an exception to Canon 1508, they must be interpreted strictly

Article 2. Mississippi Law on Acquisition

SECTION 1. THE RIGHT OF THE CHURCH TO ACQUIRE TEMPORAL PROPERTY UNDER MISSISSIPPI LAW

Consistent with its policy in the exclusion of an established church, Art. 4, sect. 66 of the Mississippi Constitution provides: "No law granting a donation or gratuity in favor of any person or object shall be enacted except by the concurrence of two-thirds of the members elect of each branch of the legislature, nor by any vote for a sectarian purpose."[104] On the other hand, Mississippi law severely limits both the proprietary capacity of religious societies as well as their capacity to take property by devise. While the latter provisions are referred to in the Codes as mortmain statutes, the former may likewise be termed such, as both have the same purpose, viz., to prevent the accumulation of property by religious societies in *mortua manu.*

A. Statutory Limitations Restricting the Proprietary Capacity of Religious Societies.

Statutes restricting the proprietary capacity of religious societies in Mississippi first appeared in the Code of 1857. Sect. X, art. 53, provided:

> Any religious society or congregation, or ecclesiastical body, may hold, at any one place, a house or tenement for a place of worship, with proper and rea-

(can. 19). Hence, movable goods pertaining to the Holy See must be reckoned according to the norms of the civil law regarding time. Moreover, moral persons spoken of in the second paragraph must be understood in the strict sense, and hence not inclusive of pious associations.—Vermeersch-Cruesen, II, n. 831, p. 584.

[104] Grants of state funds to a non-profit sectarian hospital are not violative of this section of the Constitution if such a non-profit hospital (1) has agreed with the Commission on Hospital Care to maintain at least ten per cent (10%) of its bed capacity, if needed, for charity patients; (2) will be operated with the purpose of providing maximum hospital facilities to citizens of the state at minimum cost; and (3) will be available at all times as part of the statewide hospital program. —Craig, State Auditor v. Mercy Hospital-Street Memorial, 209 Miss. 427, 45 So. 2d. 809 (1950).

> able ground thereto attached; a house or tenement as a place of residence for their pastor or minister, with proper and reasonable ground thereto attached; a house or tenement to be appropriated and used as a male school, or seminary of learning, with proper and sufficient ground thereto attached; and another house or tenement, to be appropriated as a female school or seminary of learning; and a cemetery of sufficient dimensions, and no more. *Provided,* that any religious society or denomination may own such colleges or seminaries of learning, as it may think proper, if used for such purposes.[105]

This statute was incorporated into the subsequent Codes of 1871 and 1880 without change.[106] The Code of 1892, however, extended that statute to include a place of residence for the superior clergyman of the religious society, congregation or ecclesiastical body.[107]

No further change occurred until 1930 when the statute was revised. The amended statute provided as follows:

> Any religious society, ecclesiastical body and/or any congregation thereof, may hold and own, at any one place, the following real property, but no other, viz.:
>
> (a) Each house or building used as a place of worship with a reasonable quantity of ground annexed to such building or house.
>
> (b) The house or houses used as parish house or houses, community house or houses, Sunday school house or houses, or house or houses of similar nature, as may be reasonably necessary, together with a reasonable quantity of ground thereto annexed.
>
> (c) Each house used for a place of residence for its pastor, minister, bishop or representative in charge of a district, conference or convention, together with a reasonable quantity of ground thereto annexed.
>
> (d) A hospital or infirmary and a nurses home in connection therewith, together with a reasonable quantity of ground thereto annexed.

[105] *Mississippi Code of 1857,* Ch. 35, sect. X, art. 53.

[106] *Mississippi Code of 1871,* Ch. 35, art. VII, sect. 2438; *Mississippi Code of 1880,* Ch. 38, sect. 1072.

[107] *Mississippi Code of 1892,* Ch. 25, sect. 859.

(e) All buildings used by a school, college or seminary of learning contiguous to and or a part of the college or seminary plant, for administration, class rooms, laboratories, observatories, dormitories, and for housing the faculty and students thereof, together with a reasonable quantity of land in connection therewith.

(f) All buildings used for an orphan asylum or institution together with a reasonable quantity of ground used in connection therewith.

(g) All buildings used for a camp ground or assembly for religious purposes, together with a reasonable quantity of land in connection therewith.

(h) Lands for a cemetery or cemeteries of sufficient dimensions.[108]

In 1946 the statute was again amended by a special act of the legislature so as to permit religious societies, in addition to the above property, to hold and own buildings and grounds used for denominational headquarters or administrative purposes. The provisions of the Code of 1930 and the act of 1946 are now incorporated in section 5331 of the Mississippi Code of 1942 as recompiled in 1956.[109]

The historical development of the statute as outlined has a practical as well as an academic value. In 1926, the legislature enacted a curative statute validating titles to all real estate which had been acquired up to that time by religious societies contrary to statute.[110] The statute, however, was

[108] *Mississippi Code of 1930 of the Public Statute Laws of the State of Mississippi, Revised and Annotated by the Code Commission under the Provisions of an Act of the Legislature approved April 26, 1928, and Reported and Revised, Annotated and Adopted by the Legislature at its Regular Session in 1930* (2 vols., Atlanta, 1930), Vol. I, ch. 100, sect. 4169 (hereafter cited *Mississippi Code of 1930*).

[109] *Laws of the State of Mississippi, Appropriations, General Legislation and Resolutions, Passed at the Regular Session of the Mississippi Legislature held in Jackson, 1946* (Jackson, Mississippi, 1946), Ch. 279, par. 3 (hereafter cited *Laws of the State of Mississippi*, followed by the year); *Mississippi Code of 1942, Annotated, Recompiled,* Vol. 4A, sect. 5351.

[110] "That the title to all real property now owned by any religious society, ecclesiastical body and/or any congregation thereof, be vali-

retroactive only and did not affect the titles to any property acquired by any society after the statute went into effect.[111] A similar statute was enacted in 1946.[112] This statute however, had a limited effect only; validating titles to real estate acquired by religious societies for denominational headquarters and/or administrative purposes.[113]

The Supreme Court of Mississippi has not at any time defined precisely what the phrases "in any one place" and "reasonable quantity of ground" entail. With regard to the latter phrase, it would appear that if the land is being used in connection with any of the facilities mentioned in the statute, which religious societies may own and operate, then such land constitutes a "reasonable quantity of ground". Thus the quantity of ground may extend from the lot on which a church or parish house is situated to 640 acres which a college or institution for the education of youth may hold.[114]

There are no extant cases involving what is meant by the phrase "in any one place". Consequently, it would appear that such would be explained along denominational lines. Thus in the case of the Catholic Church, the phrase would

dated and the same is hereby validated and such society, body or congregation is authorized and empowered to continue to own the same or to convey or encumber the same,"—*Laws of the State of Mississippi, Appropriations, General Legislation and Resolutions, Passed at a Regular Session of the Mississippi Legislature held in Jackson, 1926* (Jackson, Mississippi, 1926), Ch. 194.

[111] Cf. State ex rel. Knox v. Sisters of Mercy, 150 Miss. 559, 115 So. 323 (1928).

[112] *Laws of the State of Mississippi*, 1946, ch. 279, #3.

[113] Cf. *Mississippi Code of 1942 Annotated, Recompiled*, Vol. 4A, sect. 5351, subsection (i).

[114] Section 9697 of the *Mississippi Code of 1942* provides that any college or institution for the education of youth, may hold real estate to the amount of 640 acres exempt from taxation, if the property is used directly and exclusively for such purpose. It was stated in the case of Central Methodist Church v. City of Meridian, 126 Miss. 780, 89 So. 650 (1921), that it never was the purpose of the legislature to exempt from taxation any more property than a religious society could lawfully hold.—Cf. Chandler v. Executive Committee on Education, Synod of Presbyterian Church, U.S., Inc. 165 Miss. 690, 146 So. 597 (1933).

mean "in any one parish". There are a few cases which discuss the phrase "reasonable quantity of ground", but none are specific. Use and contiguity seem to be the essential requirements. Thus, in the case of Enochs v. City of Jackson, the Supreme Court held that the church lot adjoining that on which the church house was situated and not used except that a plank walk for entrance to the church annex was maintained thereon, constituted property held in contravention to the statute.[115] In the case of Central Methodist Church v. Meridian the court seemed to place emphasis on the element of contiguity. Speaking of the property that the religious society was not entitled to own, the court stated:

> It (is) further agreed that the two pieces of vacant property in block 64 and block 84 are not contiguous to each other nor are they contiguous to the parsonage site in block 43 nor to the church site in block 157, but both pieces are several blocks distant from the church site and parsonage site."[116]

Whether the court had reference here to the phrase "in any one place", or was simply indicating that since this property was not contiguous to the church or parsonage site it could not be said to constitute a reasonable quantity of ground in their regard, is not quite clear. It would seem that the latter explanation is more logical. For if contiguity were essential for the phrase "in any one place" then religious societies would have to forego the right they have to obtain much of the property mentioned in the statute, for the simple reason that it is impossible to obtain all the property needed in one place.

If a religious society acquires property in contravention to the statute the property does not escheat to the state as the statute contains no provision for forfeiture.[117] The title to the property, however, is a defeasible one at the instance of

[115] Enochs v. City of Jackson, 144 Miss. 360, 109 So. 846 (1926).

[116] Central Methodist Church v. Meridian, 126 Miss. 780, 89 So. 650 (1921).

[117] State ex rel. Knox v. Sisters of Mercy, 150 Miss. 559, 115 So. 323 (1928).

the state, which can force a sale of the property but cannot take it from the society.[118] The religious society, therefore, can continue to use and enjoy the property, unless and until the right to do so is successfully questioned in a direct proceeding by the state.[119] Neither private persons nor next of kin can take advantage of the restrictions imposed by law on the amount of property a religious society may own.[120]

B. Mortmain Statutes as Affecting the Capacity of the Church to Acquire Property by Devise

Statutes limiting the capacity of religious societies to acquire property by devise likewise have had a long and somewhat varied history in Mississippi. They appeared for the first time in the Code of 1857 and provided as follows:

> Article 55. Every devise or bequest of lands, tenements, or hereditaments, or any interest therein, of freehold, or less than freehold, either present or future, vested or contingent, or of any money directed to be raised by the sale thereof, contained in any last will and testament, or codicil, or other testamentary writing, in favor of any religious or ecclesiastical corporation, sole or aggregate, or any religious or ecclesiastical society or to any religious denomination or association of persons, or to any person or body politic, in trust either express or implied, secret or resulting, either for the use and benefit of such religious corporation, society, denomination, or association, or for the purpose of being given or appropriated to charitable uses or purposes, shall be null and void, and the heir at law shall take the same property so devised or bequeathed as though no testamentary disposition had been made.
>
> Article 56. Every legacy, gift or bequest, or money

118 State ex rel. Knox v. Sisters of Mercy, 150 Miss. 559, 115 So. 323 (1928).

119 Peeples v. Enochs, 170 Miss. 472, 153 So. 798 (1934).

120 State ex rel. Knox v. Sisters of Mercy, 150 Miss. 559, 115 So. 323 (1928); Jones v. Habersham, 107 U.S. 174, 2 S. Ct. 336, 27 L. Ed. 401 (1882).

> or personal property, or of any interest, benefit or use therein, either direct, implied or otherwise, contained in any last will and testament or codicil, in favor of any religious or ecclesiastical society, or to any religious, denomination or association either for its own use or benefit, or for the purpose of being given or appropriated to charitable uses, shall be null and void and the distributees shall take the same as though no such testamentary disposition had been made.[121]

These provisions were incorporated, practically without change, in the Code of 1871.[122] They were omitted, however, from the Code of 1880. What reasons motivated the legislature to repeal these statutes are not revealed; whatever they may have been, their omission from Mississippi jurisprudence was to be of short duration. In the Constitution adopted by the people of the state in 1890 they were given recognition as part of the fundamental law of the state by their incorporation into the Constitution as articles 269 and 270 respectively.[123]

The provisions of the articles of the Constitution as well as the statutes of the subsequent codes enacted in accordance

[121] *Mississippi Code of 1857*, Ch. 55, arts. 55, 56. Section 54 of this Code provided that lands, tenements or hereditaments, or any interest or benefit therein, or therefrom, except for the purposes provided in the foregoing article (art. 53 already discussed) which shall be granted in any manner to any religious society, denomination, or congregation shall be *ipso facto*, by such an alienation forfeited to the state. This section was incorporated in the subsequent Code of 1871 (sect. 2439), but following the omission of the mortmain statutes from the Code of 1880, it was not incorporated in subsequent codes.

[122] *Mississippi Code of 1871*, Sects. 2440, 2441. Art. 56 reads in the 1871 Code as follows:

> Every legacy, gift or bequest of money or personal property, or of any interest, benefit or use therein, either direct, implied or otherwise, contained in any last will and testament or codicil, in favor of any religious or *ecclesiastical corporation sole or aggregate*, or any religious or ecclesiastical society, or to any denomination or association, either for its own use or benefit or for the purpose of being given or appropriated to charitable uses, shall be null and void, and the distributees shall take the same, as though no such testamentary disposition had been made.

[123] *Mississippi Constitution of 1890*, Arts. 269, 270.

therewith remained unchanged until 1940.[124]

Though the interpretations of the Supreme Court of Mississippi regarding the application of these provisions are now to a great extent purely academic, it is of interest to note what the court said regarding the purposes of these provisions. The extant cases manifest a twofold purpose with varied emphasis on each. The case of Barton v. King which was decided after the enactment of the statutes in 1857 stated their purpose as follows:

> This whole section concerning religious societies or congregations was designed simply to prevent the evils resulting, as well from the efforts to accumulate vast estates in the hands of the church as from the accomplishment of such an object, and had no reference to the power of testamentary disposition.[125]

On the other hand, in the case of Blackbourn v. Tucker, which was decided five years after the adoption of the constitutional provisions, the following purpose was enunciated:

> Manifestly, the purpose of the Constitution is to prevent one who will not be charitable at his own expense from being so at the expense of his heir at law. One may yet "sell all that he hath, and give to the poor," but he may not keep his gripe [sic] on his estate until death relaxes his grasp, and then, at the expense of wife and child, devote it to religious uses.[126]

Finally, a case decided as late as 1941, stated:

> Sections 269 and 270 of the Constitution were enacted to prevent the evils and abuses which provoked the early statutes of mortmain. Although some of the evils thwarted by these statutes have been defined with reference to the dishersion of the immediate heirs, the original purpose to pre-

[124] The statutes of the codes were identical, at least materially, with the constitutional provisions and as such therefore served no purpose, as it is well settled that prohibitory sections of a constitution are self-executing.—Cf. 11 *Am. Jur.* 695, Sect. 77.

[125] Barton v. King, 41 Miss. 288 (1866).

[126] Blackbourn v. Tucker, 72 Miss. 735, 17 So. 737 (1895).

> vent the accumulation of land in *mortua manu* through grant or devise to religious or ecclesiastical bodies has been generally recognized.[127]

This twofold purpose of the mortmain statutes can be more readily seen in the amendments to the constitutional sections approved by the people of the state and adopted in 1940. In 1938, the legislature proposed amendments to constitutional sections 269 or 270.[128] The proposed amendments were approved by an overwhelming majority of the voters in November, 1939, and on January 18, 1940, the amendments went into effect.[129] Former section 269 was repealed and section 270 of the Constitution was amended to read as follows:

> No person leaving spouse or child, or descendant of child shall by will, bequeath or devise more than one-third of his estate to any charitable, religious, educational or civil institution, to the exclusion of such spouse or child, or descendants of child, and in all cases the will containing such bequest or devise must be executed at least ninety days before the death of the testator, or such bequest or devise shall be void.
>
> Provided, however, that any land devised, not in violation of this section, to any charitable, religious, educational, or civil institution may be legally owned, and further may be held by the devisee for a period of not longer than ten years after such devise becomes effective, during which time such land and improvements thereon shall be taxed as any other land held by any person, unless exempted by some specific statute.

[127] Coleman v. Whipple, 191 Miss. 287, 2 So. 2d 566 (1941).

[128] *Laws of the State of Mississippi, Passed at an Extraordinary Session of the Mississippi Legislature held in Jackson, 1938* (Jackson, Mississippi, 1938), chs. 94, 95 (hereafter cited *Laws of the State of Mississippi* followed by the year).

[128] *Laws of the State of Mississippi, Passed at an Extraordinary lation and Resolutions, Passed at a Regular Session of the Mississippi Legislature held in Jackson, 1940* (Jackson, Mississippi, 1940), chs. 325, 326 (hereafter cited *Laws of the State of Mississippi* followed by year).

At the same session the legislature enacted chapter 318, now section 671 of the Mississippi Code of 1942, which authorizes the devisee to sell the lands within ten years, and, in default thereof, creates a reverter to or remainder in the heirs or other devisees under the will. The statute repeats the constitutional provisions and adds the following section:

> Provided further, that within said period of ten years during which such land may be held, the charitable, religious, educational or civil institution holding the same shall have the power and right to sell and convey the said lands so held, or any part thereof and its deed of conveyance may be treated as passing such title thereto as was possessed by the testator, or the said land or any part thereof, may be leased for a length of time not extending beyond the expiration of the period during which it may be legally held by the lessor institution. But if such land be not sold and disposed of within the said period of ten years, then in that event at the expiration of the said ten years it shall revert to the heirs at law of the testator under whose will it was devised to the institution holding it, or to the devisees under such will as the case may be.

By virtue of these amendments the only restriction or limitation now imposed by the Constitution or statute upon the right of any charitable, religious, educational or civil institution to take a devise of land or bequest of personalty is that in the case of a devise of land the devisee may not hold the title to the land for a period of longer than ten years after such devise becomes effective, provided however that in either case the devise of land or bequest of personalty is not in violation of section 270 of the Constitution and section 671 of the Code as now written.

There have been two cases interpreting the first paragraph of amended section 270. The first case, that of Bell v. Mississippi Orphans Home, having indicated that this paragraph seems to have been modeled after section 2419 of the Code of Georgia, 1873, with the single exception that this paragraph substituted spouse for wife, stated that the ninety day clause in this paragraph applies only where the testator dies leaving a spouse or child or descendants of child.[130] To this effect it quoted from several Georgia cases.[131]

The second case involving the construction of the first paragraph of section 270 was that of the Mississippi School for the Blind v. Armstrong. In that case the testatrix left surviving her a son. After providing for stated bequests, she bequeathed and devised certain personal and real property to the Mississippi School for the Blind, to be used by that institution for the education and benefit of the blind children in attendance at that school. The will, executed more than ninety days before the testatrix's death, came within the other part of the first paragraph of section 270, viz. "No person leaving a spouse or child, or descendants of child shall, by will, bequeath or devise more than one-third of his estate to any charitable, religious, educational or civil institution to the exclusion of such spouse or child." The court

[131] Reynolds v. Bristow, 37 Ga. 283 (1867):

[130] Bell v. Mississippi Orphans Home et al., 192 Miss. 205, 5 So. 2d 214 (1941).

> The obvious intention of the legislature was to prevent testators who had wives, or children, having a just claim upon their bounty, from defeating those just claims; and therefore, in all cases of that character whenever the attempt is made by a testator to devise any portion of his estate to charitable uses, to the exclusion of his wife, or child, or descendants of a child, from its enjoyment, then the will should be executed at least ninety days before his death. The object was to protect the testator's wife, children and descendants of children, from any improper influences that might (be) exercised over him *in extremis*, thereby inducing him to devise any portion of his property to charitable uses, to their prejudice, and therefore, in all cases, when that was attempted to be done, the will must be executed ninety days before his death.

The court further stated:

> Where there is no wife, child, or descendants of a child to be provided for, the testator may make his will, bequeathing, or devising his property to charitable uses as in other cases, without any restriction as to the time of its execution.

The same principle was maintained in Wetter v. Habersham, 60 Ga. 193 (1878); Wesley Memorial Hospital v. Thomson, 164 Ga. 466, 139 S. E. 15 (1927); Jones v. Habersham, 107 U.S. 174, 2 S. Ct. 336, 27 L. Ed. 401 (1882).

held that the School could take, *pro tanto*, one-third of the estate, this clause of the will being valid to that extent; and that the balance went to the son. The gift was not void *in toto*.[132]

The meaning of this section therefore, may be stated briefly as follows: a person leaving spouse, child, or descendant of child can bequeath one-third of his estate to a charitable, religious, educational or civil institution by will executed ninety days before such person's death, and a person not leaving spouse or child or descendant of child can bequeath all his estate to such an institution by will whether or not such will is executed ninety days before such person's death.

The interpretation of the second paragraph of section 270 and of section 671 of the Code, was treated incidentally in the case of Bell v. Mississippi Orphans Home and *ex professo* in the case of Mississippi College v. May.[133] The court in the former case stated that the second paragraph of section 270 was inserted to apply without regard to whether or not the testator or testatrix left surviving him or her a spouse or child, or descendant of child. This statement, however, was rather, an *obiter dictum* than the *ratio decidendi* of the case.

In the case of Mississippi College v. May, a certain Mr. May, who had died without leaving spouse or child or descendants of child provided in the fourth item of his will as follows:

> To Mississippi College, Clinton, Mississippi, I devise and bequeath my 465 acre farm in district two, Claiborne County, Mississippi. At the proper time the same is to be converted into cash and held as a perpetual trust fund or endowment, and the proceeds therefrom shall annually go to the support of Christian Education in that institution....

[132] Mississippi School for the Blind v. Armstrong, 216 Miss. 348, 62 So. 2d 369 (1953).

[133] Bell v. Mississippi Orphans Home, et al., 192 Miss. 205, 5 So. 2d 214 (1941); Mississippi College v. May, 235 Miss. 200, 108 So. 2d 704 (1959).

The college failed to convert the land into cash within the prescribed time, and as a result the heirs of Mr. May contended that the land reverted to them.

In giving a decision for the heirs, the court held that the second paragraph of section 270 of the Constitution (the second paragraph of section 671 of the Code as now written) limiting the holding of property to a period of ten years, is applicable to any land and not merely where the testator leaves a spouse or child or descendant of child. The court likewise indicated that even if the college is recognized as a mere trustee to hold the property for the purposes indicated in the will this fact does not prevent the operation of the provisions of the statute or Constitution. For "we do not think that a bequest (sic) or devise to an eleemosynary corporation in trust for the very purposes for which it is organized prevents the operation of the provisions of section 270." Whether land in trust for purposes other than the purpose of the particular corporation would fall within the provisions of the statute or Constitution, is not indicated, but it would appear, from the emphasis that the court placed on the phrase "in trust for the very purpose for which the trustee is organized" that the provisions would not apply.[134]

Finally, speaking of the statutory provision relating to devises of land to charitable, religious, educational or civil institutions, that is, the third paragraph of section 671 of the Code as now written, the court stated that the Constitution and the statute read together create in the college an estate for ten years, with the power of disposition in the college. The heirs or the devisees of the testator have a vested remainder, subject to defeasance by the college exercising its power of disposition. The court further noted, though this was *obiter dicta,* that should another institution within the prohibited class, be constituted devisee either by direct provision or through a general residuary clause, such an institution could not take under the statute and Constitution, for "the purpose and terms of the Constitution and statute preclude the tacking of one ten-year term period of

[134] Mississippi College v. May, 235 Miss. 200, 108 So 2d 704 (1959).

ownership by a religious, charitable, educational or civil institution on to the holding by another such institution for ten more years."[135]

SECTION 2. MODES OF ACQUISITION

A. *Religious and Charitable Gifts in Mississippi*

a. The Concept of a "Charity"

The word "charity" cannot be limited to any narrow and stated formula. It must advance with the advancement of civilization and the daily increasing needs of men.[136] However, a definition, though imperfect, is of necessity, and no better definition can be given than the celebrated one of Horace Gray. According to Gray, a charity, in the legal sense, may be more fully defined as a gift, to be applied consistently with existing laws, for the benefit of an indefinite number of persons either by bringing their minds or hearts under the influence of education or religion, by relieving their bodies from disease, suffering or restraint, by assisting them to establish themselves in life, or by erecting or maintaining public buildings or works or otherwise lessening the burden of government.[137]

Due to the limitations placed on charitable gifts by the mortmain statutes prior to 1940, there is no developed jurisprudence regarding charities in Mississippi. Nevertheless, as stated in the case of National Bank of Greece v. Savarika, charities are generally favored and will be enforced if there is some pivotal point of definiteness by which or through which they may be administered.[138]

Mississippi rules governing charities are derived from

[135] Mississippi College v. May, 235 Miss. 200, 108 So. 2d 704 (1959).

[136] Zollman, *American Law of Charities* (Milwaukee, Wisconsin: The Bruce Publishing Co., 1924), p. 122.

[137] Jackson v. Phillips, 96 Mass. (14 Allen) 539, 556 (1867).

[138] National Bank of Greece v. Savarika, 167 Miss. 571, 148 So. 649 (1933). Prior to 1940 only the following charitable gifts were possible: testamentary bequests of personalty to any legatee except a religious association, and *inter vivos* dispositions of realty or personalty.

the unwritten law of England prior to the statute of Elizabeth or from the statute of Elizabeth itself.[139] It is probable therefore, that the following purposes outlined in the statute of Elizabeth would be accepted as charitable by the Mississippi courts:

> the relief of the aged, impotent, and poor people; the maintenance of maimed and sick soldiers and mariners; the support of schools of learning; free schools, and scholars of universities; repair of bridges, ports, havens, causeways, churches, seabanks, and highways; education and preferment of orphans; the relief, stock and maintenance of houses of correction; marriage of poor maids; aid and help of young tradesmen, handicraftsmen, and persons decayed; relief or redemption of prisoners and captives; aid of poor inhabitants concerning payments of fifteenths, setting out of soldiers and other taxes.[140]

There is no doubt that gifts to the Church and to moral persons within the Church come within the purview of this statute.

The courts of the United States have been divided on the question as to whether property given to charitable corporations is to be considered as being held absolutely, or whether it is to be considered as held in trust for the purposes or some of the purposes for which the corporation was organized. Some decisions have unequivocally denominated gifts to charitable corporations as conveyances of mere legal title to the corporation as trustee. Others have regarded such gifts as held by the charitable corporation without the character of a technical trust.[141]

The question has not been discussed *ex professo* by the

[139] National Bank of Greece v. Savarika, 167 Miss. 571, 148 So. 649 (1933).

[140] Statute 43 Elizabeth, c. 4 (1601). This list of purposes is demonstrative rather than exhaustive.

[141] For an excellent discussion of the varying views confer Scott, *The Law of Trusts* (5 vols., 2. ed., Boston, Toronto: Little, Brown and Co., 1956), IV, sect. 348, pp. 2553-2560 (hereafter cited Scott).

Mississippi courts; however, it would appear that where the instrument of the gift specifies the purposes for which the gift is to be used, even though such should constitute the purpose of the charitable corporation, a trust will be imposed with the corporation as trustee. In the case of the Mississippi Children's Home Society v. City of Jackson, one Thomas Gale conveyed real property to the Mississippi Children's Home Society and provided in the deed that the said property, by which is meant the physical property itself, shall be used exclusively for the eleemosynary, humanitarian and/or educational purposes of the said grantee. In holding that a trust was created the court stated:

> The owner of property may devote it to charitable purposes not only by transferring it in trust for such purposes but also by transferring it to a charitable corporation. Most of the principles applicable to charitable trusts however, are applicable to charitable corporations. Consequently, any restrictions in the instrument conveying property to a religious or charitable corporation are as valid and enforceable as they would be if the property were given to individual trustees for charitable purposes. In each case the question is whether the rule which is applicable to trustees is applicable to the particular charitable corporation with respect to the use of the property.[142]

This decision does not definitively decide that any time a gift is made to a corporation, a trust is imposed thereon. If a gift contains no specification, particularly in the case of personal property, it is probable, in view of the language of the court, that such a gift is unlimited by any trust except such as is implied by its being given to a charitable corporation.[143]

A direct gift to an unincorporated society would probably fail in Mississippi, particularly if there is question of a gift of land. For an unincorporated society cannot hold property

[142] Mississippi Children's Home Society v. City of Jackson, 230 Miss. 546, 93 So. 2d 483 (1957).

[143] Cf. 10 *Am. Jur.* 610, 611, sects. 36, 37.

in Mississippi.[144] Besides, a grantee in *esse* is a necessary prerequisite to the validity of a deed conveying land.[145] Hence, where there is a question of a gift of land to an unincorporated society it should be made through the intervention of a trustee, either natural or artificial. In the case of personal property, however, though there are no Mississippi cases in point, the objections to the vesting of title in a voluntary association are not so strong. In fact, it is generally held that a bequest for a charitable use to an unincorporated society may be enforced by virtue of the statute of charitable uses. And in jurisdictions which have adopted this statute, the rule is that trusts otherwise valid, especially when in aid of religious, charitable or educational enterprises, are not void because of lack of corporate capacity in the beneficiary.[146]

Whatever the jurisprudence of the state may be on the above question, in either case, the law on gifts, whether *inter vivos* or *mortis causa,* wills and charitable trusts, through which charitable institutions are generally benefited, will be applied as the particular case may demand. Hence, it is necessary to discuss briefly the law regarding each of these institutes.

b. Gifts

A gift may be defined as a transfer of property without any consideration or compensation in exchange being given.[147] Its principal elements are a competent donor and donee, intention to make a gift, delivery, acceptance by the donee and the gift going into effect immediately and absolutely.[148] Therefore, to establish a "gift," it must not only appear that the donor intended to make a gift, but that he

[144] Treas v. Price, 167 Miss. 121, 146 So. 630 (1933); West v. State, 169 Miss. 302, 152 So. 888 (1934).

[145] Morgan v. Collins School, 157 Miss. 295, 127 So. 565 (1930).

[146] 10 *Am. Jur.* 609, sect. 39.

[147] Black, *Black's Law Dictionary* (3. ed., St. Paul: West Publishing Co., 1933), p. 843 "gift" (hereafter cited *Black's Law Dictionary*).

[148] Maier v. Hill, 221 Miss. 20, 72 So. 2d 209 (1945); McClellan v. McCauley, 158 Miss. 456, 130 So. 145 (1930).

consummated the gift by an actual, constructive or symbolical delivery of the property to the donee; the mere declaration that the gift was made is not sufficient where unaccompanied by acts showing delivery of possession or an absolute parting with dominion and interest.[149]

Under the present law and jurisprudence of Mississippi there is nothing peculiar by way of controlling provisions in regard to gifts to the Church. Neither is it necessary to give a detailed discussion on the law pertaining to gifts as it is relatively uniform and simple. However, it is of practical interest to note the attitude of the Mississippi courts to the concept of delivery— an attitude which in regard to the delivery of specific chattels appears both inconsistent and to a degree archaic.

The concept of delivery will be discussed with regard to three classes of property. These classes are (1) real property, (2) specific tangible chattels or personal property capable of manual delivery, and (3) choses in action.[150]

With regard to the first class, that of real property, a statute was enacted as early as 1857 providing for the transfer of land by a writing signed and delivered. The provisions of this statute are now incorporated in section 831 of the present Mississippi Code.[151] Likewise, there are many cases in Mississippi now holding that a written instrument conveys the title to land whether by way of gift or upon consideration, even though there is no possession given, if prop-

[149] Allison v. Allison, 203 Miss. 20, 33 2d 619 (1948).

[150] Choses in action is a term used to denote that class of property which has no tangible physical existence and which cannot be picked up and delivered to another person. A chose in action is an intangible right which one person has against a second person, to obtain property the title or possession of which is in that second person.

[151] Any interest in or claim to land may be conveyed to vest immediately or in the future, by writing signed and delivered; and such writing shall have the effect to transfer, according to its terms, the title of the person signing and delivering it, with all its instruments (sic) as fully and perfectly as if it were transferred by feoffment with livery of seizin, notwithstanding there may be an adverse possession thereof.—

Mississippi Code of 1858, Ch. 36, art. 1; *Mississippi Code of 1942 Annotated, Recompiled*, Vol. 1A, sect. 831.

erly executed and delivered and is irrevocable, and that equity will not cancel it because there has been a complete failure of a promised consideration, or because there never was a consideration.[152]

In regard to specific chattels there appears to be some inconsistency in the opinions of the courts regarding the nature of delivery. Some of the cases, particularly earlier ones, say that the delivery of possession of the subject matter of the gift is not required, others on the contrary say that delivery is required without any of the cases saying that the others are overruled.

In the case of Wall v. Wall, the court stated: . . .

> with regard to personal estate, the rule is generally held by the courts in this country, that a deed conveying chattels to a donee, reserving the possession and use of the property to the donor during his life, is valid, though the deed be not made to a trustee for the parties in interest.[153]

Of similar import is the case of McDaniel v. Johns,[154] and that of Hiserodt v. Hamlett.[155] However, the cases requiring delivery of possession of the subject matter of the gift are numerous. Perhaps, the most significant statement in this regard is contained in the case of Gidden v. Gidden in which the court stated:

> In Thornton on Gifts and Advancements, p. 173, Mississippi is set out in the notes as standing alone in holding that delivery to the donee of a deed of gift is not sufficient alone to convey the title. Whether that be true or not, and whether the rule in this case be good or bad, according to reason, we do not think it ought to be changed now. It is not is not a mischievous, harmful rule; the donee loses nothing, the donor simply 'plays Indian' and takes

[152] Cresswell v. Cresswell, 164 Miss. 871 (1932); Campbell v. State Highway Commission, 212 Miss. 437, 54 So. 2d 654 (1951); McDaniel v. Johns, 45 Miss. 632 (1871); Graham v. Triplett, 148 Miss. 299 (1927); McMillan et al. v. Gibson, 222 Miss. 408 (1954).

[153] Wall v. Wall, 30 Miss. 91 (1885).

[154] McDaniel v. Johns, 45 Miss. 632 (1871).

[155] Hiserodt v. Hamlett, 74 Miss. 37 (1896).

> back what he attempted to give before the donee gets his hands on it.[156]

As to choses in action, there are no Mississippi cases which hold that the delivery of a written instrument alone is ineffective to convey title.[157]

c. Last Wills and Testaments

As previously indicated, the capacity of the Church to acquire property by last will and testament is limited by

[156] Gidden v. Gidden, 176 Miss. 98, 167 So. 785 (1936); The same principle was held by the courts in the following cases: Johnson v. Grice, 140 Miss. 562, 106 So. 271 (1925); Pace v. Pace, 107 Miss. 292, 65 So. 273 (1914); Meyer v. Meyer, 106 Miss. 638, 64 So. 420 (1913); Fairley v. Fairley, 34 Miss. 18 (1857); McWillie v. Van Vacter, 35 Miss. 428, 72 Am. Dec. 127 (1858).

[157] In Young v. Power, the court in approving the rule that "if the intention of making a gift exists, any language which expresses that intention is sufficient if accompanied by an abandonment of possession and control of the subject matter of the gift to the donee," continued as follows:

> This rule may be well enough with reference to gifts of specific chattels, but it has no application to the release of a debt existing in parol. This instruction and most of the others on the part of the defendant touching this point, proceed on the assumption that his was a gift of a chattel by parol, with delivery of possession of it to the donee; and many of the authorities cited by counsel have application to cases of that kind only. But this is manifest error. There is no such gift and no such delivery of possession; for the testatrix had nothing in her possession which she could deliver to the defendant.

The court approved a requested instruction which read as follows: "To make a valid legal gift of a debt due by parol or open account the creditor must in writing, release or discharge said debt or do some act by which the debt is placed beyond his legal control and dominion."—Young v. Power, 41 Miss. 197 (1886). Similarly, in the case of "In re Lewis Estate," the court citing 7 *Am. Jur.* 299, sect. 425, stated:

> If therefore the general rule applicable to gifts, that the donor must divest himself of all power over the gift, is to be applied, it seems that the gift in such a case must fail. This is the view of some cases. The majority of cases, however, hold that if the intention of the donor is to vest a present right to share in the deposits constituting the joint account, such an act constitutes a completed gift, despite a reserved power of revocation.

In re Lewis Estate, 194 Miss. 480, 13 So. 2d 20 (1943).

mortmain statutes. Consequently, in drawing up a will in which the Church or an institution sponsored by the Church is beneficiary, care must be taken that both the provisions of the mortmain statutes and the statutory law regarding wills and testaments in general be carefully observed.

The right to devolve property by will and the rights thereunder, are statutory.[158] Therefore, the exercise of testamentary power is conditioned on the observance of the formalities prescribed by statute with reference to the execution of the will.[159] In the construction of the will, however, the testator's intention is the prime inquiry, and when such intent has been ascertained, all minor, subordinate and technical rules of construction must yield thereto.[160] Thus, where facts show effort by testator in good faith to execute a will, the courts will not have resort to any technical or hard construction of the statutory law, prescribing essentials of execution, to defeat his purpose.[161]

Under Mississippi law every person twenty-one years of age, male or female, married or unmarried, being of sound and disposing mind shall have power to dispose of his property by last will and testament.[162] A person is of sound and disposing mind if he has sufficient mind and memory to understand the particular business in hand, remembers who are the natural objects of his bounty, and can recall to mind his property and make disposition of it understandingly according to some purpose or plan formed in his mind.[163] These qualifications are determinable as to the date of the will.[164]

Three types of wills are recognized in Mississippi, viz., the formal will, the holographic will and the nuncupative

[158] Woodville et al. v. Pizzati, 119 Miss. 442, 81 So. 127 (1919).

[159] Warren v. Sidney's Estate, 183 Miss. 669, 184 So. 806 (1938).

[160] Mississippi School for Blind v. Armstrong, 216 Miss. 348, 62 So. 2d 369 (1953).

[161] Better v. Hirsch, 115 Miss. 614, 76 So. 555 (1917).

[162] *Mississippi Code of 1942 Annotated, Recompiled,* Vol. 1A, sect. 657.

[163] Moore v. Parks, 122 Miss. 301, 84 So. 230 (1920).

[164] Ellis v. Ellis, 160 Miss. 345, 134 So. 150 (1931).

will. With regard to the formal will statute law provides that it must be signed by the testator or testatrix or by some person in his or her presence and at his or her direction, and shall be attested by two or more credible witnesses in the presence of the testator or testatrix.[165]

As regards the signing of the will by the testator, it is not necessary that he sign the will in the presence of the witnesses or that the witnesses sign the will in the presence of each other.[166] However, the witnesses must attest to the will in the presence of the testator, and this presence of the statute is not simply the bodily presence of the testator; it is essential that he be also mentally capable of recognizing and actually conscious of the act performed before him. To be corporally present, however, it is not necessary that the testator and the witnesses be in the same room or even in the same house where the attestation is made, or that he should actually see the act of attestation; if the attestation be within the scope of the testator's view from his actual position it will be sufficient.[167]

A holographic will, that is, a will which is wholly written by the testator in his own hand, must also be subscribed by the testator.[168] It has been held, however, that if the will is unsigned it does not affect its validity.[169]

The disposition of property by nuncupative will is also recognized in Mississippi, but only within certain specified limitations. The statute law provides that nuncupaive wills have no effect unless made at the time of the last sickness

[165] *Mississippi Code of 1942 Annotated, Recompiled,* Vol. 1A, sect. 657.

[166] Phifer v. McCarter, 222 Miss. 415, 76 So. 2d 285 (1954); Austin v. Patrick, 179 Miss. 718, 176 So. 714 (1937).

[167] Watson v. Pipes, 32 Miss. 451 (1856); Walker v. Walker, 67 Miss. 529, 7 So. 491 (1890).

[168] *Mississippi Code of 1942, Annotated, Recompiled,* Vol. 1A, sect. 657; under statute providing that all holographic wills must be "subscribed" by testator, quoted word means that testator's signature must appear after and beneath the dispositive portion of the instrument. —In re George's Estate, 208 Miss. 45 So. 2d 571 (1950).

[169] Better v. Hirsch, 115 Miss. 614, 76 So. 555 (1917).

of the deceased, at his or her residence, or where he or she resided for ten days next preceding death, except where the testator was taken sick away from home and died before returning.[170]

Interpreting the meaning of the phrase "last sickness" of the statute, the Supreme Court of Mississippi stated in the case of Schinitz v. Summers that "last sickness means that at the time of the making of the will the testator is *in extremis*, at least, so near death that he did not have reasonable time and opportunity to make a written will." In accordance with this interpretation the court declared the will invalid in the instant case, on the basis that neither the testator nor his physician considered his condition mortally serious, even though the testator was actually sick when he made the will and later died from that sickness.[171]

The statute law of Mississippi, likewise provides for the disposition of property by codicil in writing and under the same conditions as that required for written wills, whether formal or holographic, depending on what manner the codicil is executed.[172] A codicil, however, is not a will, but rather a clause or clauses added to a will by the testator after the will has been executed and may confirm, revoke, explain, alter, modify, add to or subtract from anyone or all of the provisions of the will.[173]

There is no limitation as to the quantity or quality of property that a person may dispose of by a holographic or formal will.[174] In the case of a nuncupative will, if

[170] *Mississippi Code of 1942 Annotated, Recompiled,* Vol. 1A, sect. 663.

[171] Schinitz v. Summers, 179 Miss. 260, 174 So. 569 (1937).

[172] Cf. *Mississippi Code of 1942 Annotated, Recompiled,* Vol. 1A, sect. 657.

[173] Holcomb v. Holcomb, 173 Miss. 192, 159 So. 564 (1935).

[174] "Every person aged twenty-one years, male or female, married or unmarried . . . shall have power by last will and testament, or codicil in writing, to devise all the estate, right, title and interest in possession, reversion or remainder, which he or she hath, or at the time of his or her death shall have, of, in, or to land, tenements, hereditaments, or annuities, or rents charged upon or issuing out of them, or goods and chattels, and personal estate of any description whatever." —*Mississippi Code of 1942 Annotated, Recompiled,* Vol. 1A, sect. 657.

the value of the property bequeathed exceeds one hundred dollars ($100), the will has no effect unless it is proved by two witnesses that the testator or testatrix called on some person present to take notice or hear testimony that such is his or her will, or words to that effect.[175] Moreover, real estate cannot be devised by a nuncupative will.[176]

In general, a person is free to dispose of his property to any person or purpose he may wish to benefit and such disposition will be effective subject only to its acceptance by the beneficiary.[177] However, the law imposes certain limitations affecting the capacity of a beneficiary to take under a will. Thus, where a religious, charitable, civil or educational institution is the beneficiary the statutes of mortmain must be accurately observed. Moreover, a devise or bequest to a subscribing witness is void, if the will cannot be proven without his testimony.[178] But if such a witness would have been entitled to share in the estate, if the decedent had died intestate, he may take such share up to but not in excess of the amount of the devise or bequest.[179] Likewise, if a creditor is a subscribing witness, any special provision made in favor of such creditor in the will, either by admitting the debt or by providing for its payment, or by giving it a preference, is void, and such claim stands as though the provision had not been made.[180]

A will vests no present interest and is revocable during

[175] *Ibid.*

[176] Sadler v. Sadler, 60 Miss. 251 (1882).

[177] Greely v. Houston, 148 Miss. 799, 114 So. 740 (1927).

[178] It is interesting to note that a member of a parish or religious order has been declared not disqualified by interest from being a subscribing witness to a will containing a gift to the parish or religious order.—Haven v. Hillard, 23 Pick (Mass.) 10, 53 A.L.R. 213 (1838); Loring v. Park, 7 Gray (Mass.) 42, 53 A.L.R. 213 (1838); Will v. Sisters of the Order of St. Benedict, 67 Minn. 335, 337, 69 N.W. 1090, 53 A.L.R. 213 (1897).

[179] *Mississippi Code of 1942 Annotated, Recompiled,* Vol. 1A, sect. 661.

[180] *Ibid.*, sect. 662.

the life of the maker.[181] The same degree of mentality is necessary for revocation as for the making of a will.[182] Such revocation may occur either by the testator or testatrix destroying, cancelling, or obliterating the will or codicil or causing it to be done in his or her presence, or by a subsequent will, codicil, or declaration in writing made and executed.[183]

In addition to the express revocation provided for by statute as above,[184] a will may also be revoked by implication or by operation of law.[185] Implicit revocation occurs when the testator executes another will disposing of his entire estate in a manner absolutely inconsistent with the provisions of any earlier will, though the latter contains no words of revocation or mention of an earlier will.[186]

Revocation by operation of law occurs when the statute law does not permit that certain heirs be omitted from the provisions of the will. Thus, while provisions with respect to children born after the execution of a will vary somewhat according as to whether or not the testator had children living when the will was executed, it may be stated generally, that after-born children, including posthumous children not provided for by settlement and neither provided for nor disinherited by the will, but merely pretermitted, take the share of the estate they would have taken in case of intestacy.[187] Moreover, a surviving spouse cannot be disinherited and

[181] Strange v. State Tax Commission, 192 Miss. 765, 7 So. 2d 542 (1942).

[182] Watkins v. Watkins, 142 Miss. 210, 106 So. 753 (1926).

[183] *Mississippi Code of 1942 Annotated, Recompiled,* Vol. 1A, sect. 658.

[184] Statute pertaining to revocations of wills applies only to express revocations and has no application to an implied revocation.—Holcomb v. Holcomb, 173 Miss. 192, 159 So. 564 (1935).

[185] Cf. Holcomb v. Holcomb, 173 Miss. 192, 159 So. 564 (1935).

[186] Crawford's Estate v. Crawford, 225 Miss. 208, 82 So. 2d 823, 59 A.L.R. 2d 1 (1955).

[187] Cf. *Mississippi Code of 1942, Annotated, Recompiled,* Vol. 1A, sects. 658, 659.

takes the share which would be hers or his due if the testator had died intestate.[188]

In accordance with the common law rule, the testamentary disposition of personalty in Mississippi is governed by the law of the testator's domicile and construable as though the beneficiaries were resident there.[189] The testamentary disposition of realty on the other hand, is governed by the law of the state in which the realty is located.[190]

d. Charitable Trusts

(1) The Creation of Charitable Trusts

The fundamental distinction between a private trust and a charitable trust is that in the case of a private trust, property is devoted to the use of specified persons who are designated as beneficiaries of the trust, whereas in the case of a charitable trust, property is devoted to purposes beneficial to the community and hence indefiniteness of beneficiaries is essential.[191] Moreover, charitable trusts do not fall within the rule against perpetuities.[192]

Certain elements must concur in the creation of any valid express trust, irrespective of the mode or character of the instrument by which it is created. These elements are: (1) a person competent to create the trust; (2) indication of intention; (3) property to which the trust may and does pertain; (4) a definite and complete present disposition of the property; (5) a provision, at least by implication, for the office of trustee, although the nomination of a trustee is not essential; and (6) a person capable of holding the equitable interest in the property as beneficiary, although such person may be undetermined or unborn.

[188] Cf. *ibid.*, sects. 668, 669, 670.

[189] National Bank of Greece v. Savarika, 167 Miss. 571, 148 So. 649 (1933).

[190] Hailey v. McLaurins Estate, 112 Miss. 705, 73 So. 727 (1917).

[191] Old Ladies Home Association v. Grubbs Estate, 191 Miss. 250, 2 So. 2d 593, overruling suggestion of error, 191 Miss. 250, 199 So. 287 (1940).

[192] National Bank of Greece v. Savarika, 167 Miss. 571, 148 So. 649 (1933).

With regard to the first element: the capacity of the person to create a trust will depend on the mode of conveyance adopted. Hence, where the conveyance is by last will and testament, the requirements as previously outlined must be observed. The second and third elements are self-explanatory. In the execution of the fourth element, i.e., the present and complete disposition of the property, the following provisions of the Mississippi Code must be observed:

> Hereafter, all declarations and creations of trusts, confidence of or in any land, shall be made and manifested by writing signed by the party who declares or creates such trust, or by his last will, in writing, or else they shall be utterly void; and every writing declaring or creating a trust shall be acknowledged or proved as other writings, and shall be lodged with the clerk of the chancery court of the proper county to be recorded, and shall only take effect from the time it is so lodged for record, but where any trust shall arise or result by implication of law, out of a conveyance of land, such trust or confidence shall be of like force and effect the same as it would have been if this statute had not been passed.
>
> All grants, assignments or transfers of any trust or confidence shall likewise be in writing signed by the party granting or assigning the same, or by last will and testament, or else, they shall likewise be utterly void and such grant or assignment shall also be acknowledged or proved and recorded, and shall only take effect from the time it is lodged with the clerk for record.[193]

In the nomination or appointment of a trustee (viz., the fifth element), it is a general rule that all persons capable of confidence or of holding real or personal property are qualified to act in the capacity of a trustee.[194] A corporation may likewise hold property as trustee,[195] but it is probable,

[193] *Mississippi Code of 1942 Annotated, Recompiled,* Vol. I, *The Statute of Frauds,* sects. 269, 270.

[194] Commissioners of Sinking Fund v. Walker, 7 Miss. (6 How.) 143, 38 Am. Dec. 433 (1842).

[195] Wade v. American Colonization Society, 7 Smedes & Marshall (15 Miss.) 663, 45 Am. Dec. 324 (1846).

at least, in Mississippi that an unincorporated association cannot act in that capacity.[196] Where no provision is made for a trustee, it is a general rule, aside from the statutory changes and regardless of whether the statute of uses is in force (on the grounds of public policy), that if the object of a charitable trust is lawful and sufficiently specific and definite to enable the court to execute it, it will not be permitted to fail for want of a trustee. A court of equity, by its general inherent jurisdiction over charitable trusts, will supply one.[197]

Finally, regarding the sixth element, it must be noted that though indefiniteness of beneficiaries is an essential element of a charitable trust, there must be something definite in such indefiniteness. To this effect the Supreme Court of Mississippi, in the case of National Bank of Georgia v. Savarika, stated as follows:

> Such indefiniteness cannot apply to an unlimited and indiscriminate portion of the human race without at least some vested or delegated authority for selection, but there must be some class or creed or color, or condition of mankind. Even where there is a definite class of indefinite members, the power to select such members must be vested somewhere; and if the class be indefinite and the power of selection be wanting the plan or scheme or purpose must be so definite as to admit of no conjecture by those appointed to carry it into execution. Also, there must be some trustee or executor to whom the fund is given for the charity, with discretion to complete the general scheme, and with authority to put it into execution.[198]

(2) The Doctrine of Cy pres

Cy pres is defined by Scott as the principle under which the courts thus attempt to save a charitable trust from fail-

[196] Treas v. Price, 167 Miss. 121, 146 So. 630 (1933).

[197] 10 *Am. Jur.* 611, sect. 38; cf. National Bank of Greece v. Savarika, 167 Miss. 571, 148 So. 649 (1933).

[198] National Bank of Greece v. Savarika, 167 Miss. 571, 148 So. 649 (1933).

ure by carrying out the more general purpose of the testator and carrying out approximately though not exactly his more specific intent.[199]

Cy pres as administered in England is of two kinds, prerogative and judicial. Not much is known about the common law origins of the cy pres doctrine but it is thought that the judicial power was first exercised by the chancellor under his extraordinary jurisdiction as an equity judge, while prerogative cy pres is supposed to have originated with the power of the king to insure justice to all his subjects. In time the prerogative power was delegated to the king's council and was finally taken over by the chancellor as the keeper of the king's conscience. Thus, the chancellor acted in a dual capacity, one judicial and the other ministerial. Although it is not known exactly where the line was drawn between prerogative and judicial cy pres there was a tendency to increase the judicial power at the expense of the prerogative until the chancery had encompassed most of the prerogative powers over charitable trusts. The Crown, however, as *parens patriae*, retained the power to designate a charitable purpose by means of the sign manual[200] where the object of the gift was illegal or void as contrary to public policy, and where a gift was made to charity generally without the interposition of a trustee.[201]

The power of the English King was eliminated in the United States after the Revolutionary War and as a consequence prerogative cy pres also vanished. The cy pres doctrine, however, did not disappear entirely, though for a time it appeared to have done so, as the courts in the earlier cases failed to distinguish between the judicial and prerogative cy pres. This was due in part, at least, to the fusion

[199] Scott, IV, sect. 399, p. 2824.

[200] The signature or subscription of the king is termed his "sign manual." There is this difference between what the sovereign does under the sign manual and what he does under the great seal, viz., that the former is done as a personal act of the sovereign, the latter as an act of state.—*Black's Law Dictionary*, p. 1088, "sign manual."

[201] Cf. Fisch, *The Cy Pres Doctrine in the United States* (New York: Bender and Co., 1950), pp. 56, 57 (hereafter cited Fisch).

of both powers in the English chancellor. The matter, however, is now properly settled and practically all states recognize judicial cy pres but in varying degrees.[202]

The first case in Mississippi to deal with the doctrine of cy pres was that of National Bank v. Savarika. The testator provided for a fund to be forwarded to the National Bank of Greece to be kept by it as an endowment for the benefit of a school for girls at Borgasticon, Macedonia, Greece. At the time of the testator's death the school no longer existed, and the heirs claimed that the gift had lapsed. In granting judgment for the heirs, the court held that neither the cy pres doctrine nor the statute of Elizabeth, nor the sign manual had any place in Mississippi jurisprudence. It stated:

> "... without regard to the refinement of distinction between the use of the cy pres to describe the power exercised by the English chancellors in charity cases under the sign manual of the crown, on the one hand, and that exercised under the assumed general jurisdiction of equity on the other, the practice in either case is incompatible with the public and judicial policy of this state, and repugnant to its laws of wills, and of inheritance, under the statute of descent and distribution, and the judicial decisions of the highest court on the subject."[203]

Having thus rejected the English doctrine of cy pres, Mississippi adopted what it terms the equitable doctrine of approximation, which in reality is nothing more than a modified form of the judicial doctrine of cy pres.[204] In virtue of this doctrine a court of chancery may vary the details of administration, in order to preserve the general purpose of the donor.[205]

202 Zollman, *The American Law of Charities*, p. 76.

203 National Bank of Greece v. Savarika, 167 Miss. 571, 148 So. 649 (1933).

204 "The doctrine of cy pres is the doctrine of nearness or approximation, and, as modified and applied by some of the courts in the United States, has been called the doctrine of approximation."—14 C.J.S. sect. 52.

205 National Bank of Greece v. Savarika, 167 Miss. 571, 148 So. 649

The equitable doctrine of approximation, however, cannot be applied where the donor of the property has himself declared how it shall be used in the event of the failure of the charitable use to which he in the first instance provided that it should be devoted.[206]

B. Adverse Possession

Since the passage of the various statutes of limitations, the construction and application of these statutes in reference to occupancy of land has become known as the law of adverse possession. Adverse possession may be defined as the open and notorious possession and occupation of real property under an evident claim or color of right.[207]

Under Mississippi law, ten years actual adverse possession by any person claiming to be the owner for that time of any land, uninterruptedly continued for ten years by occupancy, descent, conveyance or otherwise, in whatever way such occupancy may have commenced or continued, shall vest in every actual occupant or possessor of such land a full and complete title. There is a saving to infants and persons of unsound mind of a right to sue and set aside title allegedly acquired by adverse possession within ten years after the removal of such disability; but the saving in favor of these persons never extends beyond thirty-one (31) years.[208]

The capacity of religious societies to acquire property by adverse possession has been asserted by the Supreme Court of Mississippi in the case of Ivey v. Geisler.[209] Though this

(1933); Mississippi Children's Home Society v. Jackson, 230 Miss. 546, 93 So. 2d 483 (1957).

[206] Mississippi Children's Home Society v. Jackson, 230 Miss. 546, 93 So. 2d 483 (1957).

[207] 1 *Am. Jur.* 793, sect. 2.

[208] *Mississippi Code of 1942 Annotated, Recompiled,* Vol. 1A, sect. 711.

[209] Ivey v. Geisler, 213 Miss. 212, 56 So. 2d 501 (1952).—

> "Unincorporated religious societies are authorized by our statutes to hold and own real estate by and through their officers and trustees such as appellants here. Such religious groups may acquire title by adverse possession even as against a

case concerned an unincorporated religious society, it may be logically inferred that *a fortiori* an incorporated religious society can also acquire property by adverse possession.

In the canonical section it was stated that five conditions are generally required to establish prescription, viz., (1) a thing that is prescriptible; (2) some kind of title; (3) good faith; (4) possession; (5) continuous (possession) for the statutory period. As the Code of Canon Law canonizes the provisions of the civil law regarding some of these elements, it is best, for the purpose of comparison, to discuss the provisions of Mississippi law regarding adverse possession under these titles.

a. A Thing that is Prescriptible

In general, all lands held in private ownership are subject to the state statutes on adverse possession.[210] The statutes of limitation, however, do not run against the state in favor of one claiming title by adverse possession.[211]

b. Some Kind of Title

Obviously, when speaking of adverse possession, title does not refer to valid title but rather to what is termed color of title. Color of title is that which gives the semblance or appearance of title but which is in fact no title.[212] Thus, the Supreme Court of Mississippi when considering color of title as a basis of a claim of title to realty by adverse possession stated as follows:

> The question is not whether the instrument relied on as color of title operates to convey and continue to convey any actual title but whether it appears to do so; and when on the face of the instrument it purports to convey title to land therein described, it will constitute color of title, although because of

grantor where property is openly diverted from a use specified in the grant."

[210] Dimitry v. Jones, 149 Miss. 641, 115 So. 786 (1928).

[211] Rotenbury v. Arnold, 212 Miss. 564, 55 So. 2d 141 (1951).

[212] Sharp v. Shenandoah Furnace Co., 100 Va. 27, 40 S.E. 703 (1901).

matters *de hors* the instrument it conveys no title at all.[213]

A writing is generally required to constitute color of title.[214] However, in Mississippi it appears that a parol gift may likewise constitute color of title, but not as to persons not in privity with the donor. Hence, as between the donee in possession under a parol gift and the donor, or a person in privity with him, the parol gift is color of title and the possession is extended by construction to the boundaries fixed thereby.[215]

Color of title is a necessary element to constitute adverse possession in Mississippi only to the extent that without it adverse possession gives title only to the land actually and continuously used, cultivated, and occupied. In brief, color of title is necessary for constructive possession but not for actual possession.[216]

c. Good Faith

The element of good faith relative to adverse possession plays little or no part in Mississippi jurisprudence. The statute law does not require it and the courts seem satisfied that when the other elements required to claim title adversely are present, the claimant has acquired a good title irrespective of his good faith.

Where the courts have considered the element they have

[213] Shepherd v. Cox, 191 Miss. 715, 4 So. 2d 217, 136 A.L.R. 1346 (1941); overruling suggestion of error 191 Miss. 715, 1 So. 2d 495.

[214] v.g., a deed, Hanna v. Renfro, 32 Miss. 125 (1856); invalid tax deed, Hanner v. Yazoo Delta Lumber Co., 100 Miss. 349, 56 So. 466 (1911); forfeited taxland patent obtained from the State, Shipman v. Lovelace, 58 So. 2d 657, judgment corrected 215 Miss. 141, 60 So. 2d 559 (1952).

[215] Cf. Brooks-Scanlon Co., v. Childs, 113 Miss. 246, 74 So. 147, 2 A.L.R. 1453 (1917).

[216] Evans v. Shows, 180 Miss. 518, 177 So. 786 (1938).—

> "while color of title coupled with actual possession of part of the land would constitute constructive possession of the whole, it is equally true that without color of title by parol gift, deed, or other writing, adverse possession gives title only to the land actually and continuously used, cultivated or occupied."

described it as an honest belief on the part of the claimant that he has acquired a good title, although upon investigation it proves to be otherwise.[217]

d. Possession

Whether entry is under color of title or not, in either case, the possession to be adverse, must be actual, open and notorious, hostile, exclusive, under claim of right and continuous for the statutory period.

(1) Actual

There is no fixed rule whereby the actual possession of real property by an adverse claimant may be determined in all cases. It may be stated as a general rule, however, that the claimant's possession must be such as to indicate his exclusive ownership of the property.[218] Hence, a mere claim of title to land, unaccompanied by actual adverse possession will not bar the true owner.[219]

Actual occupation or possession includes possession by owner's tenant, agent, assignee or vendee.[220] It is not necessary, however, that someone actually occupy the land, but merely pasturing, cultivating, cutting and selling timber and other acts of ownership and control adverse to the owner of record title suffice.[221]

Neither actual occupation, cultivation nor residence is necessary to constitute "actual possession" of property in such sense as to render it adverse to the true owner where the property is so situated as not to admit of permanent useful improvement. It is sufficient in such a case if the continued claim of the party is evidenced by public acts of

[217] Kersh v. Lyons, 195 Miss. 598, 15 So. 2d 768 (1943).

[218] 1 *Am. Jur.* 865, sect. 130.

[219] Leavenworth v. Reeves, 106 Miss. 722, 64 So. 660 (1914).

[220] Cox v. Richerson, 186 Miss. 576, 191 So. 99, 124 A.L.R. 1138 (1939).

[221] Smith v. Anderson, 193 Miss. 161, 8 So. 2d 251 (1942); Chatham v. Carter, 209 Miss. 16, 45 So. 2d 841 (1950); Pasturing the land without enclosure held not sufficient to constitute actual possession.—Geoghegan v. Kraus, 228 Miss. 231, 87 So. 2d 461 (1956).

ownership, such as he would exercise over property which he claimed in his own right, and would not exercise over property which he did not claim.[222]

(2) Open and Notorious

The underlying principle on which is founded the rule requiring that possession must be open and notorious before it can be considered adverse to the real owner is that such character of possession is presumptive notice to the true owner of such possession and adverse claim. Thus, where the owner has knowledge of the adverse claim such knowledge is equivalent to a possession which is open and notorious.[223]

In each case therefore, the nature, situation, and uses of the property are to be considered in determining whether th occupation is visible and notorious.[224] If the acts of the adverse claimant are such as to arrest the attention of the true owner, and indicate to him that the land is being appropriated by another, then the possession is open and notorious.[225]

(3) Hostile

An adverse occupancy must be hostile from the inception of the period claimed in order to acquire title by adverse possession.[226] What exactly constitutes hostility depends a great deal on the circumstances of each case, and is a question of fact rather than law.[227] Thus, it has been held that a void and worthless deed may be sufficient to show the hostile character of possession.[228] In another case the court stated:

[222] McCaughn v. Young, 85 Miss. 277, 37 So. 839 (1905).

[223] Kornegay v. Montgomery, 194 Miss. 274, 12 So. 2d 423 (1943); McCaughn v. Young, 85 Miss. 277, 37 So. 839 (1905).

[224] Ford v. Wilson, 35 Miss. 490, 72 Am. Dec. 137 (1858).

[225] Leavenworth v. Reeves, 106 Miss. 722, 64 So. 660 (1914).

[226] Eddy v. Clayton, 44 So. 2d 395 (1950).

[227] Grafton v. Grafton, 8 Smedes & Marshall (16 Miss.) 77 (1846).

[228] Henry v. Henderson, 216 Miss. 252, 62 So. 2d 315 (1953); C. L. Gray Lumber Co., v. Pickard, 220 Miss. 419, 71 So. 2d 211, 41 A.L.R. 2d 920 (1954).

> not only does the law presume that he who has entered without title has done so in recognition of, and in subordination to the title of the owner, but having affixed this *prima facie* presumption to his entry, it will not allow him to convert it into an adverse one except by acts which plainly demonstrate its hostile character.[229]

The term hostile therefore implies that the claimant is in possession in contradistinction to holding in recognition of, or in subordination to, the true owner.

(4) Exclusive

An adverse possession in order to ripen into title must be exclusive,[230] that is, the claimant must hold possession of the land for himself, as his own, and not for another. Hence, permissive possession even if long continued does not confer title on the person in possession of the property.[231]

That which tends to prove the exclusiveness of a possession differs in no material respect from that which goes to prove the other elements of an adverse holding. Indeed "exclusive possession" simply means that the disseisor must show an exclusive domination over the land and an appropriation of it to his own use and benefit.[232]

(5) Under Claim of Right

The terms "claim of right," "claim of title," and "claim of ownership," are not synonymous with the term "color of title," but simply mean the intention of the disseisor to appropriate and use the land as his own to the exclusion of all others irrespective of any semblance or shadow of actual title, or right.[233] That a claim of right is essential for ad-

229 Davis v. Bowmar, 55 Miss. 671 (1878).

230 Dead River Fishing and Hunting Club v. Stovall, 147 Miss. 385, 113 So. 336, citing R.C.L. (1927).

231 Barron v. Federal Land Bank of New Orleans, 182 Miss. 50, 180 So. 74 (1938).

232 1 *Am. Jur.* 875, sect. 141.

233 1 *Am. Jur.* 897, sect. 187, 2 C.J.S. 573, sect. 55.

verse possession in Mississippi has been stated many times by the courts.[234]

It is to be noted that the rules as outlined above regarding the character of possession do not apply in the case of property used for church purposes. In the case of Ivey v. Geisler, the court stated "there is sufficient possession of such property if it is used in a way that such property is ordinarily used."[235]

(6) Continuous for Statutory Period

In addition to the necessity of having an open, notorious, exclusive and hostile possession under claim of right as stated heretofore it is also essential that such possession, in order to ripen into title should be shown to have been continuous and uninterrupted for the full statutory period.[236]

The statute runs only where the acts of the one party have notoriously given the other a cause of action which he neglected to act upon,[237] whether such be at the time of entry or later.[238] However, once the statutory period begins to run it is not suspended unless there be a physical interruption of adverse possession,[239] suit or unequivocable act of ownership inconsistent with the exercise of possession.[240]

[234] "To acquire title by adverse possession, the possession must not only continue for the statutory period, but it must be exclusive and under claim of right."—Alabama & V. Ry. Co., v. Joseph, 125 Miss. 454, 87 So. 421 (1921); "No continuance of occupation, no matter how long protracted will avail to establish title to Mississippi land by adverse possession unless accompanied by a claim of title."—Shepherd v. Mahannah, 220 F. 2d 737 (1955).

[235] Ivey v. Geisler, 213 Miss. 212, 56 So. 2d (1952).

[236] Alabama & V. Ry. Co., v. Joseph, 125 Miss. 454, 87 So. 421 (1921).

[237] Magee v. Magee, 37 Miss. 138 (1859).

[238] 1 *Am. Jur.* 885, sect. 161.

[239] "If a person abandons property before the expiration of the period of limitations and thereafter exercises no control over the land, it is an interruption precluding a claim by adverse possession."—Nixon v. Porter, 38 Miss. 401 (1860).

[240] Daniels v. Jordan, 161 Miss. 78, 134 So. 903 (1931).

Mere verbal protests, therefore, or statements are insufficient to stop the running of the statute.[241]

Two or more adverse possessions, if continuous may be reckoned together.[242] However, before one adverse possession may be tacked on to another there must be privity of possession between the holders thereof, and generally such privity may be created by a conveyance or understanding that has for its object the transfer of possession accompanied by a transfer in fact.[243]

As regards the acquisition of title to personal property by adverse possession, it is generally recognized that it rests on analogy to the law relating to real property.[244] Hence, the same prinicples apply *mutatis mutandis* except that under Mississippi law the period of time required for the prescription of personal property is three years.[245]

[241] *Loc. cit.*

[242] Benson v. Stewart, 30 Miss. 49 (1855).

[243] Crowder v. Neal, 100 Miss. 730, 57 So. 1 (1911).

[244] 1 *Am. Jur.* 846, sect. 96.

[245] *Mississippi Code of 1942, Annotated, Recompiled,* Vol. 1A, sect. 729.

CHAPTER IV

ARTICLE I. THE LAW OF THE CHURCH REGARDING

THE ADMINISTRATION OF CHURCH PROPERTY

The right of the Church to administer its property flows necessarily from its native right to acquire and own property, for the dominion of a thing carries with it the power to use that thing as one sees fit, unless the exercise of that right endangers the common good or the inalienable rights of others. It is to be noted, however, that only that property which passes into the ownership of the Church[1] is properly ecclesiastical[2] and subject to the jurisdiction of the Church. The property of associations which have not been erected as moral persons by competent ecclesiastical authority, or property dedicated to pious causes, but not in the ownership of the Church, is subject to ecclesiastical law only to the extent that it makes explicit provision concerning it.[3]

Since according to the present discipline in the Church the subjects of ownership of ecclesiastical property are moral persons, which cannot as such engage in active administration, the right and duty to administer their holdings pertains to him who has been lawfully designated as administrator. As such a status might jeopardize the property of the respective moral person, in the event of negli-

[1] "In canonibus qui sequuntur, nomine Ecclesiae significatur non solum Ecclesia universa aut Sedes Apostolica, sed etiam quaelibet persona moralis in Ecclesia, nisi ex contextu sermonis vel ex natura rei aliud appareat."—Can. 1498.

[2] "Bona temporalia, sive corporalia, tum immobilia tum mobilia, sive incorporalia, quae vel ad Ecclesiam universam et ad Apostolicam Sedem vel ad aliam in Ecclesia personam moralem pertinent, sunt bona ecclesiastica."—Can. 1497, #1.

[3] Cf. cans. 336, 344, 1515-1517.

gence on the part of the administrator, moral persons are granted by Canon Law a status equivalent to that of minors.[4] The respective administrators therefore occupy a status similar to that of a guardian, tutor or trustee in respect to the moral person and as such are subject to the same duties and obligations which such a fiduciary relationship generates.[5] As the Code expresses it, they are obliged to fulfill their office with the care and diligence of a good father.[6]

Administration as applied to ecclesiastical property is defined as the control or care of the temporal goods of the Church in order that they may serve the purposes for which they were acquired. This definition includes all acts which are necessary or useful (1) to keep the property in good condition; (2) to make it productive; (3) to derive benefit from it; and, (4) to apply, pay out and use it for legitimate purposes.[7] Of these acts some may be ordinary, others extraordinary. Acts of ordinary administration are those which the administrator may perform validly by reason of his office and without the permission of a superior. Such acts are regularly and frequently necessary for the upkeep of the property and for meeting current expenses. Extraordinary acts of administration, on the other hand, comprise all those acts which require the permission of a competent superior or other solemnities required by law, in order to be juridically valid.[8]

[4] "Personae morales sive collegiales sive non collegiales minoribus aequiparantur."—Can. 100, #3.

[5] Coronata, II, n. 1058, p. 483.

[6] Cf. can. 1523.

[7] Comyns, *Papal and Episcopal Administration of Church Property*, The Catholic University of America Studies in Canon Law, n. 147 (Washington, D.C.: The Catholic University of America Press, 1942), p. 1 (hereafter cited Comyns).

[8] McManus, *The Administration of Temporal Goods in Religious Institutes*, The Catholic University of America Studies in Canon Law, n. 109 (Washington, D.C.: The Catholic University of America Press, 1937), p. 82 (hereafter cited McManus); Beste, p. 812.

SECTION 1. THE ADMINISTRATORS OF ECCLESIASTICAL PROPERTY

A. The Roman Pontiff as Supreme Administrator

The Roman Pontiff as head of the Church is not only the supreme pastor, but also the immediate pastor of all the faithful. Consequently, all baptized persons and all ecclesiastical goods are subject to his jurisdiction. This does not mean, however, that the Roman Pontiff is the owner of all Church property; for the ownership of ecclesiastical goods, as previously indicated, pertains to that moral person which has legitimately acquired them; but rather that by virtue of his supreme jurisdiction he is the supreme administrator and dispenser of all ecclesiastical property.[9]

De facto, however, the Roman Pontiff does not exercise immediate administration over the various moral persons in the Church, but entrusts their administration to inferior administrators.[10] But by virtue of his power as supreme administrator, he issues general norms to direct inferior administrators and reserves to himself, through the Roman Congregations, more important acts of administration such as alienation in certain cases.[11] Moreover, as supreme dispenser, he does, when necessity or a proportionate utility demands, transfer, extend, limit, or otherwise circumscribe the ownership of ecclesiastical goods.[12]

B. The Local Ordinary as Administrator

The Code does not describe the administrative rights of

[9] Can. 1518.

[10] The property of the Holy See is administered by the Cardinal Camerlengo.—Cf. can. 262.

[11] Bouscaren-Ellis, p. 822.

[12] Beste, p. 812; Coronata II, n. 1059, p. 483. This power is similar to the power of eminent domain which is on occasion exercised by the civil sovereign for the common good. Thus, for example, by virtue of this power the Roman Pontiff may in special cases and for grave reasons grant a reduction of charges or debts, accept compromises, admit to composition heirs unwilling to pay in full pious legacies, renounce partially or entirely legitimate claims of confiscated property, etc.—Cf. Ayrinhac, pp. 424, 425.

the local ordinary in the same manner in which it treats those of the Roman Pontiff. It calls the latter the supreme administrator of all ecclesiastical property, while it seems to restrict the power of the local ordinary to that of supervision. Thus, canon 1519, #1, states that the local ordinary has the duty to watch over carefully the administration of all ecclesiastical property within his territory which has not been withdrawn from his jurisdiction, without prejudice to more extensive rights which he may enjoy through lawful prescription.[13]

As supreme administrator in his diocese, however, the local ordinary enjoys immediate administrative power over the following property within his territory: (1) the property which constitutes the *mensa episcopalis*;[14] (2) property which is strictly diocesan, that is, property which belongs to the diocese considered as a moral person distinct from the parishes and other juridical persons within the territory of the ordinary;[15] (3) alms given for churches entrusted to religious in those cases in which the religious have neither the dominion nor the perpetual or quasi perpetual use of them;[16] (4) property of the cathedral church;[17] (5) alms

[13] Although Vromant seems to think that the words of canon 1519, #1, "salvis legitimis praescriptionibus," refer only to prescription as used in canons 1508-1512 (De Bonis Ecclesiae Temporalibus), this phrase has a wider application and may include any enactment which has the force of law, for example, a privilege or a concordat, or the documents of a foundation. (Coronata, II, 473; Ayrinhac, p. 425).

[14] Can. 1483, #1. The *mensa episcopalis* signifies the benefice of the residential bishop.

[15] Such property includes special collections for the welfare of the diocese as such; taxes imposed on various churches and other moral persons for the same purpose according to the law of canon 1505, and property which remains after parishes have been suppressed in accordance with the norms of canon 1501.—Cf. Comyns, pp. 84, 85.

[16] Can. 630, #4; cf. Vromant, pp. 188, 205, 206.

[17] The local ordinary is the co-administrator with the cathedral chapter of the cathedral church and its possessions.—can. 1192, #1. It is to be noted, however, that the administration of the cathedral church does not pass to the *coetus consultorum.* Such a right is not given by the Code, which states in canon 427 that this group is to assist in the government of the diocese.—Cf. Comyns, p. 93.

which have been donated for charitable purposes within the territory of the local ordinary, without any specification;[18] (6) the revenue accruing from the levying of taxes.[19] In addition to the above, the local ordinary may acquire the right of immediate administration over ecclesiastical property within his territory, even though it may be exempt, by lawful prescription.[20]

With regard to other ecclesiastical property within his territory and not withdrawn from his jurisdiction, the local ordinary enjoys a supervisory power. In virtue of this supervisory power, the local ordinary enjoys the right of visitation, an accounting and the right and duty within the limits of the common law, vested rights and legitimate customs and circumstances, to issue opportune instructions for the regulation of the entire matter of the administration of ecclesiastical property.[21]

In particular the supervisory power of the local ordinary extends to the following property: (1) parochial property as distinct from that of religious; (2) religious property which is not withdrawn from his jurisdiction; and (3) non-parochial-non-religious property.

With regard to parochial property, the supervisory power of the local ordinary extends to (1) the property of all parish churches, even to those churches which are parochial churches in parishes united *pleno iure* to a religious house,[22] unless a parochial church is owned by the religious community with strict property rights;[23] and (2) the property of all parishes considered as distinct from the property of

[18] Vromant, p. 194.

[19] Such taxes are the seminary tax (cans. 1355, 2°, 1356, #1-3, 1357, #1), the cathedratic tax (can. 1504) and exactions imposed upon an ecclesiastical moral person at the time of its foundation or consecration (can. 1506).

[20] Canon 1519, #1; Cf. footnote 13, p. 157.

[21] Can. 1519, #2; Beste, p. 812.

[22] Code Comm., 25 July 1926, IV—*A.A.S.*, XVIII (1926), 393; Bouscaren, *The Canon Law Digest*, I, 699.

[23] Comyns, p. 72.

the parochial church, as for example, alms for the parishioners, for the school or for other buildings which together with the church make up the property of the parish.[24]

The supervisory power of the local ordinary over property possessed by religious extends to (1) the administration of all the property of diocesan institutes both of men and women, provided the administration is conducted by a superior who resides within the territory of the ordinary;[25] (2) all property administration conducted by nuns even though they are subject to a regular superior;[26] (3) the administration of the dowry in all institutes of women religious;[27] (4) money donated to individual religious or to religious houses for the benefit of the parish or mission, and money given directly to the parish or mission;[28] (5) trust funds given to a religious house to be applied to divine worship or to works of charity in the neighborhood.[29]

In addition to his supervisory rights over property which is parochial or which, if not parochial, is possessed by religious, the local ordinary has the right to exercise vigilance over (1) pious wills, except when made in favor of clerical exempt religious;[30] (2) pious foundations, unless they have been established in the churches, even parochial, of exempt religious;[31] (3) property which constitutes or belongs to non-collegiate moral persons, that is, hospitals, orphanages, benefices, seminaries, etc., and other institutions which have

[24] Comyns, p. 72.

[25] Can. 535, #3, 1°.

[26] Can. 535, #1, 1°, 2°.

[27] Can. 535, #1, 2; The vigilance in this matter pertains by right to the ordinary of the place where the mother general or the provincial superioress has her habitual residence, because either one or other is obliged to administer this fund.—Comyns, p. 74.

[28] Cans. 535, #3, 2°; 533, #1, 4°.

[29] Cans. 535, #3, 2°; 533, #1, 3°.

[30] Cf. can. 1516, #3; Bouscaren-Ellis, p. 819. However, where a pious will provides for the establishment of hospitals, orphanages and other non-collegiate moral persons, even though entrusted to exempt religious, they are nevertheless, subject to the vigilance of the local ordinary.—Cans. 1492, #1, 1493.

[31] Cans. 1545, 1546, #1, 1547, 1549, 1550; cf. McManus, pp. 106, 107.

a religious or charitable end and have been constituted juridical persons by competent authority;[32] (4) property given in trust to individual clerics or religious for pious causes, unless in the case of a clerical exempt religious as trustee, the donor specifies that the property be expended for the purposes of his institute;[33] (5) the property of lay associations which have been constituted moral persons by ecclesiastical authority, even when these associations are established in the churches of exempt religious.[34]

To help the local ordinary fulfill his office of vigilance, and thus provide further for the security of ecclesiastical property, the Code imposes on all local ordinaries the duty of establishing a diocesan council of administration, unless an equivalent provision has been lawfully made by law or particular custom.[35] This council should consist of the local ordinary as president and two or more qualified men, if possible experts in civil law, to be selected by the local ordinary with the advice of the board of diocesan consultors.[36] In the selection of the members of this board the local ordinary must exclude those who are related to him in the first or second degree of consanguinity or affinity, unless he has obtained an indult from the Holy See permitting it.[37] He may, however, choose laymen to serve as well as clerics, provided the laymen are Catholics.[38]

The members of the board of administration when duly appointed must take the oath in the presence of the local ordinary that they will fulfill their office well and faith-

[32] Cans. 1492, #1, 1493.

[33] Can. 1516, #2, 3.

[34] Cans. 690, #1, 2; 691, #1, 5.

[35] Can. 1520, #1. In many dioceses of the United States, by provision of the local ordinary, the board of diocesan consultors (cf. cans. 423-428) likewise constitutes the board of administration prescribed by this canon. Beste, p. 813.

[36] Can. 1520, #1.

[37] Can. 1520, #2.

[38] Blat, *Commentarium Textus Codicis Iuris Canonici* (5 vols., Vol. III, Pars Altera, Romae: Collegio Angelico, 1923), III, n. 434 (hereafter cited Blat); Bouscaren-Ellis, p. 824.

fully.[39] Although their function is generally consultative, with the exception of those particular cases in which their consent is required either by the common law or the articles of a foundation, nevertheless, it is the wish of the legislator that in all administrative acts of greater moment the local ordinary should not neglect to hear their opinions.[40]

C. Inferior Administrators

a. Appointment

Every moral person in the Church must have its own administrator, whose duty it is to administer its property in the name of the Church. Such administrators are generally provided for by law, either by direct appointment, or by allowing the moral person to choose its own administrators,[41] or provision for an administrator may be made by the charter of a foundation.[42] Where, however, neither the law nor the charter of a foundation has made provision for an administrator for some church or pious place, the local ordinary must appoint some prudent capable men of good repu-

[39] Can. 1520, #4.

[40] Can. 1520, #3. With the exception of those cases in which the consent of the board of administration is required, their intervention is not necessary for the validity of the local ordinary's acts, since the canon merely warns the ordinary "*ne praetermittat audire concilium*" —Vermeersch-Cruesen, II, n. 841, p. 592.

[41] The administrators designated and authorized by the law of the Code are the following: (1) the rector of a church or public oratory, relative to the possessions of such a church of oratory (cans. 485, 1182, #1, 1191, #1); (2) the beneficiary with regard to the property of the benefice (can. 1476, #1); since parishes are benefices, the pastor of a parish has the right to administer the property of the parish (cf. cans. 1411, 5°, 1415, #3, 1476, #1, 1182, #1; Bouscaren, *The Canon Law Digest*, I, 150; (3) the rector of a non-collegiate moral person, such as an orphanage, hospital, etc., regarding its goods (can. 1489, #3); (4) the cathedral chapter as a whole for the property which belongs to the chapter and the cathedral church (can. 415). In other instances, the Code does not directly designate the administrators of the possessions of collegiate moral persons, but gives to these entities the power to choose their own administrators, who are then sanctioned as such by the common law.—Cf. cans. 532, #1, 2; 676, #2, 691, 697.

[42] Can. 1521, #1.

tation to administer the property.[43] The term of office of such administrators is generally three years unless local circumstances make it advisable that the same men be appointed for successive terms.[44]

b. Rights and Duties

The administrators of ecclesiastical property are generally clerics; however, as indicated, laymen may be authorized to participate in the administration of ecclesiastical property either by the legitimate title of the foundation, or by the will of the local ordinary. Where such occurs, they must be given to understand that the administration must be transacted entirely in the name of the Church, and that the local ordinary has the right of visitation, of demanding an account, and of prescribing the manner of administration.[45] Moreover, before lay administrators appointed by the local ordinary enter upon their duties they must take an oath before the local ordinary or the vicar forane (dean) that they will faithfully attend to their duties.[46] Likewise, they must make an accurate and specific inventory, to be signed by all administrators, of immovable and precious movable goods and all other property, with their description and valuation; or they may accept an inventory previously made, provided that they check it and indicate those things which were lost or acquired in the interim. One copy of this inventory must be kept in the archives of the administration and another in the archives of the diocesan curia. In each copy must be noted any change which the goods of the church or institution may undergo.[47]

[43] A layman cannot be placed in sole control of the administration of ecclesiastical property, but it seems to suffice that a single cleric should be designated. It is to be further noted in this regard that the bishop need not appoint laymen to administer the property of a church or pious place for which no administrator has been provided.—Adams, "The Rights and Duties of Trustees and their Appointment," *The Jurist*, XVIII (1958), 186.

[44] Can. 1521, #1.

[45] Can. 1521, #2.

[46] Can. 1522, 1°.

[47] Can. 1522, 2°, 3°.

Acts which may be incumbent on administrators, whether ecclesiastical or lay, may, as already indicated, be ordinary or extraordinary. With regard to these latter acts, the Code provides that unless administrators obtain the previous written permission of the local ordinary, they act invalidly when they exceed the limitations and methods of ordinary administration.[48] What these particular acts are is usually determined by local legislation, with the exception of particular cases, concerning which, the common law makes explicit provision.[49]

In regard to acts of ordinary administration, the Code in canon 1523 enunciates the fundamental principle which should be characteristic of all good administrators and outlines in general the duties incumbent on them *ratione officii.* The canon states that administrators of Church property should fulfill their office with the care and diligence of a good father. Hence, they should observe the following: (1) guard against any loss or damage to the property; (2) observe the requirements of both Canon and civil law, as well as the requirements specified by the founder or the donor, or imposed by legitimate authority; (3) collect the income and profits diligently and promptly, safeguard them, and use them in accordance with the intent of the founder or with established laws or norms; (4) invest the surplus revenues of a church for the benefit of the church itself, after obtaining the consent of the ordinary; (5) keep an accurate account of receipts and expenditures; (6) arrange in proper order the documents and deeds on which the prop-

[48] Can. 1527, #1.

[49] Thus the following provisions were enacted by the Tenth Diocesan Synod of the Diocese of Natchez-Jackson:

> The following transactions shall be regarded as extraordinary administration requiring the written consent of the ordinary; (a) to sell, lease, assign, transfer, trade or in any way alienate any immovable church property, and movable property which has an estimated value of more than $1,000.00; (b) to borrow or lend parish funds; (c) to invest parish funds in new loans, bonds, stocks, etc., or in any way to change existing investments and banking of parish funds; (d) to undertake any building, maintenance or repair project which will amount to more than $1,000.00.—n. 255.

erty rights of the church are indicated, and file them in the archives of the church or in a suitable and adequate safe; and if possible deposit authentic copies of them in the archives or safe of the chancery office.[50] Moreover, even though there be no obligation on them by reason of an ecclesiastical benefice or office, administrators who have either expressly or tacitly accepted their office may not relinquish it of their own accord; and should they do so, in such manner that harm comes to the Church, they are themselves obliged to make restitution.[51]

It is to be noted, however, that though to defend the rights of the Church is in itself an act of ordinary administration, nevertheless, the common law requires that administrators shall not begin a lawsuit in the name of the Church, nor act as defenders in one, without having first obtained the written permission of the local ordinary, or in case of urgent necessity at least the permission of the rural dean, whose duty it will be to inform the ordinary at once of the permission given.[52]

In accordance with the right of the local ordinary, by virtue of his supervisory power over all administrators, to demand an account of their administration, the Code sanctions the specific performance of this duty in canon 1525. Wherefore, notwithstanding any custom to the contrary, all administrators, whether clerics or laymen of any church, even of a cathedral church, or any pious place canonically erected,[53] or of any confraternity[54] are obliged to give an account of their administration to the local ordinary every year.[55]

[50] Can. 1523, 1°-6°.

[51] Can. 1528.

[52] Can. 1526. This prohibition is effective even in the case of a suit in an ecclesiastical court.—Cf. Abbo-Hannan, p. 730. Moreover, an administrator without the requisite permission is personally liable for any damages that may result from his action.—Cf. Bouscaren-Ellis, p. 828.

[53] Can. 1489, #1.

[54] Cans. 690, 691.

[55] Can. 1525. The administrators of certain religious institutes are included among those who must submit this report to the local ordinary:

The fact that an annual accounting must be rendered to other designated persons by reason of particular law,[56] does not exonerate the administrators from rendering this accounting to the local ordinary or his delegate, even in the case in which they are released from the obligation of rendering the account to the designated persons.[57]

SECTION 2. THE ALIENATION OF ECCLESIASTICAL PROPERTY

Wishing to forestall as many conflicts as possible between Canon Law and the law of whatever country or jurisdiction is involved, the Church has ordained that whatever the secular law of the territory provides in the matter of contracts, generally or specifically either by name or otherwise (*sive nominati sive innominati*), is to be observed as enacted by Canon Law in ecclesiastical matters with the same effects, unless it is contrary to the divine law or unless other provision is made by Canon Law.[58] However, to safeguard the property of the Church, the Code prescribes the observance of certain solemnities in contracts of alienation, in addition to whatever solemnities may be required by the civil law.

Alienation at Canon Law has a twofold sense. In its strict sense, it embraces all acts and contracts by which temporal goods are gratuitously or onerously transferred from the direct ownership of some ecclesiastical moral person to another person either secular or ecclesiastical, as happens in donation, sale or exchange. In the wide sense, it embraces

(1) Diocesan Congregations, can. 535, #3, 1°; (2) Pontifical Congregations (clerical), cans. 535, #3, 2°; 533, #1, 4°; (3) Pontifical Congregations (lay), cans. 535, #3, 2°; 535, #1, 3°; (4) Pontifical Congregations (sisters), can. 535, #2; (Nuns), can 535, #1, 1°, 2°.

[56] Particular law in this case might arise either from the articles of a foundation or from civil law.—Cf. Bouscaren-Ellis, p. 827.

[57] Can. 1525, #2.

[58] Can. 1529. As indicated heretofore, the Church does not accept the provisions of the civil law which limit the capacity of an individual to donate his goods to pious causes (can. 1513, #1); or those which place limitations on trusts to pious causes (can. 1516); or sanctions of invalidity arising from the omission of civil formalities in legacies or bequests to pious causes (can. 1513, #2).

all juridic transactions by which ecclesiastical goods, although their direct ownership is retained, are exposed to the danger of loss and so the way is opened for alienation, as in the case of mortgages, leases, the contracting of debts, the admission of passive servitudes, etc.[95] Not every transaction, however, involving an outlay of money or other property is to be regarded as alienation. On the contrary, alienation enters in only when the stable capital of a moral person is affected by the transaction.[60]

Authors usually define stable capital as including all those assets which are not in ordinary circulation as mediums of barter or exchange, but which constitute the permanent basis of a church body's financial security. It is that sum which has been legitimately set aside to remain intact and be a source of regular income. This stable capital may consist of actual cash deposited at interest or in dividends, or in real estate which is rented or leased as a means of procuring steady income. The general principle is, that alienation is had only when this stable capital or patrimony is diminished.[61]

[59] Beste, pp. 818, 819.

[60] Heston, *The Alienation of Church Property in the United States*, The Catholic University of America Canon Law Studies, n. 132 (Washington, D.C.: The Catholic University of America Press, 1941), p. 72 (hereafter cited Heston).

[61] Heston, p. 73. The following categories of money or securities are parts of stable capital, and as such subject to the canonical restrictions on alienation: (1) all money that has been explicitly incorporated into the stable capital of an ecclesiastical corporation; (2) money or investments withdrawn from the fixed capital of the organization; (3) money or securities received under annuity agreements, since the principal must remain intact as long as there are regular payments to be made; (4) money or securities received from the sale of property which belongs to the stable capital of an ecclesiastical organization; (5) money or securities from bequests and pious foundations, especially, if the accompanying obligations have not yet been completely acquitted; (6) money or securities set aside by legitimate authority for the construction of buildings or for the purchase of other immovable property. —Cf. Heston, pp. 75, 76. The following list enumerates forms of money or its equivalent which do not fall within the scope of the restrictions on alienation: (a) money employed in meeting current expenses; (b)

Without prejudice to the provisions of canon 1281, #1 (requiring the permission of the Holy See for the valid alienation or transfer of images and relics of great importance),[62] to alienate imperishable Church property, whether movable or immovable, there is required: (1) a written appraisal of the property made by reliable experts;[63] (2) a just cause, that is, urgent need or evident usefulness for the Church or piety;[64] and (3) the permission[65] of the legitimate superior without which the act of alienation is invalid.[66]

money or securities borrowed without explicit contractual obligations, even though a nominal rate of interest be paid; (c) proceeds from the sale of old church furnishings used for the purpose of purchasing new equipment; (d) withdrawals from the investments pertaining to stable capital, if the withdrawals are made for the purpose of purchasing or constructing buildings which will yield income, v.g., schools, hospitals; (e) money used for the purchase or construction of buildings when this money is already available; (f) funds used for the construction of residences for ecclesiastics or religious, particularly, if this step will obviate the necessity of renting or leasing other buildings; (g) funds used for the repair of buildings already constructed; (h) resources changed from securities to simple bank deposits at interest; (i) portions of capital transferred to safer investments which are at least equally lucrative; (j) money given with the express intention that it be used for specific purposes; (k) money obtained by mortgage contract in order to construct church buildings, with the express understanding that the mortgage is on the buildings to be constructed, not on the actual stable capital of the Institute; (l) the refusal of legacies or donations.—Heston, pp. 76-78.

62 It is to be noted that the permission of the Holy See is likewise required for the alienation of all votive gifts.—S.C. Conc., 14 Jan., 1922,—*A.A.S.*, XIV (1922), 160; Bouscaren, *The Canon Law Digest*, I, 730.

63 At least two are required.—Cleary, *Canonical Limitations on the Alienation of Church Property*, The Catholic University of America Canon Law Studies, n. 100 (Washington, D.C.: The Catholic University of America Press, 1936), p. 62 (hereafter cited Cleary).

64 Piety in this context includes every pious work of religion or mercy, spiritual as well as corporal.—Vermeersch-Cruesen, II, n. 852, p. 599.

65 The permission need not be in writing; however, such is generally required by particular law.—Cf. *Tenth Diocesan Synod of the Diocese of Natchez-Jackson*, n. 255.

66 Can. 1530, #1, 1°-3°.

The contract of alienation should be executed by public auction, or at least the fact that the alienation will take place should be made public unless the circumstances should dictate otherwise; and the property should be given to him, who, all things considered, has offered the highest price.[67] However, the property may not be sold for a lower price than that indicated in the appraisal made by the experts.[68]

The money received by way of alienation must be invested carefully, safely and usefully in favor of the Church.[69] Hence, such money may not be spent,[70] unless permission to spend it was obtained at the time the authorization to alienate it was granted. Obviously, permission to use the money acquired by alienation to pay off a debt would be implicitly granted when the reason for permitting the alienation was the urgent need of paying said debt.[71]

The competent superior whose permission is required for the validity of the acts of alienation is determined by the estimated value of the property in question, as set by the experts. Canon 1532, #1, 1°-2°, provide that if the property involved be a precious object[72] or its value exceeds 30,000 lire or francs, the permission of the Holy See is required. However, on July 13, 1951, the Sacred Consistorial Congregation reduced the limit to 10,000 gold francs,[73] and

[67] Can. 1531, #2. While ordinarily the property to be disposed of should be given to the highest bidder, still circumstances might arise in which this might not be advisable, as when property near a church might be used by the highest bidder for purposes not desirable in that vicinity, for instance to build a dance hall. —Cf. Bouscaren-Ellis, p. 834.

[68] Can. 1531, #1.

[69] Can. 1531, #3.

[70] Cf. S.C. Conc., 13 July, 1919,—*A.A.S.*, XI (1919), 416; Bouscaren, *The Canon Law Digest*, I, 729.

[71] Bouscaren-Ellis, p. 834.

[72] Precious objects according to many commentators have a notable value, if they are worth more than 1,000 lire or francs ($167).—Cf., e.g., Bouscaren-Ellis, p. 834. This opinion was sustained in a case decided by the Sacred Congregation of the Council on July 22, 1919—*A.A.S.*, II (1920), 577; Bouscaren, *The Canon Law Digest*, I, 728.

[73] S.C.Consist., 13 July, 1951—*A.A.S.*, XLIII (1951), 602; Bouscaren, *The Canon Law Digest*, III, 212.

on October 18, 1952, it declared this amount to be the equivalent of 5,000 American dollars.[74]

When the value of the property to be alienated does not exceed 1,000 lire or francs,[75] the local ordinary may give the necessary permission after consulting the council of administration, unless the matter be of small moment, and after obtaining the consent of the interested parties.[76] When the value of the property to be alienated is more than 1,000 lire or francs ($167) but not over 30,000 lire or francs ($5,000), the local ordinary may likewise give the necessary permission but in this case he must obtain the consent of the cathedral chapter (diocesan consultors), of the council of administration,[77] and of the parties concerned.[78]

It is to be noted, that should the cathedral chapter (dioc-

[74] Bouscaren, *The Canon Law Digest,* IV, 391. By virtue of their quinquennial faculties, bishops in the United States are authorized to grant, in an urgent case, alienation up to $10,000. They must however, inform the Holy See within a year of the use of this faculty.—*Ibid.,* I, 66; III, 581. Besides, the Apostolic Delegate has permission, whenever there is urgent necessity, evident utility and danger in delay, to authorize alienations of ecclesiastical property or property of pious causes up to twice the amount fixed by the Sacred Consistorial Congregation on October 18, 1952, for the various countries, that is, up to $10,000 in the United States.—S. Consist. Cong., April 27, 1953, in Bouscaren, *The Canon Law Digest,* IV, 393. Bouscaren states that he has from reliable sources the information that the Apostolic Delegate has now the faculty to permit alienations up to three times the sum mentioned on October 18, 1952, that is, up to $15,000 in the United States.—Cf. *loc. cit.*

[75] The sum of 1,000 lire or francs is to be taken as a sum equivalent to one-thirtieth of $5,000, or approximately $167.—S. Consist. Cong., 18 October, 1952, in Bouscaren, *The Canon Law Digest,* IV, 392.

[76] Can. 1532, #2. Interested parties where there is question of alienation may include the founder or patron of a church, benefice, pious institute, and the like; the beneficiary in regard to the property constituting his benefice; the collegiate person owning the property under consideration.—Bouscaren-Ellis, p. 837.

[77] The convocation of both of these groups is necessary and they must act as a body. This is the general rule for both the diocesan board of consultors and the diocesan council of administration as contained in canons 101, #1,1°, and 105, 2°.

[78] Can. 1532, #3.

esan consultors) and the administrative council disagree among themselves, the ordinary cannot supply the consent of either of these bodies.[79] Nor can the local ordinary validate an act of alienation which was invalid because of the non-observance of the required formalities.[80]

If the property to be alienated is divisible then all parts already alienated must be mentioned in the petition for further alienation, if such be the case, otherwise the permission, if granted, will be invalid.[81] Moreover, divisible property must be taken together (*per modum unius*) when it coalesces for the purpose of alienation.[82] Coalescence may occur either by reason of intention,[83] the purpose of the contractor,[84] or the time within which the alienation will occur.[85]

The provisions heretofore discussed treat of the requisites for alienation in the strict sense, that is, as an act whereby the rights of ownership are completely relinquished. However, the Church can suffer loss not only from such alienations but also from contracts, which, while leaving intact

[79] S.C.Conc., Jan. 14, 1922—*A.A.S.*, XIV (1922), 160; Bouscaren, *The Canon Law Digest*, I, 731.

[80] S.C.Consist., May 18, 1919—*A.A.S.*, XI (1919), 382; Bouscaren, *The Canon Law Digest*, I, 727.

[81] Can. 1532, #4.

[82] On July 20, 1929, the Code Commission gave an affirmative answer to the following inquiry: whether in virtue or canon 1532, #1, 2°, the permission of the Holy See is required in order to alienate property belonging to the same person when the value of the articles taken together (*per modum unius*) is in excess of 30,000 lire or francs ($5,000). —*A.A.S.*, XXI (1929), 574; Bouscaren, *The Canon Law Digest*, I, 731.

[83] Once it is determined to alienate several pieces of property their total joint value must be considered in reference to the permission needed, regardless of any time intervals between sales of individual pieces of property.—Bouscaren-Ellis, p. 836.

[84] This occurs when the various items of property are alienated for the same purpose, v.g., it is decided to put up an addition to a building and there is no cash on hand.—Bouscaren-Ellis, p. 836.

[85] When several independent pieces of property are alienated within a short space of time, these acts become morally one.—Bouscaren-Ellis, p. 836.

the right of ownership, diminish or restrict the rights attendant thereto. Accordingly, canon 1533 extends to those contracts, whereby the property of the Church is in any way jeopardized, the regulations provided for alienation in the strict sense.[86]

It is altogether evident that no precautions provided by general law will cover satisfactorily all possible contingencies. Consequently, lest the Church be exposed to harm in contracts of alienation, #2 of canon 1530 empowers all competent superiors to lay down other conditions not provided for in detail in the law, in accordance as prudence and necessity may suggest. Moreover, the law itself prescribes other timely precautions to safeguard the property of the Church where there is question of particular contracts.

Thus in connection with mortgages and pledges[87] canon 1538 while extending to these contracts the formalities required for alienation in general, provides further that the superior who is to give the requisite permission must see to it that such debts are paid off as soon as possible. To accomplish this purpose, he should designate in advance the annual rate of amortization.

Similarly, canon 1541 prescribes that in leases of ecclesiastical property, the requisites prescribed for alienation in general must be observed, with the further provisions however, that the boundaries of the property be clearly indicated; that the nature of cultivation or care expected be specified; that the time and mode of payment of the rental (canon) be defined and that guarantees for the fulfillment of these conditions be secured.[88]

Moreover, because of the nature of the contract of lease

[86] Such contracts would be the following: the contracting of debts and mortgages, annuity obligations, compromise or arbitration in financial matters, renunciation of active easements, allowing passive easements, acting as security for others, and all contracts of a similar nature.—Bouscaren-Ellis, p. 837.

[87] A pledge under Anglo-American law is a contract of bailment whereby the bailer remits a chattel to the bailee in surety for a debt. —Cf. Cleary, p. 99.

[88] Can. 1541, #1.

and the possible difficulty involved in reckoning its evaluation for the purpose of determining to which superior recourse must be had, #2 of canon 1541 gives the following regulations regarding the value and duration of the lease with reference to the requisite permission: (1) If the value of the lease exceeds 30,000 lire or francs ($5,000) and the term of the lease is more than nine years, the permission of the Holy See is required; if the term does not exceed nine years, the provision of canon 1532, #3, must be observed (that is, the local ordinary's permission is required, together with the consent of the board of diocesan consultors, the consent of the council of administration and of the interested parties).[89] (2) If the value of the lease is between 1,000 lire or francs ($167) and 30,000 lire or francs ($5,000) and the term exceeds nine years the same provision of canon 1532, #3, must be observed; if the term does not exceed nine years, canon 1532, #2, applies (that is, the permission of the local ordinary after consultation with the council of administration as well as the consent of the interested parties is required.[90] (3) If the value of the lease does not exceed 1,000 lire or francs ($167) but the term is longer than nine years, the provision of canon 1532, #2, must be observed; if however, the term does not exceed nine years, the lawful administrator may grant the lease after he has informed the ordinary.[91]

Finally, if Church property is subjected to the contract of emphyteusis,[92] canon 1542, #1, provides that the grantee

[89] Can. 1541, #2, 1°.

[90] Can. 1541, #2, 2°.

[91] Can. 1541, #2, 3°. The value of the lease as indicated in the above paragraph does not signify the value of the property leased, nor the cumulative sum due or received on the termination of the lease, but the rental to be paid after each individual term has expired as expressed in the contract, namely, annual or biennial, in so far as the rent or fruit of the lease is due or matures each year or every two years.—Beste, p. 825.

[92] The contract of emphyteusis is not known in Anglo-American law. In Roman Law it was a contract in the nature of a perpetual lease, by which the owner of an uncultivated piece of land granted it to another either in perpetuity or for a long time, on condition, that he would

cannot free himself from the obligation of paying the annual rental (*canonem redimere*) without the permission of the lawful ecclesiastical superior mentioned in canon 1532; should he free himself from the obligation, the lessee must hand over to the Church a sum of money corresponding to the market value of the rent for the unexpired term.[93]

Moreover, to insure the Church against possible fraud or deception, and also against the unforeseen financial embarrassment of the lessee, #2 of canon 1542 provides that in every contract of this kind the grantee must be obliged to give all the necessary guarantees for the payment of the rent (*canon*) and for the fulfillment of the conditions inserted in the contract. Furthermore, a stipulation must be put in the contract that in case of conflict the parties shall settle their differences before an ecclesiastical court. It shall also be expressly stipulated that all improvements accrue to the property and not to the grantee.[94]

It is of interest to note, that unlike the provisions of the old law, which extended to the exchange of securities the restrictions imposed on alienations,[95] the present law permits administrators to exchange negotiable securities payable to the bearer (*tituli ad latorem*) for others which are safer and more productive, or at least, are equally safe and productive, provided that all appearance of business and trade be excluded. However, the consent of the local ordinary, the diocesan council of administration and of the interested parties is required.[96]

Before discussing the judicial remedies available to the Church against irregular alienations, the following distinction between the effects of invalid and illicit alienations must be noted. An invalid alienation, that is, one executed with-

improve it by building on it or cultivating it and that he would pay an annual rent. He had a right to sell it or transmit it to his heirs; and the grantor was restrained from entering into it as long as the rent was paid.—Abbo-Hannan, II, 746.

[93] Can. 1542, #1.

[94] Can. 1542, #2.

[95] Heston, p. 177.

[96] Can. 1539, #2.

out the permission of the competent superior, does not produce any effect, and hence, it cannot effect a real transfer of ownership. An illicit alienation on the contrary, is not voided of its natural effect. Consequently, the object in question really becomes the property of the other party. There can be no redress against what was done, although steps may be taken to remedy the irregularity arising from the manner in which the transaction was carried out.

Wherefore, if the contract of alienation was invalid, the Church has a right to a real action against any possessor whatsoever. It can, however, give the purchaser a right to claim damages against the person who sold him the object, especially if the restitution to which he himself is obliged will occasion him considerable loss or harm.[97]

An illicit act of alienation, as already indicated, does not impede the transfer of ownership. Hence, the Church has no right to sue for the object, and its only remedy is recourse against the person, physical or juristic, who was responsible for the act. This recourse can oblige the alienator to compensate the Church for the damages ensuing from the illicit contract, and thus establish her in the favorable condition which she enjoyed before the alienation. The canon provides for the permanence of this right in the Church, by extending the possibility of instituting personal action at law against the heirs of the person responsible for the illicit alienation.[98]

The following persons may institute an action to recover the property where it was alienated invalidly: the administrator responsible for the alienation, his superior and their respective successors in office. Moreover, any cleric attached to the church which has suffered the damage has a similar right.[99]

[97] Can. 1534, #1. It is to be noted, that in regard to invalid contracts of alienation the Code makes no distinction as to whether the transaction is to the benefit of the Church or to its detriment.—Cf. can. 1527, #2. The Holy See, however, will much more readily sanate such transactions if it is shown that the Church did not suffer any harm.—Heston, p. 142.

[98] Can. 1534, #1.

[99] Can. 1534, #2.

ARTICLE 2. THE ADMINSTRATION OF CHURCH PROPERTY UNDER MISSISSIPPI LAW

SECTION 1. PROPERTY ADMINISTRATION UNDER THE CORPORATION SYSTEM

There are two statutes in Mississippi under which religious societies may incorporate; the non-profit corporation statute and the religious corporation statute. In the discussion of the system of tenure adopted by the Church in Mississippi, it was pointed out that the religious corporation statute is adapted to those types of religious societies which are congregational in form and is not suitable to the hierarchical constitution of the Catohlic Church. However, because of the particular organizational status of religious orders or congregations, it is possible for them to use this statute. Hence, in the subsequent discussion the religious corporation statute, because of its applicability to these latter institutes, will also be referred to.[100]

As a preliminary, it is essential to point out the nature of American religious corporations. The corporation, as a legal entity has no concern with the church proper, or for that matter with the internal life of a religious community. It is a purely secular agency, and is as soulless as is any other corporation. Its sole purpose is to make contracts and acquire, hold and dispose of property.[101] It is as much a business corporation, therefore, within its limited powers as any other private corporation.[102]

A. The Powers of Religious Corporations

The powers and functions of religious corporations are determined by the general rules relating to other private

[100] The principles stated in the subsequent section although treating of religious corporations in particular are applicable to any charitable corporation, for example, Catholic hospitals, etc.

[101] Sale v. First Regular Baptist Church of Mason City, 62 Iowa 26, 17 N.W. 143, 49 Am. Rep. 136 (1883); McGrath, "Canon Law and American Church Law," *The Jurist*, XVIII (1958), pp. 261, 262.

[102] Cf. Zollman, *American Church Law* (St. Paul: West Publishing Co., 1933), p. 151 (hereafter cited Zollman, *American Church Law*).

corporations.[103] Religious corporations, therefore, like other private corporations, being creatures of law do not have all the rights and powers of an individual, but derive their powers solely from the law. Hence, a religious corporation possesses only those powers which are expressly granted in its charter or in the statutes under which it is created, or such powers as are necessary for the purpose of carrying out its express powers and the object of its incorporation.[104] However, with regard to the latter powers, namely, the implied powers to do whatever is reasonably necessary to effectuate the powers expressly granted and to accomplish the purpose for which it was formed, it must appear that such are necessary to the enjoyment of some specifically granted right which would fail without the possession of such power.[105]

The following express powers may be acquired by religious societies under the non-profit corporation statute: the power

(1) to determine the manner of calling and conducting meetings and the mode of voting by proxy;

(2) to elect all necessary officers and to prescribe the duties, salaries and tenure of officers;

(3) to sue and be sued, and prosecute and be prosecuted, to judgment and satisfaction before any court;

(4) to have a corporate seal;

(5) to contract and be contracted with within the limits of the corporate powers;

(6) to sell and convey real estate, and personal property;

(7) to borrow money and secure the payment of the same by mortgage;

(8) to issue bonds and secure them in the same way, and to hypothecate its franchises;

(9) to make all necessary by-laws not contrary to law, sub-

[103] 45 *Am. Jur.* 783, sect. 73.

[104] Cf. Southern Electric Securities Co. v. State, 91 Miss. 195, 44 So. 785, 124 Am. St. Rep. 638 (1907); McIntyre v. Ingraham, 35 Miss. 25 (1858).

[105] Mobile and Ohio R.R.Co., v. Franks, 48 Miss. 494 (1867).

ject to such limitations if any, as may be contained in its charter or any amendment thereto.[106]

The religious corporation statute not only indicates the powers proper to a corporation which is duly organized under the statute, but specifies certain requirements which must be observed with regard to acts relating to its property.[107]

B. Powers, Duties and Liabilities of the Officers of Religious Corporations

All corporations must of necessity act and contract through the aid of and by means of individuals. In the case of religious corporations therefore, their temporal affairs will be conducted through the agency of trustees or officers, appointed or elected depending on the terms of the statute under which the society is incorporated and the constitution of the religious society itself.[108]

The general powers of the officers of religious corporations

[106] *Mississippi Code of 1942, Annotated, Recompiled,* Vol. 4A, sect. 5325.

[107] Having dealt with the requirements for incorporation (heretofore treated) the statute provides further:

> "...the society so organized at each particular locality shall be a distinct and independent society; and any society so organized may sue and be sued, by its society name or appellation, and process may be served on its presiding or chief officer, or secretary or on the trustees or manager. Upon the completion of the organization of any such society the title to the real property theretofore owned by it shall vest in the society as hereunder organized, and shall not be divested out of the same, or encumbered, except by a deed, deed of trust or mortgage duly executed under the authority of a resolution adopted by a majority vote of the members present at a meeting duly called for that purpose, at which meeting at least twenty per cent (20%) of the members in good standing of such organized society must be present. The minutes of such meeting shall be entered in the official record book of such society, and the aforesaid resolution shall designate which officers, trustees or managers of such society are to execute deed, deed of trust or mortgage. The provisions of this section shall also apply to all real property acquired by any such society after its organization hereunder."—

Mississippi Code of 1942, Annotated, Recompiled, Vol. 4A, 1956, sect. 5350.

[108] Zollman, *American Church Law,* p. 464.

are not materially different from those exercised by managing directors of private corporations.[109] Therefore, in accordance with the principles applicable to the officers or directors of private corporations, the powers of the officers or trustees of religious corporations are governed by the same principles as those applicable to agents generally. Hence, the authority of such an officer may be actual, express or implied, or it may be an authority which is variously described as apparent, ostensible or by estoppel.[110] In either case, however, the powers of the officers of religious corporations are no greater than those inherent in the corporation itself, and are subject to the limitations of the rules and discipline of the church, which are in conformity with the laws of the state.[111]

The specific duties incumbent on the officers or trustees of religious corporations, will depend to some degree on the terms of the incorporating act. Where the officers or trustees are themselves the corporation, and the society remains unincorporated the relation of trustees or officers to the members of the society is that of trustee and *cestui que* trust. On

[109] Clark v. Brown, 108 S.W. 421, reversed on other grounds 102 Tex. 323, 116 S.W. 360, 29 A.L.R. (N.S.) 670 (1909).

[110] 13 *Am. Jur.* 869, sect. 889. It is a fundamental and well settled rule that when, in the usual course of the business of a corporation an officer or agent is held out by the corporation, or has been permitted to act for it, or to manage its affairs in such a way as to justify third persons who deal with him in inferring or assuming that he is doing an act, or making a contract within the scope of his authority, the corporation is bound thereby, even though such officer or agent has not the actual authority from the corporation to do such an act or to make such a contract. This authority is known as apparent or ostensible authority.—Cf. Bank of Holly Springs v. Pinson, 58 Miss. 421, 38 Am. Rep. 330 (1887). This apparent authority is materially the same and is based upon the same principle as authority by estoppel. Stating the rule in terms of estoppel, a corporation which by its voluntary act places an officer or agent in such a position or situation that persons of ordinary prudence are justified in assuming that he has authority to perform the action in question and deal with him upon that assumption, is estopped, as against such persons, from denying the officer's or agent's authority.—Cf. 13 *Am. Jur.* 870, 871, sect. 890.

[111] 45 *Am. Jur.* 783, sect. 73.

the other hand, where the society itself is incorporated, the relation of the officers to the society is not that of trustee, but is merely the fiduciary or trust relation, using the word in a broader sense, existing between incorporators and officers of any private corporation.[112] As the duties and liabilities of the trustee to his *cestui que* trust will be discussed in a subsequent section, only the duties and liabilities proper to the latter relationship will be discussed here.

By virtue of the fiduciary relationship which they occupy, officers or trustees of corporations, religious or private, are subject in their dealings respecting corporate interests to the general rules governing the relation of a trustee to his *cestui que* trust.[113] They are forbidden therefore, to secure for themselves any advantage which good faith and fidelity to the trust reposed in them would not in any way warrant.[114] Thus, they cannot either directly or indirectly in their dealings on behalf of the corporation with others, or in any other transaction in which they are under a duty to guard the interests of the corporation, make any profit or acquire any other personal benefit or advantage.[115]

With regard to the liabilities of the officers or trustees, it may be stated as a general rule that they are liable jointly and severally for the losses of the corporation caused by their bad faith or wilful or intentional departures from duty, their

[112] 45 *Am. Jur.* 783, sect. 73.

[113] Pioneer Oil and Gas Co. v. Anderson, 168 Miss. 334, 151 So. 161 (1933). In the case of Knox Glass Bottle Co. v. Underwood, the court citing 19 C.J.S. Corporations 105, sect. 761, stated: "A director's duties being trust duties or in the nature of the duties of a trustee toward his *cestui que* trust, his acts are subject to be tested by the rules governing the relation of a trustee to his *cestui que* trust."—228 Miss. 699, 89 So. 2d 799, sugg. of error overruled in 228 Miss. 699, 91 So. 2d 843, certiorari denied 77 S. Ct. 1060, 353 U.S. 977, 1 L. Ed. 2d 1137 (1956).

[114] Pioneer Oil and Gas Co. v. Anderson, 168 Miss. 334, 151 So. 161 (1933).

[115] Knox Glass Bottle Co. v. Underwood, 228 Miss. 699, 89 So. 2d 799, sugg. of error overruled in 228 Miss. 699, 91 So. 2d 843, certiorari denied 77 S. Ct. 1060, 353 U.S. 977, 1 L. Ed. 2d 1137 (1956).

fraudulent breaches of trust, their gross or wilful negligence, or their *ultra vires* acts.[116] However, an officer or trustee is not liable for an act complained of, unless it is shown that he participated therein or negligently omitted to perform his duty.[117]

C. *The Liability of Religious Corporations*

Religious corporations are, like all other corporations, bound by their contracts and by the principle of good faith and obligation which rest upon individuals in like circumstances.[118] However, with regard to tort liability, religious and charitable corporations have heretofore enjoyed a privileged status under Anglo-American law, being granted practically total immunity from tort liability. Today, however, there is a trend in many jurisdictions, either to limit, or abolish entirely, this immunity.

Three possible bases have been suggested for the exemption of charitable corporations from tort liability, and the circumstances under which there is an exemption depend upon which basis is accepted by the courts of the state as the ground for exemption. These bases are: (1) that the trust assets should not be diverted from the charitable purposes for which they were given; (2) that persons benefitting from the charity by the acceptance of such benefits waive any claim for damages; (3) that the doctrine of *respondeat superior* is inapplicable to charities.[119]

Prior to 1951, the cases which came before the Supreme Court of Mississippi on the subject of the tort liability of charitable institutions, involved actions for injuries received through the negligence of employees. In the decisions rendered in these cases, the court, on the basis that the doctrine of *respondeat superior* was inapplicable to charitable institu-

[116] Knox Glass Bottle Co. v. Underwood, 228 Miss. 699, 89 So. 2d 799, suggestion of error overruled in 228 Miss. 699, 91 So. 2d 843, certiorari denied 77 S. Ct. 1060, 353 U.S. 977, 1 L. Ed. 2d 1137 (1956) citing 19 C.J.S. Corporations, 825.

[117] Knox Glass Bottle Co. v. Underwood.

[118] Burke v. Wall, 29 La. Ann. 38, 29 Am. Rep. 316 (1877).

[119] Scott, IV, sect. 402, 2894.

tions, held that they were not subject to liability for the negligence of their agents where the institution had exercised due care and caution in the selection of such agents.

Thus, in the case of Mississippi Baptist Hospital v. Moore, it was held that a charitable hospital administered solely for charity and not for profit, is not liable for the negligence of its servants and physicians where the hospital has exercised due care and caution in selecting such agents. In such a case, the only remedy open to the injured party is an action against the person who inflicted the injury. Where, however, the hospital is negligent in selecting the physician or servant, then the hospital is liable for any injury caused by such agents.[120]

The same principles were applied in the case of International Order of Twelve of Knights and Daughters of Tabor in Mississippi v. Barnes. In that case a patient sued for damages because of burns allegedly received from hot water bottles while a patient in the hospital. The court held that the hospital was subject to liability, not however on the basis of the doctrine of *respondeat superior*, but on the ground that it was sufficiently shown that the hospital was negligent in the selection of particular nurses.[121]

The case of Rhodes v. Millsaps College, though involving an action for damages because of the negligence of an agent of the College, was not decided on the principles stated in the foregoing cases, as it is distinguishable from them on its particular facts. The instant case involved an injury to a child while playing on the premises of an establishment operated by Millsaps College, a charitable institution. The establishment however, was operated for profit and had no relation to the purposes of the charity except that the revenue derived therefrom was expended for the charity solely. In granting judgment for the plaintiff, the court stated:

[120] Mississippi Baptist Hospital v. Moore, 157 Miss. 676, 126 So. 465, 67 A.L.R. 1106 (1930). The same principles were applied in the case of Pace v. Methodist Hospital, 130 So. 468 (1930) (not reported in full).

[121] 204 Miss. 333, 37 So. 2d 487 (1948).

> We are thoroughly of the opinion that where a charitable institution or corporation goes into an independent business apart from its charitable purposes but to be operated solely for profit, or to secure funds for its charitable purposes, it is liable for injuries as other corporations.[122]

In 1951 the Supreme Court of Mississippi in the case of Mississippi Baptist Hospital v. Holmes, overruled the decisions of the aforementioned hospital cases and held that a hospital is liable for the negligence of its employees although it is not negligent in selecting them.[123]

The particular case involved an action brought by the survivors for the death of a paying patient at the defendant hospital whose employee technician caused death by negligently mislabeling blood used in a transfusion. In a rather lengthy decision the court effectively challenged the bases for the immunity doctrine heretofore mentioned. It is to be noted, however, that the court confined itself exclusively to the issue at bar stating:

> We are not concerned in the instant case with the question of whether or not a *charitable patient* should be entitled to recover if injured through the negligence of an employee of a hospital which is chartered and operated as a charitable institution, nor are we concerned with the question of whether or not a *student who pays tuition in an amount far below the cost of furnishing him the facilities offered by a denominational college, or other institution which is operated as a charitable one,* is entitled to recover damages for the negligence of an employee thereof, but we are concerned here with the question *alone* as to whether or not a *paying* patient who has been injured through the negligence of an employee of a hospital which is rendering service for the most part to paying patients, or rather whether the heirs at law in this case on account of the death of the patient because

[122] Rhodes v. Millsaps College, 179 Miss. 596, 176 So. 253 (1937).

[123] Mississippi Baptist Hospital v. Holmes, 214 Miss. 906, 55 So. 2d 142, 23 A.L.R. 2d 12. Sugg. of error overruled 214 Miss. 906, 46 So. 2d 709 (1951).

> of such negligence are entitled to recover where full compensation has been paid to the hospital for the room, board and other services rendered by the hospital employees, and where the patient has therefore not received the benefit of any charitable work done by the institution.[124]

In the light of this decision, it is incumbent on all administrators of charitable institutions of whatever nature to acquire sufficient liability insurance to protect their property from being seized in payment of judgments for damages. For although the decision was limited to the point at issue only, the conclusion of the opinion of the court indicates that the Supreme Court of Mississippi, like the courts of many jurisdictions, no longer looks favorably on the immunity doctrine. The conclusion of the decision reads as follows:

> And finally, it should be said that the tendency of immunity is to foster neglect, and that the tendency of imposing liability is to induce care and caution in the treatment of those for whom these institutions were established. Neither the encouragement of charity and philanthrophy nor the doctrine of immunity on the ground of public policy can dispel the fact that the primary interest and welfare of the public requires that one person should not suffer an injury to his life or limb without recompense, merely in order that all earnings of a charitable hospital should be devoted to the purpose of providing for others.[125]

SECTION 2. THE ADMINISTRATION OF CHURCH PROPERTY UNDER THE TRUSTEE SYSTEM

In the discussion of the tenure of church property in Mississippi, it was pointed out that under Mississippi law an unincorporated religious society cannot own title to proper-

[124] Mississippi Baptist Hospital v. Holmes, 214 Miss. 906, 55 So. 2d 142, 149, 23 A.L.R. 2d 12. Sugg. of error overruled 214 Miss. 906, 56 So. 2d 709 (1951). (Emphasis added by writer).

[125] Mississippi Baptist Hospital v. Holmes, 214 Miss. 906, 55 So. 2d 142, 23 A.L.R. 2d 12. Sugg. of error overruled 214 Miss. 906, 56 So. 2d 709 (1951).

ty,[126] and that, therefore, the property of the various congregations, parishes or missions which is not vested in the diocesan corporation is held in trust by the bishop for the use and benefit of the respective congregations, parishes or missions. It was likewise pointed out, in construing the nature of this trust relationship, that the bishop did not hold the property under a dry or naked trust, but was an active trustee empowered to use the trust *res*, within the limitations of the trust instrument, according to the rules and discipline of the Catholic Church. However, as all property rights are subject to the jurisdiction of the state, the bishop, as the trustee of any charitable trust, will be governed also by the general norms affecting the administration of trusts as contained in the statute law of the state and the judicial decisions of the courts.

A. The Powers, Duties and Liabilities of Trustees

a. Powers and Duties

The extent of the duties and of the powers of a trustee depends primarily upon the terms of the trust. In so far as the trust instrument expressly or by implication imposes duties or confers powers upon the trustee, the terms of the trust determine the extent of his duties and powers, except so far as the performance of the duties, or the exercise of the powers is or becomes impossible, or the provision is illegal, or there has been such a change of circumstances as to justify or require deviation from the terms of the trust. In cases where there is no provision, express or implied, in the terms of the trust, the duties and powers of the trustee are determined by the principles and rules which have been evolved by courts of equity for the governing of the conduct of trustees.[127]

Where the powers and duties of the trustee are spelled out in the trust instrument, as a general rule, he cannot deviate from these instructions.[128] However, a court of equity will

[126] West v. State, 169 Miss. 302, 152 So. 888 (1934).

[127] Cf. Scott, II, sect. 164, p. 1153.

[128] Pressly v. Ellis, 48 Miss. 574 (1873); Vernor v. Board of Police

direct or permit a trustee to deviate from the terms of a trust, if compliance therewith, because of circumstances not known or anticipated by the settlor, would defeat or substantially impair the accomplishment of the purposes of the trust.[129]

The question may be asked as to whether the trustee may deviate from the terms of the trust without the permission of the court, when such terms are not in themselves illegal? The question is one of possible conflicting policies. As a general rule, the trustee should comply with the terms of the trust. But if there is a change of circumstances such that compliance would endanger the trust property, slavish compliance with the terms of the trust should not be demanded. However, if the need of action is not immediate the trustee should not take upon himself the determination of the propriety of the deviation. If on the other hand, the emergency is so acute that he must act at once or not at all, there is a clear policy in favor of his acting.[130]

(1) The Particular Duties of a Trustee

Once a trustee has accepted the trust he cannot thereafter disclaim it; he can resign only with the permission of the court, or by the consent of the beneficiaries, unless it is otherwise provided by the terms of the trust.[131] This principle, however, applies only to a trust in which the instrument creating the trust has failed to provide for a succession of trustees, in case of death, resignation, inability or refusal of any trustee to act. Where a succession of trustees is provided for by the trust instrument, resort by a trustee to a court of

of Tippah Co., 47 Miss. 181 (1872); Rudy v. Johnson's Estate, 200 Miss. 205, 26 So. 2d 685 (1946).

[129] City of Jackson v. Trustees of the Young Women's Christian Association, 224 Miss. 298, 88 So. 2d 50 (1955). In the case of charitable trusts, greater deviations from the terms of the trust may be permitted through the use of the *cy pres* power (the equitable doctrine of approximation in Mississippi) heretofore mentioned.

[130] Cf. Scott, II, sects. 167. 1, 167. 2, pp. 1178-1184.

[131] Aldridge v. Breisch, 114 Miss. 281, 109 So. 713 (1926).

Chancery to be relieved of his duties is wholly unnecessary.[132]

The most fundamental duty owed by the trustee to the beneficiaries of the trust is the duty of loyalty. This duty is imposed upon the trustee, not because of any provision in the terms of the trust, but because of the relationship that arises from the creation of the trust. A trustee is in a fiduciary relation to the beneficiaries (of the trust), and hence, he must do nothing which can place him in a position inconsistent with the interests of the trust, or has a tendency to interfere with his duty in discharging it.[133]

From this duty of loyalty certain other duties follow as a necessary consequence. Thus a trustee cannot use trust property so as to derive personal profits therefrom. Whatever profit is made must go to the trust estate.[134] He cannot use trust funds to pay his own debts.[135] Moreover, during the continuance of the trust, he cannot acquire an interest in the trust property adverse to the interest of the *cestui que* trust.[136] He may not, therefore, purchase trust property from himself,[137] or sell his own property to himself as trustee,[138] or obtain by fraud an agreement with the beneficiary whereby he is deprived of the benefits of the trust.[139] However, the duty of loyalty does not preclude a trustee from

[132] Cf. Aldridge v. Breisch, 114 Miss. 281, 109 So. 713 (1926).

[133] Joor v. Williams, 38 Miss. 546 (1860); Gillenwater v. Miller, 49 Miss. 150 (1873).

[134] Alexander v. Hancock, 177 Miss. 590, 171 So. 544 (1937); Merchants Bank and Trust Co., v. Garrett, 203 Miss. 182, 33 So. 2d 603 (1948).

[135] Jackson v. Jefferson, 171 Miss. 774, 158 So. 486 (1935).

[136] Joor v. Williams, 38 Miss. 546 (1860).

[137] Scott v. Freeland, 7 Smedes & Marshall 409, 45 Am. Dec. 310 (1846). It is to be noted, however, that the doctrine that a purchase by a trustee is absolutely void as to the *cestui que* trust, applies only in those cases where a trustee is appointed to buy or sell property, and he buys and sells to or from himself. In such cases the purchase is always held void upon application of the *cestui que* trust.—Tatum v. McLellan, 50 Miss. 1 (1874).

[138] Stokes v. Terrell, 23 So. 371 (1898).

[139] Field v. Middlesex Banking Co., 77 Miss. 180, 26 So. 365 (1899).

asserting an interest in the trust property acquired before he became a trustee thereof.[140] Moreover, when a trust is at an end and a new trust is created to which the trustee is a party, he may make new terms and stipulations for his own security in undertaking the trust.[141]

A trustee has the duty to keep the trust *res* separate, and if he fails to do so he has committed a breach of trust.[142] Thus, where a trustee deposits the funds of the trust estate in his own name and not as trustee, and with his own private funds, he thereby becomes the debtor of the trust estate and the creditor of the bank; and if the trust funds are lost through the insolvency of the bank or otherwise, the loss will fall on the trustee.[143] In making deposits or investments, therefore, the trustee should make them to the account of the trust estate.

As a general rule the office and duties of a trustee, being matters of confidence, cannot be delegated by him to another, unless authority be conferred on him to do so by the circumstances creating the trust.[144] Thus, in the case of Gwin v. Fountain, it was held that the power to employ all persons necessary to conduct and manage the trust estate included the employment of competent counsel to advise and aid the trustee in the execution of his trust.[145]

Thus far reference has been made to the negative duties of the trustee. On the positive side, the duty of loyalty prescribes that the trustee should take such steps as are reasonable to secure control of the trust property. Thus, where the trust property includes an interest in land, he should see that the interest is recorded in his name as trustee. Where there is a question of a mortgage on land or a chattel mortgage in

140 Davis v. Bowmar, 55 Miss. 671 (1878).

141 Shirley v. Shattuck, 28 Miss. 13 (1854).

142 Bird v. Stein, 258 F. 2d 168, certiorari denied 78 S. Ct. 608, 359 U.S. 926, 3 L. Ed. 2d 628 (1958); Kern v. Laird, 27 Miss. 544 (1854).

143 Coffin v. Bramlitt, 42 Miss. 194 (1868).

144 Skipwith v. Robinson, 24 Miss. 688 (1852).

145 Gwin v. Fountain, 159 Miss. 619, 126 So. 18, 132 So. 559 (1930).

connection with the trust estate, it is his duty to see that the mortgage is properly recorded. Where choses in action are assigned to him as trustee, it is his duty to notify the obligors of the assignment, and on the maturity of the choses in action it is his duty to take reasonable steps to enforce them. Finally, in the case of shares of stock and registered bonds he should see that they are registered in his name as trustee.[146]

It is the duty of the trustee to make the trust property productive; to lend money at interest, to farm land, etc.[147] In this regard the terms of the trust may determine the precise activities required.[148]

(2) The Particular Powers of a Trustee

A trustee has such powers as are specifically conferred by the terms of the trust and such powers as are necessary or appropriate for carrying out the purposes of the trust. The former powers, that is, those conferred by the terms of the trust, may be either imperative or discretionary. Thus, a trustee may be given discretion to exercise a power or not to exercise it; and where he is directed to exercise a power, the time and manner of its exercise may be left to his discretion. Moreover, the discretionary power may relate to the business administration of the trust, or it may relate to the distribution of the income or principal.[149]

Where discretionary power is granted to a trustee, as a general rule, a chancery court will not substitute its judgment for that of the trustee, with respect to the exercise of that power. However, it will, whenever circumstances require it, review the exercise of discretion given to the trustee, and decide whether it is reasonable or unreasonable.[150] In the exercise of his discretionary power, therefore, a trustee

[146] Cf. Scott, II, sect. 175, pp. 1302-1305.

[147] Brown v. Mullins, 24 Miss. 204 (1852).

[148] Scott, II, sect. 181, pp. 1348-1350.

[149] Cf. Scott, II, sects. 186, 187, pp. 1370-1381.

[150] Yeates v. Box, 198 Miss. 602, 22 So. 2d 411 (1945). Thus in the case of Prewett v. Land, the court stated:

should have regard to the purpose of the trust and act in accordance therewith.[151]

In accordance with the trustee's duty to preserve and make the trust estate productive, certain powers are thereby necessarily implied. Wherefore, a trustee can protect the trust property by insuring it against loss by fire or other casualty. Similarly, he can properly pay out of the trust estate a premium on insurance against liability, although such insurance affords protection to the trustee individually as well as to the trust estate.[152] Moreover, a trustee may incur expenses for the repair of the trust estate, and pay taxes from the income and revenue derived therefrom.[153] Likewise, if it is necessary, he may sue for and recover property.[154]

Where the trust estate includes land, it is ordinarily the duty of the trustee to make the land productive by leasing it, and the trustee normally has the power to lease the land, even though there is no provision in the trust instrument to that effect. Unless otherwise provided by the terms of the trust, the lease may be for such periods and with such provisions as are reasonable under the circumstances, and it must appear that the lease is fair, reasonable and for the benefit of the beneficiary.[155]

With regard to the sale of trust property, the American Law Institute takes the position that the trustee of a charitable trust can sell trust property not only if the power of sale is conferred in specific words, but also if such sale is necessary or appropriate to enable the trustee to carry out the

"... when a trustee is given discretion to sell a portion of an estate held in trust for the support of the beneficiary in order to supplement insufficient income therefor, the court will compel him to sell when the interest of the beneficiaries so require."—Prewett v. Land, 36 Miss. 495 (1858).

151 Strong v. Cannon, 1 Miss. Dec. 11 (1885).

152 Scott, II, sect. 188. 1, p. 1396.

153 Martin v. Eslick, 229 Miss. 234, 90 So. 2d 635; judgment corrected 92 So. 2d 244 (1956).

154 Miller v. Bank of Holly Springs, 138 Miss. 529, 103 So. 362 (1925).

155 Cf. 10 *Am. Jur.* 621, sect. 51; Scott, II, sect. 189, pp. 1408-1422.

purpose of the trust,[156] unless such sale is forbidden by the terms of the trust or it appears from the terms of the trust that the property must be retained *in specie.*[157] However, as indicated previously, a prohibition against sale will not prevent a chancery court from authorizing the trustee to make a sale, in a case of necessity arising from unforeseen change of circumstances, and to apply the proceeds to the purposes of the trust.[158]

A power of sale, however, does not include the power to exchange.[159] Moreover, when the power of sale is conferred by the express terms of the trust instrument, the trustee, when selling, must follow the mode, manner and time prescribed by the instrument.[160]

Whether a trustee has a power to mortgage trust property depends primarily upon the manifestation of the intention of the settlor. The cases are numerous, however, in which it has been held that where there is nothing in the trust instrument, either in express words or otherwise, authorizing the trustee to mortgage land included in the trust estate, and where the purposes of the trust are not such as to justify making the mortgage, the trustee commits a breach of trust by doing so. Similarly, in numerous cases it has been held that the trustee was not empowered to pledge securities or other personal property included in the trust estate.[161]

b. The Liabilities of Trustees

As a general rule, trustees, as long as they keep themselves

[156] The power of sale will be implied whenever duties are imposed on the trustee which cannot be performed without it.—Corley v. Bishop, 101 Miss. 490, 58 So. 360 (1912).

[157] *Restatement of the Law of Trusts,* (3 vols., St. Paul, Minn.: American Law Institute, 1959), Vol. II, sect. 380; 10 *Am. Jur.* 620, sect. 51.

[158] City of Jackson v. Trustees of Young Women's Christian Association, 224 Miss. 298, 80 So. 2d 50 (1955).

[159] Columbus Banking Co., v. Humphries, 64 Miss. 258, 1 So. 232 (1887).

[160] McCaughn v. Young, 85 Miss. 277, 37 So. 839 (1905).

[161] For a thorough discussion of this topic, cf. Scott, II, sects. 191-191. 4, pp. 1444-1454.

strictly within the line of duty, and exercise reasonable care and diligence, cannot be held responsible for any loss or depreciation in the property entrusted to them. If, however, they do not strictly pursue that line and a loss ensues, they are liable to make that loss good, although such loss may have been wholly unexpected.[162]

Thus, as previously indicated, a trustee has a duty to keep the trust funds separate. Should he violate this duty, and deposit the trust funds to his own account, he would render himself liable for it on the failure of the bank.[163] Moreover, it has been held that if a trustee mingles money received by him as a trustee with his own funds, and invests it, he is liable for the interest.[164] Similarly, it has been held that a trustee is not permitted to make gain for himself out of the trust funds by involving them in trade for his own benefit, and should he do so, he is answerable for what would be a reasonable income.[165]

With regard to liability upon contracts, it may be stated that as a general rule trustees are subject to personal liability upon contracts made by them in the administration of the trust, unless by the terms of the contract it is provided that they shall not be personally liable.[166] Where, however, the contract was properly executed in the administration of the trust, the trustees are entitled to indemnity out of the trust estate.[167]

B. The Tort Liability of Unincorporated Institutions

According to Scott, the same principles of policy are applicable to charitable trusts as are applicable to charitable corporations, although the technique involved may be somewhat different.[168]

162 Coffin v. Bramlitt, 42 Miss. 194 (1868).

163 Coffin v. Bramlitt, 42 Miss. 194 (1868).

164 Kern v. Laird, 27 Miss. 544 (1854).

165 Jordan v. Rickey, 4 How. 233 (1835).

166 Peeples v. Enochs, 170 Miss. 472, 153 So. 796 (1934).

167 Clopton v. Gholson, 53 Miss. 466 (1876); Stern Bros. v. Hampton, 73 Miss. 555, 19 So. 300 (1896); Orgill Bros. v. Perry, 157 Miss. 543, 128 So. 755 (1930).

168 Scott, IV, sect. 404. 2, p. 2913.

CONCLUSIONS

1. The tenure of Church Property under the present law of Mississippi is best achieved by vesting the titles of the various properties in the bishop as trustee. The terms of the trust should clearly specify that the property is held by the bishop in trust for a particular parish, congregation or mission, and subject to be dealt with according to the rules and discipline of the Catholic Church.

2. The proprietary capacity of the Church is limited by civil statute. However, due to the curative statute enacted by the legislature in 1926, titles to property acquired before that time contrary to the statute are now valid.

3. Property acquired by the Church contrary to statute does not escheat to the state, but the state can force a sale of such property. Private persons cannot take advantage of the restrictions imposed by law on the amount of property the Church may own.

4. The right of the Church to acquire property by last will and testament is limited by mortmain statutes. Under the present statutes the only restrictions now imposed on the right of the Church to take a devise of land or bequest of personalty, are: (1) in the case of a devise of land, the Church may not hold it for a period longer than ten years after the devise becomes effective; and (2) whether land or personalty is involved a person leaving spouse or child or descendant of child can bequeath or devise only one-third of his estate to the Church, provided, that the will is executed ninety days before such person's death.

5. Land devised to the Church must be sold within ten years. If it is not sold within that time it reverts to the heirs a law or to the devisees of the testator. However, in the case of the devisees, should they fall within the classification of a religious, charitable, civil or educational institution, they cannot succeed to the devise.

6. With the exception of the statutes of mortmain, the Church can acquire property by every means permitted to others. The following comparisons may be made between the law of the Church and the law of the state as to the acquisition of property:

(1) Delivery of a deed of gift is not sufficient of itself to convey the title to specific tangible chattels in Mississippi.

(2) The right to make a will in Mississippi is not a property right or a natural or inherent right but is purely a statutory right subject to the legislature's complete control.

(3) As regards prescription, the following discrepancies exist between the provisions of Canon Law and the provisions of Mississippi law:

(a) Good faith both in the internal and external forum is an essential element for prescription in Canon Law. In Mississippi law good faith appears not to be an essential requirement.

(b) In Canon Law color of title is likewise an essential element for prescription. Under Mississippi law color of title is required for constructive possession but not for actual possession. In other words a person can acquire adversely the property he actually possesses without any color of title whatsoever.

(c) It is probable that the state would give recognition to the provisions of the Code regarding the removal of certain objects from the scope of prescription with the exception of sacred objects. However, it would not recognize the provisions of the Code regarding the element of time.

7. The administration of Church property under the trust system, though not in agreement with the letter of Canon Law, is at least in conformity with its spirit, because the beneficial interest of the property is enjoyed by the respective moral person. Moreover, the pastor of a parish as the agent of the bishop is the actual administrator of its property.

BIBLIOGRAPHY

Sources

Acta Apostolicae Sedis, Commentarium Officiale, Romae, 1909-1928; Civitate Vaticana, 1929—

Acta et Decreta Concilii Plenarii Baltimorensis Tertii, A.D. 1884, Baltimorae: Typis Ioannis Murphy et Sociorum, 1886.

Acta Synodi Natchetensis anno 1862 celebratae.

American Jurisprudence, 58 vols. and Indices, Rochester, N.Y.: Bancroft-Whitney Co., 1935-1952.

Annotated Code of the General Statute Laws of the State of Mississippi, The, Nashville, Tennessee, 1892.

Black, H.C., *Black's Law Dictionary,* 3. ed., St. Paul: West Publishing Co., 1933.

Book of Incorporations, Office of the Secretary of State, Jackson, Mississippi.

Bullarium Sacrae Congregationis de Propaganda Fide, 7 vols., Romae: Typis Collegii Urbani, 1839-1841.

Canon Law Digest, The, 4 vols., Milwaukee: Bruce Publishing Co., Vol. I, 1934, Vol. II, 1943, Vol. III, 1954, edited by T. Lincoln Bouscaren; Vol. IV, 1958, edited by T. Lincoln Bouscaren and James I. O'Connor.

Code of Mississippi: Being an Analytical Compilation of the Public and General Statutes of the Territory and State, with Tabular References to the Local and Private Acts from 1798-1848, Jackson, Mississippi, 1848.

Codex Iuris Canonici, Pii X Pontificis Maximi iussu digestus, Benedicti Pape XV auctoritate promulgatus, Romae: Typis Polyglottis Vaticanis, 1917.

Collectanea Sacrae Congregationis de Propaganda Fide, 2 vols., Romae: Ex Typographia Polyglotta S.C. de Propaganda Fide, 1907.

Concilia Provincialia Baltimori habita 1829-1849, Editio Altera, Baltimori: Apud Ioannem Murphy et Socium, 1851.

Concilium Plenarium Totius Americae Septentrionalis Foederatae, Baltimori: Apud Ioannem Murphy et Socios, 1852.

Concilii Plenarii Baltimoriensis II in Ecclesia Metropolitana Baltimoriensi habiti, Acta et Decreta, Baltimorae: Ioannes Murphy, 1869.

Concilium Neo-Aurelianense Provinciale Primum, habitum anno 1856, New Orleans, 1857.

Concilium Neo-Aurelianense Provinciale Secundum, New Orleans, 1864.

Corpus Iuris Civilis, 3 vols., Vol. I, *Institutiones,* ed. stereotypa, 15 recognovit P. Krueger; *Digesta,* ed. stereotypa 15, recognovit T. Mommsen, retractavit P. Krueger; Vol. II, *Codex Iustinianus,* ed. stereotypa 10, recognovit et retractavit P. Krueger; Vol. III, *Novellae Constitutiones,* ed. stereotypa 5, recognovit R. Schoell, opus Schoellii morte interceptum absolvit G. Kroll, Berolini, 1928-1929.

Corpus Iuris Secundum, 95 vols., and Indices, Brooklyn, N.Y.: The American Book Co., 1936-1951.

Decretales Gregorii Papae IX, suae integritati una cum glossis restitutae cum privilegio Gregorii XIII, Pont. Max. et aliorum Principum. Romae, 1582.

Hernaez, Francisco J., *Colecciòn dè Bulas, Breves y Otros Documentos Relativos a la Iglesia de America y Filipinas,* 2 vols., Bruselas: Vromant, 1879.

Laws of the State of Mississippi, Appropriations, General Legislation and Resolutions, Passed at the Regular Session of the Mississippi Legislature held in Jackson, 1926, Jackson, Mississippi, 1926.

Laws of the State of Mississippi, Passed at an Extraordinary Session of the Mississippi Legislature held in Jackson, 1938, Jackson, Mississippi, 1938.

Laws of the State of Mississippi, Appropriations, General Legislation and Resolutions, Passed at the Regular Session of the Mississippi Legislature held in Jackson, 1940, Jackson, Mississippi, 1940.

Laws of the State of Mississippi, Appropriations, General Legislation and Resolutions, Passed at the Regular Session of the Mississippi Legislature held in Jackson, 1946, Jackson, Mississippi, 1946.

Mississippi Code of 1930 of the Public Statute Laws of the State of Mississippi, Revised and Annotated by the Code Commission under the Provisions of an Act of the Legislature, Approved April 26, 1928 and Reported to and Revised, Amended and Adopted by the Legislature at its Regular Session in 1930, 2 vols., Atlanta, Ga.: The Harrison Co., 1930.

Mississippi Code 1942 Annotated: Containing Permanent Public Statutes of Mississippi to the end of the Legislative Session 1942, 8 vols., Atlanta, Ga.: The Harrison Co.; Rochester, N.Y.: The Lawyers Co-operative Publishing Co., 1942.

McKinney's Consolidated Laws of New York Annotated, 68 vols., Brooklyn, N.Y.: Edward Thompson Company; Vol. 50, *Religious Coroporations Law,* 1952, *with 1953 Cumulative Annual Pocket Part.*

Natchez-Jackson Diocesan Archives, Chancery Office, Jackson, Mississippi.

Revised Code of the Laws of Mississippi, The, in which are comprised all such acts of the General Assembly of a Public Nature as were in force at the end of the year 1823, Natchez, Miss.: Francis Baker, 1824.

Revised Code of the Statute Laws of the State of Mississippi, The, Jackson, Miss.: E. Barksdale, 1857.

Revised Code of the Statute Laws of the State of Mississippi, The, as Adopted at the January Session, 1871 and Published by the Authority of the Legislature, Jackson, Miss.: Alcorn and Fisher, 1871.

Revised Code of the Statute Laws of the State of Mississippi, The, Prepared by J.A.P. Campbell and Reported to and Amended and Adopted by the Legislature at its Biennial Session in 1880, Jackson, Miss.: J. L. Power, 1880.

Shearer, Donald C., *Pontificia Americana, Documentary History of the Catholic Church in the United States (1784-1884)*, The Catholic University of America Studies in American Church History, Vol. XV, Washington, D.C.: The Catholic University of America Press, 1933.

Synodus dioecesana Natchetensis Prima, habita a Gulielmo Henrico Elder.

Synodus dioecesana Natchetensis habita diebus 19, 20, 21 mensis Ianuarii 1874, a Gulielmo Henrico Elder, in monasterio cui nomen "St. Theresa's Retreat" patrum congregationis SS. Redemptoris apud Chatawa.

Synodus dioecesana Natchetensis quinta habita, diebus 16, 17 mensis Septembris, 1886 a Francisco Janssens.

Synodus dioecesana Natchetensis sexta habita, mense Aprilis, A.D. 1892, a Thoma Heslin.

Synodus dioecesana Natchetensis septima habita fine Aprilis principioque mensis Maii, 1897 a Thoma Heslin.

Constitutiones Dioecesios Natchetensis quae in Synodo Dioecesana Octava Die 14 Julii, 1922 habita in Ecclesia Parochiali Bay St. Louis, a Ioanne Edwardo Gunn, Jackson, Mississippi, 1922.

Tenth Diocesan Synod of the Diocese of Natchez-Jackson, Jackson, Mississippi, 1957.

REFERENCE WORKS

Abbo, J.—Hannan, J., *The Sacred Canons,* 2 vols., St. Louis: B. Herder Book Co., 1952.

Andre, G., *Une Page d'Histoire sur les Associations Cultuelles,* Paris.

Ayrinhac, H. A., *Administrative Legislation in the New Code of Canon Law,* London-New York-Toronto: Longmans, Green and Co., 1930.

Baart, Rev. P. A., *The Tenure of Catholic Church Property in the United States of America,* Authorized copy, 1900.

Baudier, Roger, *The Catholic Church in Louisiana,* New Orleans, 1939.

Beste, Udalricus, *Introductio in Codicem,* 4. ed., Neapoli: M. D'Auria, 1956.

Biever, Albert H., *The Jesuits in New Orleans and the Mississippi Valley* New Orleans, 1924.

Biographical and Historical Memoirs of Mississippi, 2 vols., Chicago: The Goodspeed Publishing Co., 1891.

Blackstone, William, *Commentaries on the Laws of England,* 4 vols., New York, 1852.

Blat, Albertus, *Commentarium Textus Codicis Iuris Canonici,* 5 vols., Vol. III, Pars Altera, Romae: Collegio Angelico, 1923.

Bouscaren, T. L.—Ellis, A. C., *Canon Law: A Text and Commentary,* 2. revised ed., Milwaukee: Bruce Publishing Co., 1951.

Brown, Brendan, *The Canonical Juristic Personality with Special Reference to its Status in the United States of America,* The Catholic University of America Canon and Civil Law Studies, n. 39, Washington, D.C.: The Catholic University of America Press, 1927.

Byrne, Harry J., *Investment of Church Funds,* The Catholic University of America Canon Law Studies, n. 309, Washington, D.C.: The Catholic University of America Press, 1951.

Capello, Felix, *Summa Iuris Canonici,* 3 vols., Vol. II, 4. ed., Romae: Apud Aedes Universitatis Gregorianae, 1945.

Chapman, Charles E., *Colonial Hispanic America,* New York, 1933.

Claiborne, John F., *Mississippi as a Province, Territory and State with Biographical Notices of Eminent Citizens,* Jackson, Mississippi, 1880.

Clarke, Richard H., *Lives of the Deceased Bishops of the Catholic Church in the United States,* New York, 1872.

Cleary, Joseph F., *Canonical Limitations on the Alienation of Church Property,* The Catholic University of America Canon Law Studies, n. 100, Washington, D.C.: The Catholic University of America Press, 1936.

Comyns, Joseph J., *Papal and Episcopal Administration of Church Property,* The Catholic University of America Canon Law Studies, n. 147, Washington, D.C.: The Catholic University of America Press, 1942.

Conte a Coronata, Matthaeus, *Institutiones Iuris Canonici,* 5 vols., Vol. II, 4. ed., Taurini-Romae: Marietti, 1951.

Curley, Michael J., *Church and State in the Spanish Floridas (1783-1822),* The Catholic University of America Studies in American Church History, Vol. XXX, Washington, D.C.: The Catholic University of America Press, 1940.

De Castillo, Antonio, *La Luisiana Española y el Padre Sedella,* San Juan, Puerto Rico, 1929.

Delanglez, Jean, *The French Jesuits in Lower Louisiana (1700-1763),* The Catholic University of America Studies in American Church History, Vol. XXI, Washington, D.C.: The Catholic University of America Press, 1935.

De Martinis, Raphael, *Iuris Pontificii de Propaganda Fide,* 5 vols., Romae: Typographia Polyglotta S.C. de Propaganda Fide, 1892.

Desrochers, Bruno, *Le Premier Concile Plenier de Quebec et le Code de Droit Canonique,* The Catholic University of America Canon Law Studies, n. 152, Washington, D.C.: The Catholic University of America Press, 1942.

Dignan, Patrick J., *A History of the Legal Incorporation of Catholic Church Property in the United States,* New York: Kenedy & Sons, 1935.

Doheny, William J., *Church Property: Modes of Acquisition,* The Catholic University of America Canon and Roman Law Studies, n. 41, Washington, D.C.: The Catholic University of America Press, 1927.

Easterly, Frederick J., *The Life of Right Rev. Joseph Rosati, First Bishop of St. Louis (1789-1843),* The Catholic University of America Studies in American Church History, Vol. XXXIII, Washington, D.C.: The Catholic University of America Press, 1942.

Fisch, E., *The Cy Pres Doctrine in the United States,* New York: Bender & Co., 1950.

Gams, Pius, *Series Episcoporum Ecclesiae,* Ratisbon, 1873.

Gayarre, *History of Louisiana,* 4 vols., Vols. I, II, *The French Domination,* New York, 1866.

Gerow, Most Rev. R. O., *Catholicity in Mississippi,* Natchez, Mississippi, 1939.

———, *Cradle Days of St. Mary's at Natchez,* Natchez, Mississippi, 1941.

Gierke, Otto F.—Maitland, F., *Political Theories of the Middle Ages,* Cambridge: The University Press, 1900.

Hamilton, Peter J., *Colonial Mobile*, New York, 1898.

Hannan, Jerome, *The Canon Law of Wills*, The Catholic University of America Canon Law Studies, n. 86, Washington, D.C.: The Catholic University of America Press, 1941.

Hertling, Ludwig, *A History of the Catholic Church*, Westminster, Maryland: The Newman Press, 1957.

Heston, Edward L., *The Alienation of Church Property in the United States*, The Catholic University of America Canon Law Studies, n. 132, Washington, D.C.: The Catholic University of America Press, 1941.

Hughes, Thomas, *History of the Society of Jesus in the United States*, 4 vols., New York, 1917.

Journal of Father Paul Du Ru, Feb. 1—May 8, 1700: Missionary Priest to Louisiana, Chicago, 1934.

Kenny, Michael, *The Romance of the Floridas*, Milwaukee: The Bruce Publishing Co., 1934.

Lowry, Robert,—McCardle, William, *A History of Mississippi from the Discovery of the Great River to the Death of Jefferson Davis*, Jackson, Mississippi, 1891.

Martin, Thomas D., *Adverse Possession, Prescription and Limitation of Actions. The Canonical "Praescriptio"*, The Catholic University of America Canon Law Studies, n. 202, Washington, D.C.: The Catholic University of America Press, 1944.

Marcellino, P., Da Civezza, *Storia Universale delle Missioni Francescane*, XI vols., Firenze, 1895.

Meline, Mary M.,—McSweeney, Edward, *The Story of the Mountain*, Emmitsburg, 1911.

Mereness, Newton D., *The Journal of Diron d'Artaquette, 1722-1723, in Travels in the American Colonies*, London: Macmillan Co., 1916.

Michiels, Gommarus, *Principia Generalia de Personis in Ecclesia*, 2. ed., Parisiis-Tornaci-Romae: Desclee, 1955.

Mode of Tenure: Roman Catholic Church Property in the United States, a Survey by the Legal Department of the National Catholic Welfare Conference, Washington, D.C.: National Catholic Welfare Conference, 1941, and Supplement—1954.

Murphy, Joseph P., *The Laws of the State of New York Affecting Church Property*, The Catholic University of America Canon Law Studies, n. 388, Washington, D.C.: The Catholic University of America Press, 1957.

McManus, James E., *The Administration of Temporal Goods in Religious Institutes*, The Catholic University of America Canon Law Studies, n. 109, Washington, D.C.: The Catholic University of America Press, 1937.

Noldin, H.—Schmitt, A., *Summa Theologiae Moralis*, 3 vols., 30. ed., Oeneponte: Typis et Sumptibus Feliciani Rauch, 1954.

Philipps, Paul C., *The West in The Diplomacy of the American Revolution,* University of Illinois Studies in Social Sciences, II, 1913.

Restatement of the Law of Trusts, 3 vols., St. Paul, Minn.: American Law Institute, 1959.

Scott, Austin, *The Law of Trusts,* 5 vols., 2. ed., Boston, Toronto: Little, Brown & Co., 1956.

Shea, John Gilmary, *History of the Catholic Missions Among the Indian Tribes of the United States (1529-1854),* New York: Edward Dunigan and Brother, 1885.

———, *The Catholic Church in Colonial Days,* New York: John G. Shea, 1886.

———, *Life and Times of Archbishop John Carroll,* New York: John G. Shea, 1888.

———, *A History of the Catholic Church within the United States from the First Attempted Colonization to the Present Time,* New York: John G. Shea, 1890.

Sketch of the Catholic Church in the City of Natchez, Mississippi, on the Occasion of the Consecration of its Cathedral, September 19, 1886, Natchez, Miss.: The Natchez Democrat Print, 1886.

Sohm, Rudolph—Leddie, James E., *The Institutes: A Textbook of the History and System of Roman Private Law,* 3. ed., Oxford: At the Clarendon Press, 1907.

Vermeersch, A.—Creusen, J., *Epitome Iuris Canonici,* 3 vols., 7. ed., Mechliniae-Romae: H. Dessain, 1949.

Vromant, G., *De Bonis Ecclesiae Temporalibus,* 3. ed., Brugis-Paris: Desclée de Brouvier, 1953.

Wernz, F.—Vidal, P., *Ius Canonicum ad Normam Codicis Exactum,* 7 vols. in 8, Romae: Apud Aedes Universitatis Gregorianae, Vol. II, 3. ed., 1943; Vol. IV, Pars II, 1935.

Zollman, Carl, *American Law of Charities,* Milwaukee, Wisconsin: The Bruce Publishing Co., 1924.

———, American Church Law, St. Paul, Minn.: West Publishing Co., 1933.

ARTICLES

Adams, Donald E., "The Rights and Duties of Trustees and Their Appointment."—*The Jurist,* XVIII (1958), 175-190.

De Villiers, Terrace Marc, "A History of the Foundation of New Orleans (1717-1722)," Warrington Dawson Transl.—*The Louisiana Historical Quarterly,* III (1919), 175-281.

"Documents from our Archives: Diary of Bishop Rosati; Rosati to Cardinal Consalvi, April 2, 1823."—*St. Louis Catholic Historical Review,* III (1921), n. 313.

McGrath, John J., "Canon Law and American Church Law: A Comparative Study."—*The Jurist,* XVIII (1958), 260-278.

Shea, John Gilmary, (ed.) "Instruciòn para el Gobierno de los parroccas de la Luisiana."—*United States Catholic Historical Magazine,* I (1887), 418-443.

"Spanish Documents Relating to the Founding of the Church at Natchez, Mississippi."—*American Catholic Historical Researches,* IV (1887), 149-151.

Visser, J., "De Solemnitatibus Piarum Voluntatum in Iure Canonico." —*Apollinaris,* XX (1947), 59-136.

Vogel, Claude L., "The Capuchins in French Louisiana (1722-1766)." —*Franciscan Studies,* VIII (1928), 1-201.

PERIODICALS

American Catholic Historical Researches, Philadelphia, 1884-1912.

Apollinaris, Romae, 1928—

Franciscan Studies, St. Bonaventure, New York, 1924-1940.

Jurist, The, Washington, D.C., 1941—

Louisiana Historical Quarterly, New Orleans, 1917—

St. Louis Catholic Historical Review, St. Louis, 1918-1923.

United States Catholic Historical Magazine, New York, 1887-1892.

ALPHABETICAL INDEX

BIOGRAPHICAL NOTE

James P. McGough was born in County Limerick, Ireland, on July 24, 1933. He received his primary and secondary education in the local parochial schools. He entered Mungret College, Limerick, in September, 1949, and graduated in 1953. In September, 1953, he was admitted to St. Bernard Major Seminary, St. Bernard, Alabama, and was ordained to the priesthood on May 25, 1957. He was enrolled in the School of Canon Law of the Catholic University of America in the fall of 1958, where he received the degree of Bachelor of Canon Law in June, 1959, and the degree of Licentiate in Canon Law in June of 1960.

416. Cunningham, Rev. Thomas M., O.S.M., J.C.L., The Canonical Suppression of Religious Houses.
417. McGough, Rev. James P., J.C.L., The Laws of the State of Mississippi Affecting Church Property.
418. Nace, Rev. Arthur J., A.B., M.A., J.C.L., The Right to Accuse a Marriage of Invalidity.
419. Renati, Rev. Charles G., A.B., J.C.L., The Recipient of Extreme Unction.
420. Song, Rev. Raphael H., M.A., J.C.L., The Sacred Congregation for the Propagation of the Faith.

* For a complete list of the available numbers of this series apply to the Catholic University of America Press, 620 Michigan Avenue, N.E., Washington (17), D.C. for a general catalogue.

www.ingramcontent.com/pod-product-compliance
Lightning Source LLC
LaVergne TN
LVHW050240080826
844660LV00012B/568

* 9 7 8 0 8 1 3 2 2 5 7 4 6 *